The Politics of Beginning

The Politics of Beginning

The Origin of Private Authority
in the Process of Translation

Alejandro Esguerra

UNIVERSITY OF MICHIGAN PRESS

Ann Arbor

Published in the United States of America by the
University of Michigan Press
First published September 2025

A CIP catalog record for this book is available from the British Library.

Library of Congress Control Number: 2025011010
LC record available at https://lccn.loc.gov/2025011010

ISBN 978-0-472-07765-6 (hardcover : alk. paper)
ISBN 978-0-472-05765-8 (paper : alk. paper)
ISBN 978-0-472-90524-9 (open access ebook)

DOI: https://doi.org/10.3998/mpub.14540336

Support for this publication was provided by the Open Access Publication Fund of Bielefeld University.

The University of Michigan Press's open access publishing program is made possible thanks to additional funding from the University of Michigan Office of the Provost and the generous support of contributing libraries.

Cover image courtesy Shutterstock.com / captureandcompose

Authorized Representative: Easy Access System Europe, Mustamäe tee 50, 10621 Tallinn, Estonia, gpsr.requests@easproject.com

Contents

Digital materials related to this title can be found on
the Fulcrum platform via the following citable URL:
https://doi.org/10.3998/mpub.14540336

Illustrations

Foreword

While there is a lot of existing scholarship on how private authority functions in practice, particularly in the environmental area, there is strikingly little on where private authority comes from and how it is maintained. The dominant approaches either regard private authority as a proxy for public authority, looking for the state or state agency that stands behind a set of private arrangements to play enforcer, or to assume that private authority is already a coordination game of some kind. Both of those approaches skip over the intriguing question of how a private entity comes to have anything like *authority* in the first place: how it becomes capable of making pronouncements that others consider binding. As Max Weber would put it, this is ultimately a problem of legitimation rather than of raw coercion or rational coordination. But the vast majority of our existing conceptual tools for interrogating this problem presume the existence of actors rather than asking how they emerge, and further, treat authority as an attribute that those actors subsequently acquire.

This is where Alejandro Esguerra's excellent study enters the stage. By looking closely at how a variety of voices contributed to the negotiation and stabilization of private authority in the case of the Forest Stewardship Council, and in particular at how they were able to perform authority by translating knowledge from one domain to another, Esguerra is able to disclose the complex process by which a novel authoritative actor came into being. His careful tracing of a novel archive of documents from those negotiations helps bring the story to light, and his analytical sensibility allows him to present an account that can travel—not in the way of an empirical generalization, but in the way of an analytical specification of general processes and mechanisms that unfold differently in different cases.

Especially noteworthy is Esguerra's focus on translation and dramaturgy. By treating translation not so much as the conservation of meaning across domains, but more as the forging of meaning anew in a target domain, he is able to disclose the ways that situated actors draw on their positions in one realm in order to shape their capacities to act in another. Treating these actions as parts of an impactful performance allows him to situate each in the overall process by which a novel actor came into being— with its authority as a constitutive part of its very existence. The result is a marvelous configurational account that I am pleased to have in the series.

Patrick Thaddeus Jackson
Series Editor, Configurations

Acknowledgments

The environmental crisis requires a transformation in the ways societies value and govern human–nature relations. This book walks a fine line. It is written with a firm belief in new political beginnings and their transformative potential for governing the Earth. It explores the conditions under which even formerly antagonistic actors start developing a common political project in the realm of forest governance. How do people create a new means of governing the forest? What existing knowledge resources do they mobilize, and what new insights can be made productive? How do they convince others of their future vision? While addressing this set of questions on political innovation, one must keep in mind that political beginnings are not equally desirable for everyone. Whose visions find entrance into the new political project, and which concerns are shifted into the sphere of ignorance? How do people come to an agreement when their daily experiences are worlds apart? It is equally important to address these more critical questions because they point to the exclusions and contingencies of new political beginnings. One simply does not know for sure whether and how an untried arrangement for governing will have the intended effect.

The representatives of nongovernmental organizations (NGOs) and indigenous communities, foresters, timber retailers, and many others whom I describe in this book were well aware of the contingencies of their project to develop a certification mechanism for timber. In the late 1980s forest politics were highly politicized. Timber boycotts and radical protests existed next to experiments with forestry practices that were designed to be less harmful for people and the environment while human rights violations and deforestation continued. This book screens this landscape and follows the people who became the founding members of the Forest Stewardship Council (FSC)—the most authoritative private organization for forest certification that exists today. In establishing the FSC, the founding members co-initiated a major trend in global governance: nonstate actors practicing rule setting and implementation. I speak of this as the emergence of private authority or private authority in the making.

In abstracting from the concrete practices involved in developing a private governance organization, I make two arguments. On the theoretical side, I work with the concept of translation as developed in Actor-Network Theory (ANT) and introduce it to the theory of International Relations (IR). The concept of translation sensitizes to the ways in which new (actor) networks are formed, pointing to the changes in things and people taking part in the process. More specifically, I develop an ideal-typical translation mechanism to explain the emergence of private authority. This mechanism embodies a process in which knowledge of governance is continuously recontextualized in a different context. To study this mechanism in action, I outline a dramaturgical approach to transnational politics. This choice of methodology mobilizes metaphors of theater and terms such as "performance," "stage," and "script" to study the making of private authority.

The book's title, *The Politics of Beginning*, is inspired by Hannah Arendt's work. As the preeminent theorist of political beginnings, Arendt wrote beautifully about political action and how people come, as she termed it, "to act in concert" (Arendt 1958, 179). For Arendt, acting in concert is the moment of the political in which people envision what it could mean to live together with others in a "world whose reality is guaranteed for each by the presence of all" (243). For reasons of clarity, I have abstained from intertwining Arendt's thoughts with my analysis. But the Arendtian spirit remains when I explore how people articulate attainable futures and how they manage to turn them step by step into a governance arrangement. I believe that this aim resonates well with Arendt's work; but showing as much would require another project.

Like all beginnings this book has no single origin. A first trace leads to the University of Massachusetts at Amherst and to Peter M. Haas who introduced me to the framework of epistemic communities. I thank Peter for his encouraging comments throughout the years. At Amherst, I took a class with Ann Ferguson on feminist theory that complicated theories of knowledge: knowledge became "situated" and something that needed to be performed. I was hooked. In Bremen I met Klaus Dingwerth, who had worked intensively on the FSC. He was so kind as to give me a wicked piece of data: the audiotapes of the FSC Founding Assembly, which are central for this book.

A second trace leads to Berlin and its many intellectual centers. Under the supervision of Thomas Risse at the Freie Universität Berlin and Hubert Knoblauch at the Technical Universität Berlin, I worked on my PhD dissertation, which forms the basis of this book. Thomas is a wonderful advisor who is willing to "think with" his students even, or perhaps especially, when they challenge his own theoretical assumptions. His comments on earlier versions of the text gave me the necessary guidance, and his enthusiasm about doing research has been inspiring ever since. Hubert Knoblauch welcomed me to his sociological research group when I felt that I had to go beyond conventional political science research practices. In data sessions Hubert taught me the creativity of doing interpretive research while developing theory at the same time. I owe him the many aspects of the empirical analysis that are infused by the sociology of knowledge. Also in Berlin, Jan-Peter Voss's "Innovation in Governance" group with Nina Amelung and Arno Simmons developed an approach that used theories from Science and Technology Studies (STS) to study transnational politics. The working group "Political Ethnography" at Humboldt University assembles some sparkling minds with a sensibility for empirical details and rigorous theorizing. I profited immensely from these encounters. Anna Holzscheiter became a role model for addressing the IR community while staying true to interpretive commitments. The Myxa research group—Tobias Berger, Benjamin Faude, Lea Hartung, Alexander Kleibring, Anne Koch, Nicole Helmerich, Alexandros Tokhi, and Daniel Voelsen—provided the weekly structure for writing and reading each other's work. The intensity of these discussions, the laughter and joy of thinking in Berlin Neukölln whisper between the lines of this book.

Further traces span the globe: the Cornell University Department of Science and Technology Studies was an intellectual refuge, when I needed to be away from Berlin. I thank Michael Lynch for a profound introduction to STS and Steve Hilgartner for amazing comments; Holly Case and Vlad Micic for their hospitality, dry humor, and intellectual forays; and Christopher Hesselbein for his companionship in Ithaca. Fabian Scholtes was a reassuring mentor making sense of my writings when I could not. I have received valued feedback and encouraging comments from many colleagues: Luis Aue, Annett Bochmann, Maud Borie, Christian Bueger, Benjamin Cashore, Endre Danyi, Nicole Doerr, Frank Fischer, Richard Freeman, Katja Freistein, Frank Gadinger, Katharina Gnath, Anja Görnitz, Anna Leander, Rolf Lidskog, Andrea Liese, Annabelle Littoz-Monnet, Eva Lövbrand, Hilde van Meegdenburg, Tahani Nadim, Laura Pantzerhielm, Sigrid Quack, Nina Reiners, Thomas Scheffer, Sebastian Schindler, Ole-Jacob Sending, René Tuma, Esther Turnhout, Theresa Wobbe, Lukas Ziebell, and Michael Zürn.

I owe special thanks to Silke Beck who introduced me to the world of environmental STS. Talking to Silke feels like taking the pulse of cutting-edge research on environmental knowledge politics; I highly value her intellectual generosity and continuous support of my work throughout the years. I thank Holger Strassheim for believing in my academic projects and building a wonderful research and teaching environment at Bielefeld University. I am indebted to Marion Karmann from FSC and the interview partners whom I met in part at a FSC general assembly in Kota Kinabalu in Malaysia. I acknowledge funding from the Fritz Thyssen Foundation for a doctoral stipend, and the Dahlem Research School (Freie Universität Berlin) and the German Academic Exchange Program for various travel grants.

The "Configuration" Series of the University of Michigan Press is most fitting for my project. I thank Patrick Jackson for his initial curiosity about the manuscript; his comments were indispensable for strengthening the arguments and better structuring the text. Two anonymous reviewers provided encouraging feedback while outlining precisely where there was room for improvement; I am grateful for their time and advice. Madison Allums at the University of Michigan Press was instrumental in navigating me through the final steps of publishing the book.

Many friends helped in forming early ideas for this project: I thank Katharina Bauer, Bastian Balthasar Becker, Judith Blume, David Löw Beer, Caroline Merkel, and Toni Weis. I owe David Moses and Leonie Silber for the idea for the cover design, and for a lot more. I am particularly grateful to Linda Waack; her originality in thinking and writing has been immensely stimulating and her full-hearted support allowed me to finalize an earlier version of this text. My extended family has always encouraged my academic ambitions but cared more about me than about my book—which is healthy, I believe. They are Katharina Sakou, Doris in der Schmitten-Tuke, Joachim Tuke, Jürgen, Sibylle, and Kilian in der Schmitten, Luisa Esguerra, Miguel Esguerra and Cristina Rodríguez, Sabine Knappe, and Henrike Schepers. And, finally, I am grateful to my closest family—Henrike, Emilian, and Jonah—for sharing thoughts and emotions on the state of this world and our place within it.

Abbreviations

ANT	Actor-Network Theory
COFYAL	Cooperative Forestal Yanesha
FAO	Food and Agriculture Organization of the United Nations
FoE	Friends of the Earth
FSC	Forest Stewardship Council
IPBES	Intergovernmental Platform on Biodiversity and Ecosystem Services
IPCC	Intergovernmental Panel on Climate Change
IR	International Relations
ITTA	International Topical Timber Agreement
ITTO	International Tropical Timber Organization
IUCN	International Union for the Conservation of Nature and Natural Resources
MSC	Marine Stewardship Council
NGO	nongovernmental organization
SCS	Scientific Certification Systems
STS	Science and Technology Studies
TFAP	Tropical Forest Action Plan
UN	United Nations
UNCTAD	United Nations Conference on Trade and Development
UNEP	United Nations Environmental Programme
UNESCO	United Nations Educational, Scientific and Cultural Organization
WARP	Wood Workers Alliance for Rainforest Protection
WWF	World Wildlife Fund

1 | Introduction

Governing the Earth is an activity not confined to parliaments and government commissions. Social and environmental groups, businesses, scientists, foundations, in short, a range of nonstate actors, not only lobby states but promote their own voluntary regulations. Despite disparate backgrounds, diverging goals, and historically grown conflicts, they make rules and create standards for issues as diverse as labor and indigenous rights, carbon emissions, and the internet. These rules are subsequently adopted by large brands and even by states themselves.

This book is about the politics of beginning. It deals with the stage where a new political project is gaining momentum but has not yet assumed form. It investigates in particular how the various actors involved in forest operations negotiated a new private institution into existence. In doing so, it raises questions about the ways in which different actors come up with alternative governance arrangements; it explores how nonstate actors construct knowledge about problems; and it examines how they manage to agree on procedures and institutional designs, rules, and standards. In other words, it provides an answer to the question: How do nonstate actors negotiate novel private institutions?[1]

This question is gaining in relevance because of states' inability to respond adequately to the headlines of our time—for example, climate change, biodiversity loss, migration, and financial regulation. As I write this introduction, the Amazonian rainforest is burning at a record rate, threatening both the living space of local communities and measures to counter global climate change. Calling on private actors to provide regulation because of multilateral gridlock has become fashionable, but it comes with immense problems.[2] What is a forest? The logging industry tends to view a forest as a resource for timber, often denying the interests of other humans or other species that populate the "biodiversity hotspots" of this planet. Climate scientists and others emphasize forests' potential for decreasing CO_2 concentration in the atmosphere. Social NGOs, especially those from the Global South, have insisted that forests are habitats for humans as they provide shelter, food, and security. Farmers burn trees, turning forests into land for agriculture to make a living, while big business makes a fortune. And across cultures, poets and religious leaders have celebrated the spirituality of forests as something that goes beyond any value ascribed to them for human living. Thus, despite nonstate actors' diverging views on forests, analysts and practitioners suggest that private institutions have the potential to regulate effectively, partly because of their expertise and their creativity in governing.

Negotiating private institutions can be tense. Representatives from the logging industry who may have a record of human rights violations, indigenous peoples who have fought for the rights to their ancestors' land, and concerned wood users have to begin working with each other. Tackling these deep-rooted conflicts is complex because the transnational sphere knows few standardized rules for interaction that could provide a basis for negotiations. Intergovernmental negotiations are highly formalized, especially in the context of the United Nations (UN); such rules do, however, allow states to negotiate even when they are in severe conflict. Private negotiations are exempt from the intergovernmental protocol and the sometimes-paralyzing multilateral politics.[3] One result is that participants have conflicting ideas as to how to organize the institution-making process and have to negotiate clear and generally accepted rules for decision making.[4] In other words, timber merchants, human rights activists, and environmental NGOs may not only disagree about the nature of a forest, they may also lack shared norms and rules for conducting politics. For these reasons, this book treats the rise of private authority as improbable, as something that requires explanation.

The Argument: The Origin of Private Authority in the Process of Translation

The aim of this book is to develop and apply a theoretical framework that will explain the emergence of private authority in world politics. Private authority is defined as situations in which nonstate actors "make rules or set standards that other actors in world politics adopt" (Green 2014, 6). As this book is concerned with the politics of beginning, it concentrates on private authority *in the making*. Private authority exists here only as potential; it is a project that is oriented toward the future, an outcome that is anticipated but not yet realized.

My endeavor is to theorize how an envisioned political project of this kind comes to be constituted over time: How does it become possible for antagonistic actors with conflicting views on forest operations and few rules for interaction to create a new political order? The guiding assumption of this book is that creating a new form of governance—private authority—requires investigation into new governance practices and, thus, knowledge about governance or governance knowledge.[5] The knowledge in question concerns sustainable forestry practices, institutions, rules that allow for governance, and, finally, the art of practicing governance such as how to negotiate competing interests or create convincing narratives and frames. What I am after is a social mechanism that explains how this knowledge about governance is generated and turned into a governance arrangement.

Throughout this book, I show the explanatory power of the *mechanism of translation*. Translation is commonly associated with language interpretation. Skilled interpreters at UN conferences transfer a speech delivered in Chinese into other UN languages. This practice seems smooth at first sight. But think back to an occasion when you tried to tell a joke in a language other than your mother tongue. Perhaps the punch line did not surprise your audience the way you are used to. Jokes are admittedly a tough example because they are so interwoven with the cultural codes of specific communities. We often end up having to explain why the joke is funny in a particular community. This example is meant to illustrate that translation is a contingent practice because concepts carry different meanings in different languages and for different communities. Translation sensitizes us to the complex task of transferring meaning from one language to another. This task necessarily requires changing the original (the joke) so that it resonates with the new context (the other language community). In this process of recontextualization, both the original and the context need to be transformed. This includes decisions regarding what to emphasize, what to leave out, and how to create new combinations. Agency and interpretation figure prominently here because translation is not an automated technical process but one that allows for maneuver and creativity. Insofar as it involves inserting an agent, it becomes clear that translation is about "conscious choices: translators choose between alternatives, among which some are better and some are worse" (Freeman 2009, 434). In a first approximation, translation describes a process in which a linguistic entity (e.g., a joke or concept) is recontextualized and made to fit into another context (e.g., a different language community).

I integrate into this notion of translation two core insights from Actor-

Network Theory (ANT) that is also known as the sociology of translation (Best and Walters 2013; Callon 1986).[6] First, ANT suggests that the objects of translation should be extended beyond linguistic entities. Political concepts, global norms, even soil samples, all these entities qualify as objects of translation. This move makes it possible to integrate socio-material entities into the analysis, and to study how they are transformed and adapted to another context. Carbon dioxide emissions are an intriguing example because they have become the central indicator in governing the climate crisis. A translational perspective investigates efforts to make CO_2 emissions measurable and to translate them into nationally determined contributions displaying states' efforts to fight climate change.[7] Thus, through a chain of translations the socio-ecological phenomenon of a global climate has been transformed into an instrument for governing climate conduct.[8] In other words, ANT sensitizes us to the socio-material dimension of knowledge about governance.

Second, ANT emphasizes that translation creates new relations or a network encompassing formerly disparate entities. Remember how I mentioned interpreters who translate a speech by a Chinese delegate into other UN languages. ANT argues that the practice of interpreting connects parties because it creates equivalences between concepts that were previously distinct. In the climate example, translational work renders carbon knowable and governable: it constitutes carbon as an object of governance to which global governance actors can orient themselves. For ANT translation has *constitutive effects* as it brings two (or more) entities into relation with one another.

In sum, this book shows a mechanism whereby private authority can emerge. *In its basic functioning, the mechanism of translation is a process in which knowledge about governance is continuously recontextualized.* This practice has a constitutive effect, as translation creates equivalences between entities that were previously distinct. Translators actively transform knowledge about governance and, since they thereby necessarily choose between alternatives, translation involves politics. Thus, we should study translation not only because it unveils the ways in which a new entity emerges but because it also shows the practices of inclusion and exclusion that appear during this process.

In this book, the mechanism of translation unfolds empirically in the negotiation trajectory that led to the formation of the Forest Stewardship Council (FSC), a transnational private certification organization for sustainable forestry. The nascent FSC was negotiated at a critical juncture for private governance in the late 1980s as it was one of the first global, multistakeholder certification initiatives. Klaus Dingwerth and Philipp Pattberg (2009, 17) stress that a "clear organizational model for making transnational rules did not yet exist" when the FSC emerged. Other transnational organizations have copied the FSC's institutional design, and states have partly converted FSC standards into their forestry legislation. To explore how concerned wood users, timber merchants, human rights activists, and environmental NGOs engaged in private institution-making, this book's most distinctive feature is a zooming in on a particular site—the three-day founding assembly of the FSC in Toronto in 1993 as documented through live audio recordings (chapters 4, 5, and 6). This research method allows for an unprecedented, in-depth analysis of a constitutive moment for private authority in the making.

Why Does It Matter?

Recent work in IR has paved the way for a more sociologically informed study of world politics that emphasizes the knowledge politics of environmental change (Allan 2017; Jernnäs and Lövbrand 2022; Sending 2015). This book offers three distinct contributions to this body of constructivist work that cover theory, methodology, and empirics. As its theoretical contribution, this book advances a microfoundation for private authority emergence.[9] Scholarship on private authority points to the legitimizing force of expertise (Hall and Biersteker 2002b) and argues that expert knowledge creates the "possibility of emergence" of private authority (Green 2014, 16).[10] This book enters the trajectory of emergence earlier, at a stage when claims to expertise are contested and the legitimizing force of expert knowledge is unclear. I ask *how* expert knowledge becomes consensual and *whose* knowledge is rendered authoritative and institutionalized into mechanisms of governance. This line of inquiry is particularly prominent in Science and Technology Studies (STS) (Beck, Forsyth, and Mahony 2024) and STS-inspired IR literature (Littoz-Monnet 2025; Leander 2021; Bueger 2015). This scholarship examines the interaction between knowledge and power as well as the preconditions for claims to expertise, especially in global environmental politics (Allan 2017; Jernnäs and Lövbrand 2022). I contribute to this literature by mobilizing a key STS concept—translation. I speak of a mechanism of translation to describe the active transformation of knowledge about governance in preparation for claiming authority on the world stage. In the spirit of the work by social movement scholars, the endeavor of this book is to provide a "smaller-scale mechanism" (McAdam, Tarrow, and Tilly 2001, 26) that explains the emergence of private authority.

Methodologically, this book develops a dramaturgical perspective in which the negotiation trajectory of the emerging FSC is viewed as a sequence of staged performances. Actors *perform* entrepreneurial *roles* in a specific *setting* and according to implicit and explicit *scripts*. These theatrical metaphors have increasingly entered the analytical toolbox of scholarship when analyzing global environmental meetings (Death 2011; Campbell et al. 2014; Aykut et al. 2022). Whereas the above literature focuses on governmental settings with established rules, I examine stages of global environmental politics that are in the process of emerging and are shaped by private actors. Likewise, my focus on micro-interactions shows how the founding members of the FSC had to improvise and find ad-hoc solutions to procedural issues that would otherwise have been given by UN rules. The dramaturgical perspective advances an STS-view of documents that acknowledges what documents *do*, not only what they *say* (Asdal and Reinertsen 2022; Hilgartner 2000; Riles 2006). Documents perform a social role, linking meetings and actors with one another. A document is not simply the outcome of one meeting, it is also a preparation for the next. It binds meetings together.

Empirically, the FSC is often portrayed as a prime example of a participatory model of rule-making (Quack and Malets 2014). This book nuances these findings by pointing to the legitimation struggles accompanying emergence. If a distinct form of private authority gains momentum, other visions are excluded. The microanalysis in this book especially shows up the conflicts over representation. I trace how a few participants circumvented the failure of the negotiations by excluding voices that envisioned an FSC with less corporate influence. This is illuminating because the founding of the FSC also co-established a model of participatory environmental governance that has been increasingly shaped by corporate interests (Jernnäs and Lövbrand 2022; Jacques 2016; Uribe 2024).

A New Institution for the Earth

The field of global environmental governance constitutes a privileged site for studying political experiments and emerging orders in world politics (Green and Hale 2017). For this reason, this book turns to the FSC as a case that matters in terms of the history of global governance as well as how this history has had formative effects up to the present day. FSC standards for sustainable forestry govern forests globally and affect states' forestry legislation (Auld 2014). Transnational organizations, among them the Marine Stewardship Council, have copied the FSC's institutional design and rules (Dingwerth and Pattberg 2009).

A "Constitutional Moment" of Private Authority

Historical institutionalism suggests examining "critical junctures" in order to study the political origins of important institutional arrangements and broader structures of governance (Capoccia and Kelemen 2007; Fioretos 2011). As I argue in chapter 2, the late 1980s and early 1990s represent such a period in which private authority was developed as a distinct mode of governance (Green 2014, chap. 3). While not the first private multistakeholder organization (Auld 2014; Pattberg 2007), the FSC's Founding Assembly represents what Sheila Jasanoff calls a "constitutional moment" of private authority. In Jasanoff's terms, a "constitutional moment" is a brief period in which basic rules of political practice are rewritten, which includes "renegotiating the manner in which states and other authoritative institutions employ the power of expertise" (Jasanoff 2011, 624). It is in this sense that the emergence of the FSC and its Founding Assembly represents a constitutional moment as far as private authority is concerned. In developing a new perspective on the emergence of private authority, this book provides a "conceptual innovation" that justifies selecting an already well-researched case (Bennett and Elman 2007, 178).

Empirical Findings

This book begins its story in the late 1980s. At that time, social movements addressed international organizations such as the World Bank, demanding "popular participation and people-centered development" (Abraham 2022, 7); they experimented with initiatives to create governance arrangements with and without public involvement. A few years later, ideas and practices of participation had already been turned into mechanisms of governance. The Earth Summit in Rio in 1992 institutionalized "multistakeholderism" to make global governance more inclusive (Bäckstrand 2006), the FSC had its founding assembly in 1993, and, more generally, data shows a rapid growth of transnational institutions in the early 1990s (Westerwinter 2021). Thus, the FSC's founding members operated within a relatively short time frame in which nonstate actors were molded as global political subjects.

Entering this period, this book shows three sets of empirical findings.

The first revolves around *practices of innovation.* Whether sustainable management of tropical forests was possible and what form could this take were questions to which there were no clear answers. Neither foresters from universities in the Global North nor social movements in the Global South had applicable solutions at hand (Anderson 1990). Similarly, governing instruments such as certification were perhaps known from the fair-trade coffee sector, but when discussing the sustainable use of timber FSC founding members had only limited knowledge of how such a labeling system could work in the forestry sector (Thomas, Ken, and Connor [pseud.] 1989; Poore et al. 1989). Multi-stakeholderism was a term that was gaining traction within transnational expert communities (Taggart and Abraham 2023), but it remained unclear how conflicting parties could work together in practice. As a result, actors across the globe experimented with various models of forestry and its governance that would integrate economic, social, and ecological concerns; some of the initiatives remained locally embedded while others aimed to scale up, presenting their findings at transnational meetings (Anderson 1990; Counsell and Rice 1992b).

Second, *struggles over representation* are central. A bird's-eye view of the early trajectory of the FSC reveals that representation of groups from the Global South was neither a given at the early meetings nor something that happened automatically. It required continuous pressure from such groups. Throughout this book, I show instances in which especially social and environmental NGOs from the Global South questioned representation practices and demanded more formal participation. This occurred from early conferences to the 1993 Founding Assembly itself. I show the importance of translators at the founding conference who helped social groups to articulate their views in a way that fitted the agenda of the meeting; I also show how themes that were not picked up by translators simply vanished. For instance, at the Founding Assembly environmental and social groups suggested that business actors should not serve on the board of directors to avoid conflicts of interest. Here, an "alternative FSC" was looming that was not even put to a vote thanks to some skillful chairing of the FSC interim board. Pointing to these struggles over representation and translation does not preclude acknowledging the relative balance of represented groups in the FSC's final institutional design (Quack and Malets 2014). But it is important to emphasize that groups from the Global South had to continually intervene to arrive at balanced representation and to trace themes and voices that were excluded, since they tell stories of unrealized trajectories.

A final set of findings concerns *narratives of neoliberalism*. Studies of the recent climate regime describe how nonstate actors were systematically enrolled as key players (Jernnäs and Lövbrand 2022). Narratives associated with neoliberalism shift governance responsibility to nonstate actors, foster voluntary mechanisms closely related to measuring, and emphasize partnerships between business and NGOs (Turnhout 2018). This book shows how the negotiational trajectory toward an FSC was one site among others at which neoliberal ideas were negotiated and for the first time turned into mechanisms of global governance in the early 1990s. At that time, FSC initiators describe consumers as "expressing a preference for sustainable" timber (Thomas, Ken, and Connor [pseud.] 1989) with little evidence for this claim. Others see the voluntary instrument of certification as a double-edged sword especially in authoritarian countries. The concept of sustainable development discursively paves the way for the idea of business and NGOs working together; actors refer to this as the "new paradigm." In other words, narratives of neoliberalism were tested, met with caution, or appropriated for convincing skeptics. It was the beginning of what Juanita Uribe (2024) describes as "processes of normalization" that established private actors as deemed legitimate. The trajectory toward an FSC is a site at which nonstate actors experimented with and brought about models of governing that have significantly influenced the landscape of world politics until today.

The Politics of Beginning: A Framework for Analysis

The politics of beginning describe how diverse people articulate attainable futures and how they manage to turn them step by step into an arrangement for governance. This section develops a framework for analyzing the politics of beginning in the tradition of a process-centered, interpretive constructivist research agenda (Yanow and Schwartz-Shea 2015). Scholars working within this tradition aim to unearth the meaning-making of people while simultaneously abstracting from it to arrive at theory (Jackson 2015). Inductive empirical investigations are intertwined with continuous theoretical reflection and interpretation. What has emerged from this research practice is the mechanism of translation. Translation, in this book, figures as an "ideal-typical social mechanism" (Jackson 2010, 153); it is an analytical construct that aims to capture "the essence of a social phenomenon" (Meegdenburg 2023, 408).

To develop the argument, I first establish private authority as being in the making. I argue that expert knowledge as a source for legitimizing private authority cannot be assumed a priori; instead, the making of expert knowledge itself must be investigated. When private authority is in the making knowledge of governance is liquid and conflicting. So, second, I specify the argument by drawing distinctions in governance knowledge for analytical purposes between the content of the problem, institutional structures, and the process or doing of governance. Third, I devote the remaining part of this section to introducing translation as a mechanism that describes the stepwise process of stabilizing governance knowledge.

Private Authority in the Making

Authority is a relational concept that explains why one actor *defers* to an authoritative claim made by another (Kustermans and Horemans 2022). It is based on some form of recognition on the part of those who are subject to it. Somebody must acknowledge an authoritative claim made by someone else without being forced to do so. Max Weber (1921) introduced this idea as *Legitmitätsglaube*, belief in the legitimacy of authority, because it rests on different sources of legitimation (Raz 1990).

IR scholarship has transferred this conceptualization of authority to world politics, arguing that "international *institutions with authority require legitimation*" (Zürn 2018, 11, emphasis in the original). For instance, the authority of international organizations is in part authority delegated from states (Barnett and Finnemore 2004), while epistemic communities enjoy authority because of their claim to policy-relevant knowledge (Haas 1992, 2017).[11] Ole Jacob Sending (2015) has problematized this body of work because the sources of legitimation are theoretically set rather than empirically researched. How and by what means an epistemic community gains its authoritative claim to policy-relevant knowledge remains in the dark.

Turning to the scholarship on private authority—situations in which nonstate actors "make rules or set standards that other actors in world politics adopt" (Green 2014, 6)[12]—one finds a similar problem: the existing literature argues that the legitimation of private authority is predominantly "acquired through the special expertise" of private actors (Cutler, Haufler, and Porter 1999a, 4).[13] Private actors are seen as "credible providers of technical expertise or information that is difficult to acquire, compile, organize, or analyze" (Hall and Biersteker 2002b, 14). If firms, social movements, and engaged scientists collaborate in making rules and setting standards, they can become authoritative "owing to the expertise of the private actors" (Green 2014, 7). Thus, expert knowledge is described as the key source for legitimizing private authority (Abbott and Snidal 2009; Büthe and Mattli 2013, 43). It is the social basis for recognizing the rules and standards that private actors have set without the explicit backing of the state.

However, the extensive literature on private authority tends to treat expert knowledge as preexisting and consensual rather than something that is negotiated and highly contested.[14] For instance, when Jessica Green discusses the crucial role of expertise in enabling private authority to emerge, she speaks about "preexisting" knowledge, uses terms such as "technical experience," and evokes a picture of "a scientist with an understanding of the atmospheric chemistry" (Green 2014, 31). Yet, in the multipartite arrangements so typical of private authority, fights over problem definition and disagreement about framing strategies are more likely than consensus. Or, as Sigrid Quack (2016) rightly concludes, "struggles over knowledge claims are rarely taken fully into account" when theorizing about private authority (but see Graz 2019).

Against this background, this book shows the construction and performance of expertise when private authority emerges. I suggest that expert knowledge cannot be understood as an attribute of private authority a priori but needs to be subject to empirical research. Especially when the emergence of authority is at stake, "we need to study the social processes" by which authority is stabilized (Krisch 2017, 249). For this reason, this book enters the scene before any governance arrangement is ready to claim authority on the basis of its expert knowledge. I define private authority as *in the making* when knowledge of governance is liquid and constantly being renegotiated with regard to the content of the problem, institutional structures, and the process or doing of governance. In such a situation, private actors are confronted with their conflicting interests, convictions, and visions; they have little in the way of rules for addressing these conflicts and are thus challenged to generate and negotiate governance knowledge.

Governance Knowledge: Knowledge of Policy, Polity, and Politics

If private authority is in the making, it is uncertain what counts as credible and relevant expertise and to whom. Often these emerging organizations unite a diversity of actors—firms, NGOs, scientists—with their potentially conflicting claims to relevant knowledge. A forester certainly has expert knowledge about forestry, but that knowledge may differ fundamentally from the expertise of indigenous peoples. An activist has experience in campaigning, but may know little about how to create a narrative that convinces firms to join an institution. My point is not to couple specific forms of knowledge to particular types of actor but to point to potential knowledge controversies (Barry 2012) and to different forms of knowledge about governance that become relevant when designing new institutions. I operationalize knowledge about governance as policy knowledge, polity knowledge, and politics knowledge.

Policy knowledge accounts for the content of a governance problem, anything from an HIV/AIDS crisis to the highly technical issue of respirable dust particles in air-polluted cities. Most concepts of knowledge frame policy knowledge as a set of statements about the world, carefully crafted in the institution of science, which enter the policy process either through an epistemic community (Haas 1992), or national and international advisory bodies (Hel and Biermann 2017). Investigations into the contestation of policy knowledge have made clear that knowledge-making itself needs to be examined: policy knowledge of environmental problems is in itself productive of a political order and not just a set of neutral statements concerning a socio-physical reality (Allan 2017; Beck, Forsyth, and Mahony 2024; Esguerra 2024). For instance, a forest can be many things—a unit to be managed, a resource for timber, a living space, a carbon sink. Each of these interpretations entails implicit policy assumptions about how the forest should be used and which governance structures would be deemed appropriate (Mathews 2011; Scott 1998; Turnhout 2018).

Polity knowledge refers to institutions. In established international institutions this knowledge is materialized in the practices and forms of organizations and explicated in their rules of procedure. Actors have to be familiar with these rules if they want to participate in world politics. This is true for diplomats as well as for nonstate actors who have gained some access to the formerly exclusive circles of international power (O'Neill and Haas 2019; Sending, Pouliot, and Neumann 2015). Polity knowledge in the shape of organizational forms and practices travels globally and becomes recontextualized in new organizations (Ahrne and Brunsson 2014; Czarniawska and Sevón 1996). When innovating governance, actors draw on already existing practices and forms, may experience contestation and misfit, and may have to negotiate this knowledge anew.

Politics knowledge is concerned with the process or doing of politics (Voß and Freeman 2016). Ruth Wodak's study of an EU parliamentarian is illuminating when she discusses forms of politics knowledge:

convincing and persuading others of one's opinion, lobbying, debating, arguing, struggling to win in motions, forming alliances, advising (and persuading) outsiders of one's ideas, and preparing and influencing decision-making. This knowledge . . . presupposes the knowledge of tactics and strategies, of ideologies and positions, of the strengths and weakness of colleagues; in sum, one has to know the "rules of the game." (Wodak 2009, 46)

Knowing and following these "rules of the game" is intertwined with the arena in which these rules apply. To be a diplomat comes with an entire apparatus of knowledge pertaining to the art of doing international politics in various locations or arenas (Neumann 2013; Pouliot 2016; Sending, Pouliot, and Neumann 2015). In the transnational sphere, doing politics remains a field of experimentation and contestation. In the 1980s, when the FSC was negotiated, knowledge of doing transnational politics was fragmented at best and, more often, highly contested. Actors, whether indigenous representatives or businesspeople, came to the arena with very different assumptions about systems of ordering; it was unclear what roles were available to them, which rules they had to follow, and what communicative codes were (in)appropriate.

In sum, knowledge about governance did not exist prior to the emergence of private authority; it was generated and negotiated during the very process through which authority emerged. For analytical purposes I therefore distinguish knowledge about governance, as mentioned previously, into knowing the content of the problem (policy knowledge), institutional structures (polity knowledge), and the process or doing of governance (politics knowledge).

On Translation

Translation evokes metaphors of travel and change. Literary translation comes first to mind when reflecting on the task of the translator. A translator is at home in two or more languages and recognizes the subtle changes in meaning when translating a text from one language into another. Susan Sontag (2002) has argued that translation in this sense is not so much a search for equivalences as a conscious choice between alternatives that evoke different meanings. IR scholars have drawn on these insights to study how diplomats struggle to express arguments and concepts in more than one language (Stritzel 2014; Wigen 2018). Emphasizing how world politics is about "interlingual relations" is important because it unveils the power effects of translation and those who are tasked with functioning as mediators (Wigen and Caraccioli 2026). Postcolonial scholars foreground the epistemic violence that emerges in the translation of "vernacular" idioms into dominant discourses and analyze IR as a colonial field of knowledge production and racialized hierarchies (Berger and Esguerra 2025; Davis, Thakur, and Vale 2020).

The literature on global norm diffusion and private standards has applied translation beyond linguistics (Graz 2021; Risse 2017a). This scholarship uses the concept to explain how global norms are translated so that they resonate with local contexts (Berger 2017; Knappe 2022; Zimmermann 2017). It is only then that these norms can unfold their transformative effects in contexts beyond their origin; translations change both the meanings of international human rights norms as well as the local context in which they are performed (Berger 2017). Thus, the concept of translation sheds lights on the *transformation of meaning* that occurs when systems of knowledge travel from one context to another (Berger and Esguerra 2018c; Capan, Dos Reis, and Grasten 2021). In studying how local translators change global human rights, translation turns into a concept of difference in which the "original" changes in unexpected ways. Yet the concept of translation holds an enormous potential not only for exploring difference but for explaining the production of (precarious) unity, the making of relations, the "stitching together" (Zwingel 2016), or what I term the "constitutive effect" of translation.[15]

ANT and the Constitutive Effect of Translation

To theorize this *constitutive* effect of translation, I mobilize STS literature and in particular ANT.[16] By entering the laboratories of natural scientists in the 1980s, ANT scholars paved the way for an ethnographic approach to the study of science and discovered that laboratory practices look much like mundane activities, including improvisational playing with equipment and ad hoc explanations of phenomena (Knorr-Cetina 1981; Lynch 1985). This early work was already able to put forward a handful of provocative claims that had great resonance across the social sciences and the humanities (Esguerra 2023).

Two claims are particularly important for highlighting the constitutive effect of translation. First, ANT expands on the objects involved in translational practices.[17] Because it originated in the study of scientific practices, it has a long history of integrating matter and artifacts in its analysis. Soil, carbon, and viruses as well as algorithms, data sheets, and meeting rooms are considered important for translational practices and the formation of governing. To illustrate this argument, Bruno Latour's (1999) study of an expedition to the Amazonian forest is instructive. Latour joined a field trip of French and Brazilian scientists, which had the objective of studying whether the Amazon forest was advancing or retreating in a particular area. As an anthropologist, Latour traced how scientists collect soil samples and document their data in field logs and dossiers in order to eventually publish their findings in a journal; he describes in detail the transformation of "a clump of earth" into a scientific fact (Latour 1999, 51). This transformation becomes possible because of a "chain of translation" (Latour 1999, 27) in which each step in the process refers back to a prior object and this object then forms the basis of the next. To set this chain in motion, the scientists have to take countless decisions as to what to focus on and how to proceed. As a result of their sedulous scientific practices, they are able to transform the forest eventually into an expedition report discussing the change in its formation. The steps in between are traceable but contingent, unfolding as "a risky intermediary pathway" of translation (Latour 1999, 40). In other words, Latour describes a translational process or a chain of translation in which scientists single out, package, and transform the object of knowledge (the Amazon) and eventually, after many intermediary translational steps, reconstitute this knowledge in a new context (an academic journal).

For IR, Marieke de Goede has deployed Latour's concept to examine rather reluctant security actors such as banks, airlines, and social media companies. While Latour follows scientific specimens, Goede follows "the life of a €326 wire transfer to Turkey"; in doing so she unpacks "the ways in which financial data(sets) are carved off, reported, shared, and combined, to enable security interventions" (Goede 2018, 40). Thus, her work radically expands the objects that IR closely studies. The conflicts that appear in the translational chain become apparent in the work by Lisa Campbell and her colleagues. They have studied diplomats and nonstate actors ethnographically in global environmental meetings. Participants translate, that is, "negotiate, contest, and defend," environmental knowledge in meetings trying to push specific versions of nature representations and ways of governance (Campbell et al. 2014, 5).

Second, ANT understands the concept of translation as the study of how actor-networks are constituted and formed (Callon 1986). It emphasizes the continuous translational work of bringing diverse actors into relation with one another; to translate is to associate (Law 2009). Richard Freeman (2009, 435) notes: "What is significant about this process is the way in which a new relationship (or 'actor-network') changes the properties or characteristics of those things or people party to it. Such relationships are not essential or given: they have to be made and maintained, or 'performed.' This directs attention to the process of creating networks and the politics involved; it suggests researching translation where it is enacted.[18] In IR, recent work on global object constitution draws on this dimension of translation (Corry 2024; Esguerra 2024; Pantzerhielm 2024). For instance, Christian Bueger (2015) asks how the epistemic object of "piracy" is rendered knowable. He shows how international organizations are sites of specific translational practices such as quantification that together generate knowledge regarding various instances of piracy. Instances and practices that fall under the category of piracy are translated into numbers or reports that collectively construct how the UN knows about piracy. Bentley Allan (2017) outlines the constitutive effect of translation in his study on the coproduction of the climate as a distinct object of global governance. Complex social and physical phenomena are translated into tables, charts, models, and other scientific inscriptions so that these portable entities can travel all over the world.

In sum, ANT is a source of inspiration for integrating socio-material entities into the analysis as well as for exploring the constitutive dimension of translation. In the next section, I operationalize these insights by outlining the mechanism of translation.

The Mechanism of Translation: Recontextualization and the Productivity of Enclosure and Disclosure

In its basic function, the mechanism of translation is a process in which knowledge about governance is continuously recontextualized and emerges in a different context. This becomes empirically observable when actors package socio-material knowledge about governance (e.g., new forestry or voting practices) into knowledge objects (e.g., draft standards for sustainable forestry or procedural rules). This operation requires displacing knowledge from a given context, transforming it, and re-presenting it, that is, making it "(con)textually visible and available" in a new context (Bueger 2015, 7). For instance, recontextualization can operate as a movement from written to verbal, from monologue to dialogue, from meeting notes to a research paper, or from a plenary talk to a group discussion. These operations allow for a transformation through "adding, rearranging, deleting, and substituting contents and formulations" (Wodak 2000, 78). The important premise is that the new context co-constructs the object and allows for a different kind of work. Think of the context of a

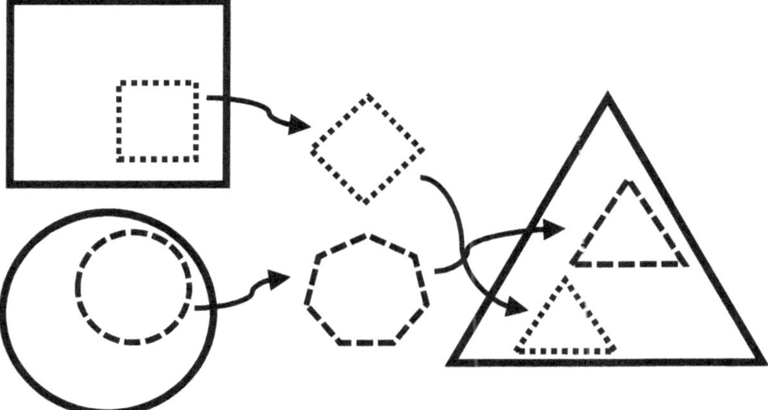

Fig. 1. A visualization of the basic functioning of the mechanism of translation

small-group meeting, where active listening and sharing experiences are easier than in a larger setting.

Translators set the mechanism of translation in motion. They actively transform knowledge about governance by making choices as to what and how to translate. Their power is subtle and productive as they turn diffuse and opposing sets of knowledge into seemingly coherent categories.[19] In so doing they "mobilize support for particular understandings of" problems, relevant actors, and "necessary actions" (Campbell et al. 2014, 5). To act as a translator is to take on a specialized role. Facilitator, mediator, honest broker, or expert are common descriptions applied to a translator. All of these labels suggest a neutral or even perhaps "a disruptive third" position (Doerr 2018) that is independent of vested interests. But because their translation practices give voice to some worldviews while silencing others, translators are heavily involved in the politics of private authority making.

Figure 1 visualizes the process of recontextualization. The forms with the bold lines indicate the contexts whereas the dotted forms represent the translated objects. The triangle in the figure emerges as a new entity. The translated object changes in shape (from a square/circle to a triangle), but "a fine line of seeming continuity" (Berger 2017, 25) is indicated through the type of dotting. This fine line is important because it ensures that the continuous chain of translation remains traceable in the new entity.

I specify the basic functioning of the mechanism of translation by introducing the productive interplay of enclosure/disclosure.[20] Enclosure is an act that aims to stabilize knowledge claims by trying to fix meanings, to remain constant, to provide established forms and templates, to rely on proxies and working assumptions. It is an attempt to achieve closure. This performance leads "a statement away from its conditions of production" (Latour 1987, 23). The core idea is to arrive at statements whose credibility will not be challenged further; it is a move from weaker to stronger qualification, from sentences such as "I guess/suppose/suggest that x is the case" to "x is the case." Disclosure, by contrast, is an attempt to reopen an issue. It problematizes what seems given and embraces uncertainty. Actors may question the credibility or quality of a claim. They criticize the framing of an issue or point to the negative implications of envisioned practices. Disclosure can be said to lead a statement "towards its conditions of production" (Latour 1987, 23) by emphasizing the uncertainty of a claim.[21]

The interplay of these two practices is the engine in the creation of political novelty (see Rheinberger 1997). I suggest that translators set some elements as technical and stable (enclosure) while leaving others open for contestation and debate (disclosure); the two operations depend on each other. There is struggle over performing these operations. To render something technical and functional is to exclude it from the political debate; to render something political is to open up a controversy and perhaps put carefully negotiated agreements at risk.

As figure 2 visualizes, the interplay of enclosure/disclosure specifies the mechanism of translation in an important dimension. It shows not only *that* recontexualization matters but specifies *how* it is done. If a translator engages in enclosure/disclosure practices, he or she recontextualizes already known elements—problem descriptions, governance templates, established practices—in the new context in such a way that they appear as fixed (enclosure) while simultaneously rendering other entities uncertain and in need of further debate (disclosure). The interplay of both practices is productive because it allows actors to explore what they can already agree on and what requires further negotiation.

To summarize, the book starts from the premise that the emergence of private authority requires explanation because the various actors involved have conflicting interests, convictions, and visions for regulation; in addition, the transnational sphere has few established rules for negotiating these conflicts. As a result, the central source for legitimatizing private authority—expertise—is scattered and conflicting. Private authority, at this stage, appears as *in the making*: that is, knowledge about governance has to be stabilized regarding the content of the problem (policy knowledge), the institutional structures involved (polity knowledge), and the

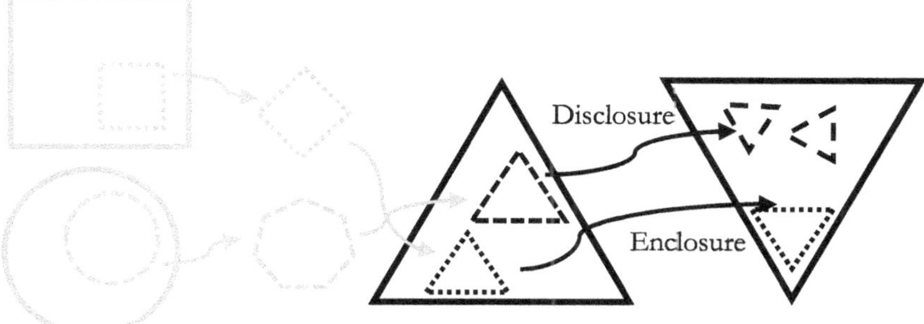

Fig. 2. A visualization of the productive interplay of enclosure/disclosure

process or doing of governance (politics knowledge). The step by step stabilization of knowledge about governance happens when the mechanism of translation is set in motion. Translators recontextualize governance knowledge. As they do so, knowledge about governance becomes transformed and constituted into a new object (e.g., a list of aims). More specifically, translators have to set some elements as stable (enclosure) while opening up others for debate (disclosure). These translational practices ensure the stepwise constitution of private authority.

Dramaturgy as Methodology

To study the mechanism of translation in action, I turn to dramaturgy as a methodological framework. A methodology refers to "those basic assumptions about the world we study, which are prior to the specific techniques adopted by the scholar undertaking research" (Fierke 2004, 36). In a dramaturgical register, these basic assumptions about the world are expressed in metaphors of theater; an actor "performs" a specific "role" in front of an "audience." Dramaturgy fits comfortably within the "family" of practice theory accounts in constructivist IR (Bueger and Gadinger 2015) that study the "socially organized and meaningful patterns of activities" (Pouliot and Thérien 2018, 164). Also, dramaturgy as a specific type of practice theory is increasingly being used to analyze global environmental meetings (Death 2011; Campbell et al. 2014; Aykut et al. 2022) and to examine innovative environmental governance (Hajer and Pelzer 2018; Oomen, Hoffman, and Hajer 2022). The sociology of Erving Goffman has been influential in providing a dramaturgical vocabulary across the social sciences.[22]

TABLE 1. Theoretical Framework for Private Authority Emergence

Why does private authority emergence require explanation?	The presence of diverse actors with conflicting interests, convictions, and visions, as well as the dearth of rules for addressing these conflicts, makes private authority emergence improbable. The legitimizing source of private authority—expertise—is scattered and conflicting.
What has to be stabilized?	Knowledge about governance operationalized as (*a*) policy knowledge: the content of the governance problem, (*b*) polity knowledge: institutions and their design, (*c*) politics knowledge: the process or doing of governance.
How does the mechanism of translation function?	In its basic function, the mechanism of translation is a process in which knowledge about governance is continuously recontextualized. In its more specific function, translators set some elements as technical and stable (enclosure) while others remain open for contestation and debate (disclosure); the two operations depend on each other.
What does the mechanism of translation explain?	The mechanism explains the stepwise process of authority emergence as a new entity is formed.

Goffman (1959, 40) suggests that actors do not have an authentic self but that they rather try to make a specific impression by putting on a mask; they perform what they wish to convey and hide in front of an audience. This is how a performer enacts a role. This role can regulate access to institutional settings and organize the setting itself by allocating the right to speak and participate. Goffman was fascinated by the orderly nature of this interaction that seems distinctively structured and yet constantly emerging (Goffman 1983, 2). Goffman's interaction order revolves around systems of enabling conventions that lift the burden of always having to renegotiate social situations anew (Knoblauch 2020). Greeting practices are a good example as they are shared within communities and differ between cultures. Performers draw on these repertoires of actions and slightly change them when they reinterpret them. Thus, in performing, actors put their and their society's shared knowledge into action, and "display for others the meaning of their social situation" (Alexander 2004, 529). They interpret and negotiate existing knowledge—whether of systems for cutting timber or rules for decision-making—and "recreate those meanings and rules" that aid as well as constrain their actions (Ringmar 2012, 3).[23]

My reading of this process explores the creativity of performances in contrast to accounts that emphasize the constraining effects of practices (Gadinger 2023; Pouliot 2016). In setting the mechanism of translation in motion, actors "bring events and structures into existence . . . , producing constraints and opportunities that were not there before they took action" (Hajer 2009, 7). Thus, performances are performative in the sense that they create and alter social reality. Actors' performances may subvert established systems of knowledge, inventing new forms of framing problems and articulating "how such transformations might be realized" (Benford and Hunt 1992, 48). World politics then, as Ringmar (2012, 3) puts it, "provides a quasi-theatrical setting—a 'world stage'—where states and other actors are often said to act and interact 'before the eyes of the world.'" In studying how this "play" unfolds, we learn how existing discourses are appropriated, which new ideas about governing emerge, and on what terms authority claims are recognized or dismissed. In what follows, I operationalize a dramaturgical methodology by specifying practices of scripting and staging a performance as well as arguing for meetings and documents as settings of world politics.

Scripting: Identifying the Cast and Cues for Appropriate Behavior

Maarten Hajer (2009) describes scripting as efforts to determine the characters and cues for appropriate behavior. A script, then, provides actors "with roles and goals, with lines to read, with instructions for how to act and for 'how to go on'" (Ringmar 2012, 7). In the politics of beginning, scripts are emergent and contested since roles and goals are unclear, the lines to be read remain to be detailed, and often the instructions for how to act and "how to go on" have to be negotiated. What is the "cast of characters" that participates in the dramaturgical cooperation, who could be enlisted as a supporting cast, and which audiences need to be impressed (Benford and Hunt 1992, 39–40; Goffman 1959)? For instance, NGOs may suddenly be confronted with a script that identifies certain business actors no longer as antagonists (those to blame for environmental degradation and social injustice) but as protagonists (those to have the capability of solving a problematic situation). Such a script may evoke efforts at counterscripting, actors twisting the meaning of a particular script.

In scripting, actors reenact already existing scripts for communication in meetings—the "interaction order" (Goffman 1983).[24] Scripts vary from context to context. In more formal conference settings, a keynote speech is probably delivered, followed by dinner or drinks. This format differs from that of a small meeting, for instance in an office, at which an issue like sustainable forestry is collectively discussed. But even in a very informal meeting, actors expect some kind of order such as a beginning and ending. Meetings are "normal things: participants almost invariably know what to do there" (Freeman 2008, 16). Especially in situations in which actors do not share the same frame of reference, participants use metaphors and storylines to build trust and create the basis for action even if they do not "fully understand one another" (Hajer 2009, 62). A metaphor permits a situation to be imagined in terms of another situation (e.g., we need a roadmap so that we can have certainty about the direction we are taking). A storyline condenses narratives of action and links them to discourses (e.g., sustainable development tells us that business interests and environmental concerns are reconcilable).

Staging: Ordering Space, Ordering Time

Staging refers to the socio-material dimension of organizing the interactions of the cast including various artifacts that participants use in accomplishing the meeting (Benford and Hunt 1992). Staging practices aim to order the space and time in which performances unfold. With regard to the ordering of space, Erving Goffman divides the stage into backstage and front stage (Goffman 1959, 32). The backstage is carefully concealed from the audience and the front stage is deliberately displayed. In the realm of politics, the front stage of a meeting is structured by the official agenda and explicit or implicit procedural rules. By contrast, side conversations in small meeting rooms, informal talks during coffee breaks, or a late-night chat at a bar can be seen as the backstage. Political scientists have frequently stressed the significance of the backstage while granting the front stage only theatrical importance.[25] A dramaturgical approach values the front stage analytically because at the front is precisely where knowledge about governance is enacted and deliberation turns into binding decisions.[26] The formal procedural rules that structure the front stage create legitimacy for an emerging political project involving antagonistic actors.

With regard to the order of time, there are different acts with related functions (for instance, introduction, discussion, resolution). The notion of acts in a play permits us to think of an overall theatrical performance in which each act serves a purpose and, consequently, each act has a script that suggests appropriate speeches. One can think of this interplay between structural forces and singular speech acts in terms of resonance. One and the same speech act may resonate well in one act, but will be dismissed in another.[27] Staging these acts and knowing and enforcing their specific scripts is a form of politics knowledge. The knowledge of how to facilitate and structure a negotiation process enables actors to exercise power productively as well as restrictively. This means that actors will have some kind of structure that permits communicative interaction; at the same time, it excludes actors, issues, or speaking modes that do not fit into the structure determined by those who "know the rules of the game." In other words, the dramaturgical framework shows how controversies appear and exclusions are performed not only at the level of content but also with regard to process—the staging of the meeting.

Settings of World Politics: Meetings and Documents

The performances described above take place in settings that are the physical and organizational situation in which the interaction takes place (Hajer 2009). Some of these settings have clear, predefined roles—for example, the priest in church; in other settings roles are emergent and overlapping, particularly in transnational governance. In the interaction speakers interpret their scripts and may develop specialized roles such as facilitating a discussion or engage as "teams" in mutual cooperation (Goffman 1959, 83).

A feature that *meetings* have in common in world politics is that performers have to travel "to the appropriate place and must terminate their performance when they leave it" (Goffman 1959, 33). Hotels are often the temporally bounded settings that function as quasi parliaments for a period of some days, before they again become spaces for leisure time or host another conference. In these settings, which "involve furniture, décor, physical layout, and other background items" (Goffman 1959, 32), performers make appearances in front of a critical audience aiming to affect its interpretation of reality. While international negotiations have emerged as study sites of world politics (Aykut et al. 2022; Hughes and Vadrot 2023; O'Neill and Haas 2019), little is known about negotiations involving private actors. Rules of procedure are not derived from international law and the practices of the United Nations (Johnstone 2011) but are, at least in the early stage of an organization, combinations of various negotiating practices. The dramaturgical perspective examines performances within meetings as well as the formatting role of meetings: performers narrate the recent history of an emerging governance arrangement as a chain of meetings.

Documents—letters, memos, feasibility studies—are settings in their own right. This book not only looks at "what documents say" but "what documents do," that is, the social role they play (Riles 2006). As Kristin Asdal and Hilde Reinertsen (2022, 40) explain, documents "can make something happen, help realise an idea . . . and put an issue in motion." Following this line of inquiry, Steve Hilgartner (2000, 19) sees documents as emerging "not just as semiotic assemblages, rhetorical constructions, or forms of discourse, but also as crucial parts of systems for organizing." Faxes and emails, studies and memoranda, consultation reports, and manifestos connect meetings with one another. These documents mediate between actors who are no longer together but aim to continue their discussion. "Meetings invariably generate documents; in being written down, committed to paper, a policy concept is both fixed and made mobile" (Freeman 2012, 14). Thus, a document collects and represents voices in a meeting, brings them into an order, and thereby transforms what has been said. This chain per se represents a reiterative structure—meeting–document–meeting–document and so forth. It creates an emerging group membership through a suggested shared vocabulary for the project in question, and functions temporarily as the institutional structure for establishing a novel governance arrangement.[28]

Staying within a dramaturgical register, documents are "a device for self-presentation that the performer uses to project his or her 'voice' and create the desired impression" (Hilgartner 2000, 16). The emerging organization circulates documents not only among its own members but also among potential allies to solicit critique as well as request feedback. In so doing, prototypes of institutional design or sets of standards for an emerging governance arrangement are iteratively tested, reworked, and presented again. Through this "ping-pong," performers aim to convince a global audience of their expert knowledge, which legitimizes a specific model of governance (Voß and Simons 2018).

This study takes the above insights seriously and turns to meetings and documents as the basic unit of analysis. Much work goes into the preparation of meetings; reports and fact sheets are drafted, which essentially translate the messiness of "macrocosms" into the structured "microcosm" of a meeting (Callon and Latour 1981). Thus, successful meetings are those in which the scale of phenomena is reduced so that performers are in fact able to negotiate (Callon, Lascoumes, and Barthe 2009, 49). This is an ongoing task of translation in which performers prepare scripts for their future actions. Meetings, like documents, always have a double function: they are the working units of transnational politics in which an emerging arrangement is specified. At the same time, they are a means to showcase expertise in order to convince an audience of authoritative claims. From a

TABLE 2. Dramaturgy as Methodology

Performance:	describes the act of putting shared knowledge into action; performances are performative in the sense that they create and alter social reality.
Interaction:	revolves around systems of enabling conventions (scripts); they lift the burden of always negotiating social situations anew.
Scripting:	efforts to determine the characters and cues for appropriate behavior by mobilizing metaphors and storylines.
Staging:	the spatial and temporal dimension of organizing the interaction of the cast including various artifacts.
Settings:	the physical and organizational situation in which the interaction takes place; meetings and documents are the central settings to consider.

dramaturgical perspective, social actors compete for private authority by staging meetings globally and producing expert documents.[29]

In sum, dramaturgy provides a methodology for studying the mechanism of translation in action. It uses metaphors of theater to describe interactions that are ordered and yet emergent, creating and altering social reality. With the help of dramaturgy, this book identifies meetings and documents as central settings in which performers engage in translational practices.

Method and Data

When politics is conceptualized as a sequence of staged performances, the approach ideally requires one to take a seat in the front row and become a spectator. Ethnography, the method of "being there" and "getting close," is a default choice because it is sensitive to the socio-material context in which interactions unfold (Pachirat 2018). This method has gained relevance in global environmental politics because researchers have immersed themselves in meetings involving state and nonstate actors, turning them into study sites (Aykut et al. 2022; Campbell et al. 2014; Hughes and Vadrot 2023). The limited duration of environmental summits does not align with an ethnography based on "casually hanging out" with someone that may require months or even years. Instead, it demands a "focused ethnography" that produces "a large amount of data in a relatively short time period," typically through audio or video recordings (Knoblauch 2005, para. 16). After a field trip, such recordings can be collectively interpreted in data sessions with colleagues.

Since ethnographers at summits have little time to carry out their observations, focused ethnography has to be specially attuned to the "imports" and "exports" that become relevant in meetings (Scheffer 2023). Imports include preparatory documents for negotiations as well as invited and noninvited participants, whereas exports refer to the texts that are adopted as well as themes that do not find expression in a text. The imports and exports link staged performances with one another. Thus, focused ethnography demands a "trans-sequential analysis" (Scheffer 2023) that follows the collectively generated products through a series of staged performances to study the becoming or making of the entity in question.

Given that the emergence of private authority and the FSC in particular took place in the late 1980s, I had to develop an ethnography that was "focused" and "trans-sequential" but also historical. The practice of such an ethnography is "a form of disciplined reading in which one engages in a kind of 'participant-observation' of the textual records of some legitimation struggle, jotting 'fieldnotes' as one reads—much as one would when studying the social practices of some group of people" (Jackson 2015, 276). Interviews and, increasingly, audio and video recordings allow one to diversify the dataset.

This book deploys a broad range of data to trace the emergence of the FSC. But where to start? Patrick Jackson (2015, 274) recommends one should "begin at the point at which a legitimation struggle concretely takes place, then move 'backward' in time to sketch out the specific historical context, and finally come back 'forward' in time to the resolution of the concrete legitimation struggle itself." Following this advice, my entry point into the research process was the three-day Founding Assembly of the FSC in Toronto lasting from Friday evening to Sunday afternoon in October 1993 (chapters 4, 5, and 6). It marks a relevant situation because struggles over the process and aims of the FSC were still taking place while at the end of the weekend participants agreed to found the organization and temporarily settled conflicts. This process of closure can be traced in detail because this book features rare empirical data—sixteen hours of audio files out of a two-and-a-half-day conference. The audio files required a reflexive analysis because only the speeches that were uttered into the two microphones were recorded; the microphones prestructured the assembly since they represented legitimate speaking positions. In situations in which the recorder was switched off—as was the case during breaks (coffee, lunch, dinner), or when delegates met in smaller groups—nothing was recorded.

From the assembly, I moved "'backward' in time" to examine the making of the specific "'imports" for the assembly such as the emerging organizational structure (chapter 3) and to "sketch out the specific historical context" (Jackson 2015, 274) in which private authority and the FSC emerged (chapter 2). To move backward in time, I examined primary sources that founding members of the FSC circulated between 1988 and 1993.[30] These documents consist of letters, meeting notes and memorandums, study proposals, country reports that were conducted on behalf of the emerging FSC, and drafts of the Principles and Criteria for sustainable forestry (for a full list, see the appendix). To acquire further background knowledge, I visited the hotel in Toronto in which the Founding Assembly took place. To triangulate the data, I conducted eight interviews with key founding members who represent different interests within the FSC. The semistructured interviews lasted between 25 and 45 minutes.[31] I moved "'forward' in time" (Jackson 2015, 274) by attending the seventh General Assembly of the FSC in Kota Kinabalu, Malaysia in 2011. I used this assembly as a contrast to the "politics of beginning" as represented by the Founding Assembly in 1993. Finally, I consulted the scientific literature on forest politics of the late 1980s as well as the secondary literature on the FSC to collect more empirical details on the case and the historical context of global environmental politics.

Adhering to the practice of ethnography, I worked with the emerging set of data in iterative cycles, coding with pen and paper as well as with the computer software MaxQda. In my coding practice I followed Kathy Charmaz's notion of constructivist grounded theory. Coding is the first step on the "analytical stairway" that entails "naming segments of data with a label that simultaneously categorizes, summarizes, and accounts for each piece" (Charmaz 2006, 43). While reading transcripts one asks oneself which theoretical category (code) this statement might belong in. In so doing, one moves beyond the data on the one hand without losing touch with them on the other.[32] I presented data at joint sessions in which colleagues engaged in the collective interpretation of the material.[33] Such sessions make the subjective interpretation intersubjectively accessible, open the room for peer-group critique at an early stage of the research process, and count as reliability and validity tests (Knoblauch 2005).

In line with the methodology of dramaturgy and ethical research practice, this book refrains from using the real names of the FSC founding members. Instead, I developed first name pseudonyms to refer to the actors. For instance, they appear in the text as Maria, I cite them as (Maria, 1990), and they can be found in the bibliography as Maria [pseud.] 1990. Also, when I quote my interview partners, I disclose their professional activity or organization. The in-text citation is, for instance, (interview, FoE activist, 08/12/2011).

The Chapters Ahead

Chapter 2 elaborates on the epistemic context of forests and governance in the late 1980s. I will show that the narrow vision of scientific forestry was broadened to include political, social, and cultural concerns (policy knowledge). The emerging international organizations governing forests focused mainly on the timber trade and remained dominated by North–South conflicts. As a consequence, NGOs and concerned wood users explored new avenues and institutions for saving the forests, including mobilizing various forces from the market (polity knowledge). Finally, I will show how, at the peak of the environmental movement, the discourse of sustainable development partly tamed the confrontational tactics of NGOs. The belief in win–win options and deliberation made possible a turn from confrontation to cooperation (politics knowledge). The reconstruction of these knowledge structures is essential, since participants in the Founding Assembly (chapters 4, 5, and 6) continuously referred to events, metaphors, and storylines from these three frontiers of governance knowledge.

It is against this background that chapter 3 begins by following actors who eventually became founding members of the FSC. It revisits the islands of innovation where actors experimented with novel forms of forestry. On these islands, governance knowledge was produced that provided the epistemic foundation for the emerging FSC. Introducing the translational mechanism in action, the chapter examines practices of *recontextualizing* knowledge about governance and explores how, in meetings and documents, actors outlined what they constructed as known and established (practices of *enclosure*), and what they thought of as requiring further work (practices of *disclosure*). The dramaturgical perspective foregrounds the instrumental character of documents and meetings for negotiations; the emerging organization circulated documents not only among its members but among potential allies to increase the legitimacy of the novel governance arrangement as well as to request feedback.

Chapter 4, 5, and 6 form the empirical centerpiece of the book. They examine in a detailed microanalysis the three-day-long FSC Founding Assembly in 1993. The assembly is presented as a drama with different characters, acts, and a reflective chorus. Throughout the assembly dissenting voices were excluded, since they did not resonate with the script as constructed by the interim board and the facilitator. The main argument is that, through a series of translations, the assembly was finally able to manufacture a consensus and found the FSC. Polity and politics knowledge became of particular importance in the process, given the institutional ambiguity in which the participants were operating.

The concluding chapter, chapter 7, opens with a reflection on "constitutional moments" (Jasanoff 2011) and the ways in which the FSC has shaped private authority ever since. It then outlines the implications of the book with regard to three major themes of world politics—authority, expertise, and negotiations.

2 | Knowing the Global Forest

Epistemic Frontiers of the Late 1980s

It is early in the morning; you draft a few thoughts in your diary. Most likely, the paper on which you write, the coffee you have freshly brewed, and even the shirt you are wearing have been subject to governance. Private certification schemes formulate standards for sustainable forestry (your diary) and agriculture (your coffee), or they aim at protecting workers' rights in the garment industry (your shirt) (Esguerra 2023). Certification instruments pervade our daily life.

It was different in the 1980s. Back then, certification and other rules governing consumer products were just emerging (Green 2014, chap. 3). Across sectors, people began to search for alternatives to products that give rise to ecological devastation and social injustice. Early initiatives in the coffee sector inspired those who were concerned about sustainable forestry, while alternative trade organizations nurtured market awareness (Auld 2014, 157). Community forest projects in Latin America developed methods that aligned the economic use of tropical forests with their social and political visions. Thus, the 1980s can be characterized as a time in which concerned wood users, timber retailers, and members of social and environmental NGOs began researching alternatives to state governance (Bartley 2007b). They faced the tremendous challenge of inventing a new system of governance, one that would operate largely independently of the political and epistemic authority of state bureaucracy (Cutler, Haufler, and Porter 1999b; Hall and Biersteker 2002a; Pattberg 2007; Dingwerth 2007).

This making of private authority required the production of specific governance knowledge. I show throughout this book that the construction of sustainable forest certification was also an exercise in creating knowledge about nonstate governance. Since its inception, the rules and norms of forest certification have served as a script for other arrangements

(Dingwerth and Pattberg 2009; Auld 2014; Green 2014). In other words, to follow actors in the creative process of innovating transnational forest governance is to explore how nonstate actors generated knowledge to convince others of their claims to authority.

This chapter concentrates on the knowledge structures of forestry governance in the late 1980s. It is an exercise in translation and dramaturgy because it prepares the ground for "investigating the ways in which agents draw on discourse and employ it in their deliberations" (Ringmar 2012, 2). When NGOs, timber retailers, concerned wood users, and others engaged in the making of the FSC, they enacted, appropriated, and in fact changed established structures of knowledge and meaning about global forest governance (Arts and Buizer 2009).

I argue that we can observe the emergence of three epistemic frontiers, which enabled the emergence of private authority. (1) On the level of policy knowledge, I will show that the narrow vision of scientific forestry was broadened by integrating political, social, and cultural concerns; the notion of policy knowledge answers the question "What is to be governed?" (2) On the level of polity knowledge, the emerging international organizations governing the forest focused mainly on the timber trade and remained dominated by North–South conflicts. As a consequence, NGOs and concerned wood users explored the idea of establishing new institutions for saving the forest including using market forces. Polity knowledge answers the question "Who governs?" (3) On the level of politics knowledge, I will show how, at the peak of the environmental movement, the discourse of sustainable development partly tamed the confrontational tactics of NGOs. The belief in win–win options and deliberation made possible a turn from confrontation to cooperation; politics knowledge answers the question of how governance is performed.

The reconstruction of this sociopolitical context is essential, since participants in the Founding Assembly (chapters 4, 5, 6) continuously referred to events, metaphors, and storylines relating to these three frontiers of knowledge and, in their performances, translated broader structures of knowledge into the microsituation in which they negotiated the nascent FSC.

Sustained Yield Management, Tropical Deforestation, and Social Injustice

The history of the forest is closely intertwined with the emergence of forestry as a science. As a distinct system of meaning, it has strongly influenced how humans in the Global North (though less so in the Global

South) think of and try to manage forests (Hölzl 2010). In the late eighteenth century, forestry science was developed in Prussia and Saxony (Germany), and traveled from there to France, England, the United States, and throughout the Global South. Forestry, like any other science, did not develop outside politics; its emergence needs to be understood "in the larger context of the centralized state-making initiatives of the period" (Scott 1998, 14). The forest was as much an administrative category, with serious implications for land rights and land use, as it was a description of an accumulation of trees on a piece of land.

The continuing popularity of eighteenth-century forestry is due to the concept of "sustained yield management," which essentially prescribes that no more timber should be removed than a forest is capable of regenerating (von Carlowitz and von Rohr 1732). Since then, foresters have continued to be preoccupied with forest growth rates, and their models have focused on the volume that can be harvested. Regardless of the narrowness of this view, "sustained yield management" as a concept is still evoked in the competing discourses on sustainable development and their institutionalization (Sachs 2015; Bernstein 2001; Beder 1994; Arts and Buizer 2009).

In the late nineteenth century, the narrow and economically motivated vision of forestry became challenged. In Europe and North America, a plurality of conservation movements emerged that emphasized the protection of nature. In California, the Sierra Club was founded in 1892 to campaign for the preservation of "forests and other natural features of the Sierra Nevada Mountains" (Sierra Club, cited in Falkner 2022, 86). In Europe, initiatives were formed that linked environmental protection and cultural identity. Also at that time, conservation scientists experienced an intensive professionalization and organized the first international meetings of scientific associations. Colonialism became a driving force as biologists and zoologists traveled to the colonies to explore the diverse flora and fauna. Similar to other governance practices, the colonies became the "an incubator for new ecological thinking and conservation practices that were later applied in Europe and North America" (Falkner 2022, 88). Thus, the late nineteenth and early twentieth century witnessed the rise of an elite-driven environmentalism that was to some extent already internationalized but lacked broad societal support.

A breakthrough for the environmental movement in general and issues of forest protection more specifically appeared in the 1970s. The global implications of many environmental issues were formulated, while the local origins were emphasized. For instance, conservationist scientists began inquiring into deforestation with a specific focus on deforestation in the tropics. In 1972 the International Union for the Conservation of Nature and Natural Resources (IUCN) and the World Wildlife Fund (WWF) raised concerns in a letter to the Brazilian president, pointing out "the need for careful consideration of the environmental problems involved in Amazonian development" (cited in Keck 2001, 35). In 1986 renowned biologists, philosophers, and economists met at the National Forum on BioDiversity in Washington, DC, and coined the term biodiversity—back then spelled with a capital B (Wilson 1988). The idea of biodiversity was not only an attempt to make the biological diversity of the planet a present reality and a means to create an inventory of all species, it also conveyed the concerned scientists' hope to increase their say in policy decisions (Höhler 2014; Takacs 1996). Thus, one of the themes of the conference was to collect data on deforestation in areas rich in biodiversity, namely the tropics, and to map what nowadays are called "biodiversity hotspots" (Nadim 2016, 76).

As I will outline in greater detail below, the 1980s saw the rise of environmental and social movements that politicized the conservationist framing of tropical deforestation. These movements called attention to the social and customary implications of logging practices. Not surprisingly, NGO campaigns refused to rely solely on the policy knowledge of scientists to accurately describe the practices and consequences of deforestation. For instance, Vandana Shiva (1993) described the practices of "scientific forestry" as reductionist or a "monoculture of the mind" and contrasted these practices with local knowledge systems. Similarly, Margaret E. Keck and Kathryn Sikkink (1998, 161) pointed out that NGOs "insisted on different criteria of expertise" and "demanded equal time for direct testimony about experience." But how did knowledge travel from the local practices of people living in tropical regions to the local yet transnational site of a World Bank meeting room?

Knowledge does not travel freely but relies on translators who can bridge different worlds and thus account for the movement of knowledge (Tsing 2005). A number of Western activists played a key role in this transnational translation process; they often joined communities in the Amazon or Southeast Asia for their doctoral research. Consider the following interview passage:

> In the early 1980s, I was living in Venezuela in the Amazon living with a very remote Indian tribe. . . . And I got very concerned on what was happening on the frontier, the racism, and the diseases,

and the suffering of the people on the frontier and I changed from being an academic to being an activist in my mentality and finished off my doctorate to get out of it as quick as possible to dedicate myself to activism. (interview, World Rainforest Movement activist, 06/29/2011)

Often highly educated, these activists built close ties with influential NGOs in the US and the UK, and linked them back to local struggles. Two cases have become transnational metaphors to show the unity of environmental and equity struggles—the rubber tappers in western Brazil and the Penan people in Sarawak, Malaysia (Keck 1995). Since participants in the FSC Founding Assembly referred to the rubber tappers' movement repeatedly, I will outline this case and in doing so exemplify the ways in which translation operates.

The rubber tappers' movement began as a social movement in Acre, western Brazil in the mid-1970s. What started as a spontaneous resistance to "deforestation, expulsion of local communities, assassinations, working conditions similar to slave labor" was institutionalized into the National Council of Rubber Tappers in 1985 (Schwartzman 1992, 207). The National Council of Rubber Tappers successfully proposed the creation of *extractive reserves* as a way of legally occupying land in the Amazon. It became a governance instrument that allowed local communities to use the land while simultaneously preventing deforestation. The creation of the reserves was the result of their successfully joining forces with national and international NGOs. However, the journey from a local struggle to a topic of international concern required a series of translations that can be exemplified by the following transnational actors.

Stephan Schwartzman conducted fieldwork as an anthropologist in the Amazon region and returned to the US in 1984 where he eventually started working for the Environmental Defense Fund. Schwartzman, together with Mary Allegretto and Tony Gross, anthropologists with Oxfam, operated as a "translator" between the local social movement and campaigners from environmental NGOs in the US who had decided to target World Bank projects in the Amazon region. For the alliance between a social movement and environmental NGOs to become successful, a translation process had to be carried out that required the transformation of the original object of concern. The NGOs convinced Chico Mendes, the charismatic leader of the rubber tappers' movement, to frame social "demands for justice within an appeal to save the rain forest" (Keck 1995, 416). Environmental and equity struggles were now communicated as belonging together. In March 1987, environmental NGOs invited Chico Mendes to Washington, DC, to speak with members of Congress and with World Bank staff. Thanks to his visit to the US, and his involvement in the campaigns by the NGOs, he became a well-known figure on the international level. While the rubber tappers' movement was barely known in Brazil itself, Chico Mendes received the UN Environment Program's Global 500 award for his contribution to environmental protection. In December 1988 Chico Mendes was assassinated in Acre, Brazil by landowners who had good reason to expect impunity due to the passivity of the Brazilian authorities. However, his death led to an international outcry: the *Washington Post* ran a headline "Thousands in Brazil Attend Slain Ecologist's Funeral" (Washington Post 1988), and within two years a series of newspaper articles, books, and even a film on his life appeared in the United States (Brook 1990). In collaboration with international media, NGO campaigns created an ecological martyr. Ecological and social struggles personified in the figure of Chico Mendes appeared as one struggle taking place in the Amazon region. The struggle led to the setting up of the governance instrument "extractive reserves" that proved the ability of poor local communities to become protagonists in the creation of solutions rather than being the recipient of solutions "imagined elsewhere" (Keck 1995, 417).

The dramaturgical perspective developed in this book suggests that documents and meetings played a pivotal role in transforming a union, social, and local struggle into an ecological and transnational concern. Schwartzman and other fellow activists have reflected on their actions in writing, and thus translated action into a medium that can easily be circulated. In so doing they did not necessarily resolve any of these conflicts, but they did create a distinct form of visibility. Consider the list of publications between 1984 (when Schwartzman started publishing) and 1993. Schwartzman published his first article in the *International Journal of American Linguistics* on linguistic humor in 1984. It discusses aspects of his fieldwork in the Amazon area and focuses on a single issue in linguistics. Yet, when he returned to the US in 1984, his publications began to address the struggle of the rubber tappers in the region (Schwartzman 1986, 1988, 1989, 1991, 1992; Arnt and Schwartzman 1992; Clement, Nepstad, and Schwartzman 1993; Nepstad and Schwartzman 1992). Schwartzman has been able to use the codes of both academia and activism in becoming a translator. He has spoken on behalf of the rubber tappers' movement in a variety of arenas in the Global North to which Brazilian rubber tappers did not have access. As a result, the narrow focus on sustained yield management has been challenged, and power as the ability to represent has become a fundamental issue in the travel and circulation of knowledge.

Emerging Institutions for the Global Forest

In the early twentieth century, Theodore Roosevelt made nature conservation an integral part of his domestic program and also initiated an international conservation agenda that led to a few international cooperation agreements on conservation matters (Falkner 2022, chap. 4). But it was not before the mid-twentieth century that states created international institutions for the global forest (Pülzl 2010). Back then, the issue of "who governs" was clearly associated with states. In 1966 the United Nations Conference on Trade and Development (UNCTAD) proposed that a tropical timber bureau should be established.[1] But it was not until 1983 that 36 producer countries and 34 consumer countries, under the auspices of UNCTAD, drew up the International Tropical Timber Agreement, which entered into force in 1985 (Pattberg 2007, 104). The decision-making body of the agreement is the International Tropical Timber Organization (ITTO), headquartered in Yokohama, Japan. The ITTO council met for the first time in March 1987. Its meetings became venues in which NGOs such as the IUCN and the WWF lobbied for more awareness of tropical forest degradation (Auld 2014, 64). Although the aim of the organization was to ensure both sustainable use and conservation, Steven Bernstein and Benjamin Cashore (2004, 46) point out that the forest negotiations were seen very much in the context of "international trade and economic development, not primarily [that of] environmental protection or conservation."

This assessment is congruent with the voting system within the organization since the votes of consumer countries are apportioned according to the amount they import, and similarly, those of producer countries are calculated on the basis of the amount they export. Marcus Colchester from the World Rainforest Movement[2] concluded in 1990:

> *The net result is that the more a country destroys tropical forest, the more votes it gets.* The voting structure ensures that the ITTO's primary role of promoting the timber trade heavily outweighs its secondary conservation role. (Colchester 1990, 167, italics in the original)

The quote illustrates a broader dissatisfaction on the part of the NGO community with the structure of the ITTO and their attempts to influence ITTO negotiations (Finger and Princen 1994; Humphreys 2004). Despite their continuous lobbying, the groups felt that the ITTO did not sufficiently address the urgent problems of deforestation; and yet the meetings of the ITTO had a community-building function. As a WWF official recalls, "I think ITTO, whether it intended to or not, played a role as a kind of forum where lots of people came together, and quite a number of those same people ended up being involved in FSC" (cited in Auld 2014, 71).

A second attempt by the World Bank and the World Resource Institute to deal with the international problem of deforestation was the Tropical Forest Action Plan (TFAP). The plan is designed to allocate development aid to tropical countries by creating national forest programs (Pattberg 2007, 104). In 1990, three years after the plan became operational, the World Rainforest Movement conducted a detailed study of nine national plans, and concluded that the TFAP "is systematically failing to achieve its objectives. . . . The national plans are promoting a massive increase in logging in primary forests" (Colchester and Lohmann 1990). Also, more academically orientated assessments argue that the TFAP is overly centralized, removed from the political realities on the ground, and too dependent on the priorities of donors (Humphreys 2012).

In the run-up to the Earth Summit in Rio de Janeiro, the issue of biodiversity and deforestation gained further attention. Members of the United Nations Educational, Scientific and Cultural Organization (UNESCO), the United Nations Environmental Programme, and scientific organizations introduced biodiversity as a central policy issue for the Rio Agenda; it became further institutionalized with the Convention on Biological Diversity, which entered into force in 1993. Similarly, NGOs lobbied extensively for a text that would encompass both boreal and tropical forests, and include the full range of forest values with an emphasis of indigenous peoples' rights.

With the Declaration of Rio de Janeiro in 1992, the international community formulated a "first global consensus on forests" that was expressed in 15 principles (United Nations 1992). The preamble to the Declaration stresses that "forestry issues and opportunities should be examined in a holistic and balanced manner . . . taking into consideration the multiple functions and uses of forests, including traditional uses" (United Nations 1992). At first glance, the declaration appears to have been a success for the environmental and social movement. Yet the consensus was degraded to a "non-legally binding authoritative statement" that therefore rather reflects the deep political conflict between northern states and southern states.

Southern states, notably Malaysia and India, "feared that northern states would dictate how forests within the jurisdiction of southern states should be managed" (Bernstein and Cashore 2004, 47; Bernstein 2001, 102). As a result, developing countries did not even consider agreeing to any legally binding statements in Rio. Thus, NGO efforts to advocate for a strong international agreement on forests had failed. While NGOs continued lobbying in the corridors of international organizations such as the ITTO (Humphreys 2004), they also directed their creative potential to private regulation initiatives bypassing states.

From Confrontation to Cooperation

The 1980s experienced an interesting shift in how politics is done. The politics knowledge of that time was defined by two developments that together enabled the creation of a new form of governance. First, social and environmental NGOs engaged in very confrontational politics. The rising global environmental movement of the 1980s politicized environmental politics and created public support for a variety of concerns. The depletion of the ozone layer, nuclear tests and catastrophes, and, indeed, tropical deforestation were the most prominent themes that NGOs put onto the (inter)national agenda. With their campaigns covering the front pages of newspapers they experienced a rapid growth in membership in the US. Whereas in 1979 the total membership of environmental NGOs stood at about two million, by 1990 membership had grown to nearly seven million (Van Der Heijden 1999, 201). Western Europe experienced a similar rise in environmental concern that led to the founding of green parties and to growth in the membership of Greenpeace, the WWF, and Friends of the Earth (FoE) in particular (Huber 2011).

While the more conservationist community had focused on deforestation and biodiversity loss, the advocacy networks in the 1980s "deliberately politicized the issue," and thus brought "new urgency to older concerns" (Keck and Sikkink 1998, 161). The tactics and techniques of NGOs differed, following the classic "carrot and stick logic." The WWF, as a more traditional NGO, engaged in dialogue with companies over sustainability guidelines, which led to some symbolic claims about the sustainability of their products (Upton and Bass 1996, 139). For instance, WWF-UK conducted a seminar with large do-it yourself retailers entitled "Forests Are Your Business" that led to the setting up of the WWF 95 group. The ten companies in this group agreed to phase out of the purchase and sale of nonsustainable wood and wood products by 1995 (Pattberg 2007, 106). At the same time, the Rainforest Action Network and Greenpeace in the United States and Friends of the Earth in Europe launched visible campaigns and called for boycotts targeted against the private sector (Domask 2003). Well-known companies such as Scott Paper, the British home improvement retailers B&Q, and Home Depot in the United States saw themselves exposed to "symbolically dramatic strategies, like bringing giant inflatable chainsaws to protests in stores' parking lots" (Bartley 2007a, 237).

The call for boycotts found resonance. In 1988 the European Parliament voted to "recommend Malaysian Timber bans to European Union members until its logging became sustainable" (Keck and Sikkink 1998, 158). Although the decision was later overturned by the European Commission, it indicates that the call for boycotts did not remain at the level of private governance but had consequences even for intergovernmental politics. Survival International and the World Rainforest Movement "called for boycotts from Malaysian timber specially, and called for boycott to tourism to Malaysia" (interview, World Rainforest Movement activist, 06/29/2011). Activists in the US and Europe had also begun to publicly accuse the World Bank for its projects in Latin America and Southeast Asia that were harmful to the local populations and indigenous communities.

The controversy over practices of deforestation led then in the early 1990s to the politicization of international institutions. Representatives from Malaysia, Indonesia, and also Brazil attacked European countries for their policy proposals with regard to tropical timber. They threatened to summon European countries before a panel of the General Agreement on Tariffs and Trade (GATT) "for infringing international free trade agreements and discriminating against Third World countries" (Kolk 1996, 44).

Tim Bartley (2003) shows the rise of public attention in the *New York Times* and *Los Angeles Times* regarding rainforest deforestation between 1980 and 2000. The discourse peaked around 1989/90, which underlines that the controversy was prominent at the time when the founding members of the FSC were beginning to constitute the organization. A founding member of the FSC described the controversy in the United States in particular as so "polarized and emotionally loaded that it was really hard to even get people to sit down and have a constructive dialogue" (interview, forester and consultant, 06/28/2011).

If polarization and politicization describe one dimension of politics knowledge, a new paradigm of cooperation and integration defines a second dimension. This second dimension became prominent with the rise of the contested concept of sustainable development (Jacobs 1999). The environmentalists of the 1970s had used the notion of sustainability to declare that exponential growth could not simply be continued because of the planet's finite resources (Beder 1994). The United Nations Conference on the Human Environment in Stockholm in 1972 had also framed development and environmental protection as "different, often competing tasks" (Bernstein 2001, 47). By contrast, the concept of sustainable development as specified and institutionalized in the 1980s and early 1990s sought ways to make economic growth sustainable.

The Brundtland Report, *Our Common Future* (1987), and the subsequent Rio Earth Summit (1992) are paradigmatic for this shift as they played a key role in the establishment of "sustainable development" as a "widely approved and at the same time vague" political norm (Höhler and Ziegler 2010, 422). They cemented what Steven Bernstein has labeled the compromise of liberal environmentalism, a compromise that "predicates environmental protection on the promotion and maintenance of a liberal economic order" (Bernstein 2001, 4). Three aspects are of special importance for understanding the kind of politics knowledge that emerged.

First, the report and the subsequent Rio Summit framed sustainable development as the successful integration of social, environmental, and economic needs in current and future societies. To have a healthy environment and a healthy economy are not contradictions; in fact, they condition one another. At the end of the day, "pollution prevention pays" (Hajer 1995, 26). This "belief in 'win-win-options' is one of the core assumptions of the (mainstream) sustainability discourse" that was essential in structuring the discourse on global forestry (Arts and Buizer 2009, 344). It discursively paved the way for environmental and social NGOs to work together with industry.

Second, the Rio Summit started to institutionalize the norm of participation by various societal groups and deliberation into a number of principles (Bernstein 2001, 107). Participatory modes of governance and broad public inclusion in decision making were termed a "prerequisite for the achievement of sustainable development" in the preamble to Agenda 21, which was also adopted in Rio (United Nations Conference on Environment and Development 1992, chap. 23). Thus, deliberative ideals have not only featured in scholarly discourses (Habermas 1981), but have been promoted in multilateral as well as local contexts (Bäckstrand et al. 2010, 7). From participating in state institutions to creating private institutions that claim authority beyond the state itself is only a small, though essential, step.

A final aspect concerns the management of the environment. The Brundtland Report already suggested that economic instruments and market-based solutions were the mechanisms best able to achieve a synthesis of growth and environmental protection; the Rio Declaration further strengthened this claim, promoting a "preference for market-based instruments over purely regulatory methods" (Bernstein 2001, 108). Thus, the premodels and experiments with certification or alternative trade initiatives that emerged in the 1980s (see next chapter) were legitimated by an emerging normative consensus institutionalized at the Rio Summit (Bartley 2003). However, contestations over these instruments existed in the late 1980s, as I will show in chapter 4, and they still exist today (Turnhout 2018). Knowing how to cooperate despite antagonistic positions is essential for the success of these instruments.

Conclusion: Policy, Polity, and Politics Knowledge Concerning the Global Forest

In the late twentieth century, knowledge of the global forest was contested, and this chapter has outlined the epistemic frontiers relevant for the emergence of a new form of governance. The analytics of policy, polity, and politics knowledge can be summed up in three questions. First, "What is to be governed?" encapsulates the policy issue of the global forest (policy knowledge). Within a decade the meaning of the global forest changed considerably. The paradigmatic scientific forestry of sustained yield management of the eighteenth century had simplified the biological composition of forests. While this narrow vision was never without contestation (Hölzl 2010), the emergence of the biodiversity concept in 1986 revealed a more nuanced picture (Takacs 1996). A community of conservationist scientists and NGOs pointed to the rich biodiversity of (mostly) tropical forests and lobbied for international agreements to stop deforestation (Falkner 2022). However, transnational activists claimed in the late 1980s that deforestation was not only a scientifically countable loss of biodiversity but also a political problem to do with land rights and displacement. They proposed a holistic understanding of the nature–human relationship that would in principle value divergent understandings of using and engaging with the forest. Activists from the Global South challenged the notion of tropical deforestation by referring to the huge deforestation that already had taken place in boreal regions.

Second, the question of "Who governs?" prompts an inquiry into the institutions of the global forest (polity knowledge). The most important international fora, the ITTO, the TFAP, and the Rio Earth Summit remained deadlocked by North–South conflicts as well as focused on trade rather than the protection of biodiversity and indigenous peoples. In the early 1990s environmental and social NGOs were increasingly able to redefine the issue (Humphreys 2004). International institutions began incorporating a language recognizing the multiple values of forests, yet this language lacked binding authority. Thus, the opening up of international institutions did not sufficiently address the concerns of civil society; state power remained an essential blocker of innovative forms of governance. Market instruments promised a more flexible and needs-based form of governance. Little polity knowledge was, however, available on how such instruments could work in practice.

Finally, the notion of "how to govern" addresses the means and tactics of actors (politics knowledge). Deforestation emerged as an international environmental challenge through the continuous lobbying of a community of conservationist scientists and NGOs. Transnational activists turned it into a global public issue in the mid-1980s. They targeted states and the timber industry for their practices of deforestation and their displacement of local and indigenous peoples. Aggressive campaigns, boycotts, and extensive lobbying were part of the repertoire of politics knowledge, until the emerging sustainable development discourse introduced a new cooperative notion to it. The promise of the win–win rhetoric suggested that the power of the market could integrate social and environmental concerns. This (com)promise of liberal environmentalism (Bernstein 2001), however, was anything but consensual when FSC founding members began practicing, researching, and mapping alternative governance models in the late 1980s. The founding of the FSC took place at the beginning of a process of normalization of private governance that caused conflicts (Uribe 2024). I turn to these disputes in the next chapter.

3 | Translating Governance Knowledge

Toward a Certification System for Sustainable Forestry

Having discussed the discursive changes in the field of forestry, my aim in this chapter is to explain the social interactions in a situation where private authority is in the making—where knowledge controversies are ongoing, institutional structures are liquid, and those who are already in the cast still have to convince potential members and others to adopt rules and standards. The chapter introduces the translational mechanism in action; it shows practices of *recontextualizing* knowledge about governance, and it explores how in meetings and documents actors outlined what they constructed as known and established (practices of *enclosure*), and what they thought of as requiring further work (practices of *disclosure*). All in all, this translational mechanism was the engine of a negotiation process that stabilized or constituted a new political project.

I begin the analysis by revisiting some of the "islands of innovation." Foresters, NGOs, activists, and others who eventually became founding members of the FSC practiced new forms of forestry (policy knowledge) and developed models of governance beyond the state (polity knowledge). I show how this knowledge of governance was created and how specific actors started to ask if it could be applied beyond its local context. To travel, it had to be packaged and performed at transnational conferences (practices of recontextualization). I show how these translational practices created controversies over representation, and how the very idea of sustainable forestry was met with skepticism. Despite this skepticism, however, people working in forest operations engaged in a politics of beginning: they enclosed uncertainty and disclosed issues that deserved further thought. In so doing, they laid out various paths toward a certification organization.

In a second step, I introduce the Certification Working Group, which consisted of concerned wood users and members of environmental NGOs. This "team," to borrow Goffman's (1959) term, engaged in impression management. To create the impression of a global endeavor addressing all sectors, the team worked on its own composition: in its institutional design it recontextualized southern representatives and carefully balanced all interested parties. It also recontextualized the emerging governance knowledge on sustainable forestry (policy knowledge) and private governance (polity and politics knowledge) into a set of standards and the FSC charter.

The final section elaborates on the global consultative process of the emerging FSC. This was essentially a test of whether the proposed governance structure as well as the principles and criteria for sustainable forestry would resonate with various audiences across the globe. In other words, the emerging FSC tested whether their newly constituted governance knowledge could be recontextualized elsewhere. Thus, these documents were a means to showcase governance knowledge in order to convince others of the FSC's claims to authority.

Islands of Innovation

Throughout the 1980s deforestation in conjunction with social injustice was an object of campaigning. Actors around the globe searched for alternative means to protect as well as to use timber (Auld 2014). I outline some of these projects in which founding members of the FSC were involved out of an interest in the knowledge about governance that arose from these cases and was translated into documents and meetings.

The Yanesha Forestry Cooperative in Peru

The Yanesha Forestry Cooperative in Peru is one of the islands of innovation on which foresters, indigenous peoples, and activists experimented with new forestry practices. Anthony, founding member of the FSC, worked at the cooperative in the 1980s. In an interview, he recalls that, until the mid-1980s, the general paradigm was that natural tropical forests are not manageable since they are too complex and too diverse (interview, forester and consultant, 06/28/2011).[1] Having this paradigm in mind, he started working in natural tropical forests in Paraguay and Ecuador where he experienced an "eruption of new information, new understanding of the dynamics of natural forest management" (interview, June 28, 2011). In

1984, he moved to Peru where he cofounded the first indigenous forestry cooperative, Cooperative Forestal Yanesha (COFYAL), in the Palcazu Valley of eastern Peru in May 1986. Being located in the Amazon region, the area is wet and the valley alone contains over 1,500 tree species. The cooperative originated from a transdisciplinary project between the Pichis-Palaczu Project that had administered a road-building project for the Peruvian government, the Costa Rican research institute Tropical Science Center, and the native communities, the Yanesha, living in the area (Simeone, Pariona, and Lázaro 1993).[2]

What started as a series of workshops on land use, concepts of sustainable development, and ways to organize a community-run enterprise grew into an applied research project in which foresters from the Tropical Science Center, together with the Yanesha, developed the "strip shelterwood system." This system was characterized by "harvesting trees in long, narrow strips and leaving natural forest in the adjacent areas to naturally regenerate the strips" (Simeone, Pariona, and Lázaro 1993, 50). The system mimics the Yanesha's traditional "cut-and-fallow" gardening system, but was further professionalized by the Tropical Science Center ecologists. Local practices of using draft animals remained in place to prevent destruction caused by big machinery. A portable sawmill, light machinery, training, and salaries for operating them were introduced. The overall aim was proclaimed to be to design a forest management model that

> integrates ecological, economic, and social principles into a production system designed for sustainable development of tropical forest resources. From an ecological perspective, the opportunity to use tropical forests without destroying them is an exciting challenge. Thus, basic research on tropical forest dynamics and gap theory can lead to economically viable and socially attractive management of tropical forests that contributes significantly to the conservation of biological diversity. (Hartshorn 1989, 569)

As the quote shows, the project was an attempt to break with the paradigm of the unmanageable natural tropical forest and to find systems that would lead to both "economically viable and socially attractive management of tropical forests." To preserve biological diversity and the integrity of indigenous communities, the project not only developed transdisciplinary knowledge practices but also created an organizational structure, the COFYAL. The community-run COFYAL was a governance arrangement that assembled different governance knowledges and practices. It operated under the assumption that natural tropical forests could remain intact through usage and native communities could profit from their forests by applying a mixture of traditional and "Western" knowledges and practices. An article written by some of the practitioners involved praises the project as exemplifying "an alternative in which Western technology provides the 'hardware' and indigenous knowledge the 'software'" (Simeone, Pariona, and Lázaro 1993, 50). Despite this positive evaluation, the article also points to large social and economic problems that have occurred since the cooperative changed the socioeconomic structure of the native communities.

COFYAL illustrates the search for new forest management practices in tropical natural forests and the core belief that economic prosperity can evolve together with social and ecological justice. It already entailed the notion of local knowledge and expertise with a strong emphasis on community ownership in conjunction with scientific forestry practices. Like the rubber tappers' movement discussed above, the cooperative arose out of a social struggle, but stressed the economic dimension to a greater extent. The core of the project was a business idea that was intended to foster both economic viability and ecological and social well-being.

To become known beyond its local field of application, the cooperative had to be made mobile. The ecologists not only engaged with the project at a local level but also publicized innovative practices in journals and spoke on the topic at a number of conferences (Hartshorn 1990, 1989; Stocks and Hartshorn 1992; Simeone, Pariona, and Lázaro 1993). At one of these conferences in Berlin, the founders of the Ecological Trading Company (Christopher and Tom) learned from the Yanesha Indian Cooperative, and visited it in 1989 (Cox 1992). As concerned wood users they were searching for tropical timber from sustainable sources, found in the cooperative a trustworthy project, and shipped the first container of sustainable timber from Peru to Europe in 1989 (interview, forester and consultant, 06/28/2011). The aim of the company was to ensure that the sustainably produced timber from Latin America could find a market in Europe. In 1990 Christopher spoke at a conference in London on his first experiences of trading sustainable rainforest timber. In his talk he stressed that "any forestry enterprise must be able to pay its way in the real commercial world" (Cox 1992, 112). The statement illustrates the interest in creating a viable business option that could compete with others in the "real commercial world." Thus, the logic of the Ecological Trading Company was that sustainable forestry can be achieved and sustained by creating and using markets.

The Ecological Trading Company established a direct link between consumer countries in Europe and the project of sustainable forestry in South America; the sustainably produced timber became mobile, and linked to the international market. Anthony, Christopher, and Tom started to create a network that would result in a working group constituting the FSC. The WWF became financially involved in the cooperative in 1988 as well through the Peruvian Foundation for the Conservation of Nature; both organizations are founding members of the FSC.

Making Alternatives Mobile

While the Yanesha Cooperative was surely a unique project, similar islands of governance innovation existed in South America. As was the case with the cooperative in Peru, founding members of the FSC worked in natural tropical forest projects since they felt that "natural forests were being ignored" in forest management (interview, WWF US activist, 06/25/2011).[3] In the late 1980s, scientists, professionals, and activists more generally organized meetings on the topic. Three books, by Anthony Anderson, by Simon Counsell and Tim Rice, and by Duncan Poore and his colleagues, are indicative of the search for governance knowledge on how to foster alternatives to deforestation. Also, founding members of the FSC were either coauthors or participated in the conferences that led to these books.

First, the proceedings of an international conference held in Belém, Brazil in 1988 published with Columbia University Press underline that alternatives to deforestation are possible:

> Yet, this text is based on the firm conviction that the current scenario *is* reversible, and that viable alternatives to deforestation . . . *do* exist. . . . In Amazonia, sustainable forms of land use are currently limited to a small minority of the rural population under highly specific conditions. Developing such practices for the population as a whole—including small farmers and ranchers, as well as private and public companies—has only just begun. (Anderson 1990, 10–11, emphasis in the original)

Noting further that the "search for successful forms of tropical forest management should begin in traditional communities," the edited volume provides 14 case studies. Mostly these studies discuss examples of indigenous groups and small farmers who offer alternative forms of using and preserving tropical forests. Among other things, the "extractive reserves" of the rubber tappers' movement and the Yanesha Cooperative are outlined together with a country report on Brazil by Gabriel who later became a founding member of the FSC (Anderson 1990, 13). A review acknowledges the book to be "the most useful and comprehensive of a number of recent books which have pushed various forms of forest management as a 'sustainable' and economically viable development option in the Amazon basin" (Cleary 1993, 408).

Second, a similar project to the one in Belém was a conference organized by members of Friends of the Earth. The conference took place in London in 1990 with the presence of the Prince of Wales (now King Charles III) who delivered a keynote speech, and a number of participants who had also joined the conference in Brazil (Counsell and Rice 1992b).[4] In addition to these conferences with their "practical and visionary" agenda (Counsell and Rice 1992a, 5), a frequently cited volume, *No Timber without Trees: Sustainability in the Tropical Forest*, is the third book of importance. The study, led by Duncan Poore with the involvement of Thomas (FSC founding member) and John Palmer, covers all continents that have forest coverage and was based on a research project commissioned by the ITTO (Poore et al. 1989). The authors conclude, with regard to good examples of forest management:

> They are still pitifully puny and infrequent in relation to the scale of the problem; and often, good though they may be, they are of only local relevance. The challenge is to extract from these local successes some general principles and to apply these widely and rapidly at a scale which will have some real impact. (Poore et al. 1989, 1)

These three books together sketch the following picture. Governance knowledge is restricted to the tropical forest, which is mostly envisioned as being in danger; the understanding of the tropical forest is holistic, encompassing various ecological, economic, social, and cultural values. Despite the threat of deforestation and bad practices, islands of sustainable management are singled out, named, and delineated at conferences and in publications.

These "good examples" are nonetheless tagged with depreciatory comments: they are "still pitifully puny and infrequent," only of "local relevance" (Poore et al. 1989, 1), and they work only under "highly specific conditions" (Anderson 1990, 11). Hence, to varying degrees actors propose "to extract from these local successes some general principles" (Poore et al. 1989, 1), or to develop such "practices for the population as a whole" (Anderson 1990, 11). While on the one hand recognizing successful local practices of sustainable management, they press, on the other, for more universal principles to be drawn from them. This desire can also be read in the review of the proceedings of the conference in Brazil. The reviewer concludes that

> it is difficult to avoid the conclusion that unless certain conditions apply—living near a large urban market, being Japanese, having capital and secure title to land—the forest management and agroforestry strategies presented so competently in this book do not come anywhere near providing an alternative development strategy for the region. (Cleary 1993, 409)

It is a call for more transnational criteria for sustainable forestry that at best are not entangled in local practices or conditions.

Yet there is also conflict and contestation to be found with regard to whose knowledge is being articulated by whom. At first glance, the best-practice examples often describe systems that have been created in tropical forests in developing countries. The forest management practices have emerged on a local or community level (sometimes in coproduction with professionals from "outside"). These "good examples" do not travel freely but need to be translated to transnational arenas. This exercise has been mostly carried out by translators who use a variety of communicative codes. For instance, the proceedings of the conference organized by Friends of the Earth in London include the question-and-answer session so that traces of a controversy remain on the surface. The president of the Instituto de Estudos Amazonicos makes the following statement:

> It is Brazilians who are creating extractive reserves, but we are not asked to make presentations at this conference. This gives me the impression that people think that others can speak better for us than we can for ourselves and that is a kind of colonialism that I do not like very much. . . . Originally, extractive reserves were conceived as a solution for people who lived by utilizing certain resources. They were not invented by us, but were created out of social demand from the local level. Anthropologists and researchers were then called in, but the concept of extractive reserves was born of local and social demand. (Maria Allegretti, in Counsell and Rice 1992b, 258–59)

In these hybrid spaces in which science and activism intersect, the speaker challenges the role of anthropologists and other researchers who, despite their contributions to the success of the movement, seem to actualize "a kind of colonialism." Issues of representation and authenticity—"we are not asked to make presentations"—emerge as criteria for the robustness of a knowledge claim. Allegretti, then, underlines that the new instrument, extractive reserves, is not some kind of innovation out of the governance toolbox but has emerged from social and local struggles.

The example is indicative of the tension that existed within the emerging discussion on sustainable forest management. On the one hand, actors worked toward criteria for sustainable forestry that would not be specific to local conditions but could be applied to other regions and contexts. Seeing the market as a potential driver of this process was part of this approach. Thus, sustainable forestry had to be developed in a way that would make it attractive as a viable business option. On the other hand, actors continuously stressed the deeply political issues of land rights and social struggle more broadly. Instead of creating a transnational viable business option, these actors were much more concerned with real change on the ground. This tension continued to be present in the early experiments with certification.

Experimenting with Certification as a Governance Instrument

Certification as a new form of doing governance emerged in various contexts. Pioneer work in this regard was done by FoE England, Wales and Northern Ireland, which launched its tropical rainforest campaign in 1985 (interview, FoE activist, 08/12/2011).[5] It was in the context of the campaign that FoE published its first *Good Wood Guide* in 1987, "emphasizing the direct link between forest destruction and the retail sales of tropical timber" (Thomas 2005, 8). Shortly after, FoE issued its own certificate, the Good Wood Seal of Approval, which was discontinued in 1990 (Counsell 1995).[6] It is important to stress that these early attempts to create a tentative labeling system came out of the laboratory of a campaigning organization. Indeed, "it was an experimental scheme," as one of the campaigners recalls, that grew out of dissatisfaction with international governance efforts (interview, FoE activist, 08/12/2011).

Like FoE, other NGOs produced guidelines. Most notably, the Rainforest Action Network published *The Wood Users Guide* in the US in 1991 to provide consumers with information on sustainable wood purchase (Wellner and Dickey 1991).[7] The Rainforest Action Network and, more prominently, WWF UK worked together with companies. In 1991, WWF launched Group 1995, which assembled companies dedicated to using timber products that came only from credibly certified, well-managed forests.[8] Early attempts at certification can also be found. As mentioned above, FoE engaged in such projects with its Good Woods Seal of Approval. In addition, the Smart Wood Program of the Rainforest Alliance is often referred to as the "first independent forest management certification effort in the world" (Donovan 1996, 105). Its first certification took place in Perum Perhutani (Indonesia) in 1990, recognizing Perum Perhutani's unique agroforestry practices. Scientific Certification Systems (SCS), based in California, began to work toward the certification of forests as well in 1991 with no in-house knowledge on forestry (interview, forester and auditor, 06/25/2011).

Others thought of transferring alternative trading models to the forest sector. A prominent example is Tom, who made bagpipes and relied on tropical hardwood imports for his work. He felt there "had to be a way to buy wood from companies and landowners who practiced sustainable forest management" (cited in Cashore, Auld, and Newsom 2004, 4). Tom had ties to the fair-trade coffee project (Max Havelaar), and their alternative trading models influenced his early thinking about certification (Auld 2014, 135). Thus, generating knowledge of governing outside of traditional government institutions appeared across a variety of sectors.

To engage more closely with knowledge practices, I turn to a specific effort, a pre-project proposal for a certification system on a global scale. In search of expertise FoE activists visited the Oxford Forestry Institute on July 26, 1988, since Oxford was the main center for tropical forestry. Here, they met with Thomas who was working for the British government forestry aid program at that time (interview, forester and consultant, 06/30/2011). Trained as a forester in Oxford, he conducted research in the 1970s on the effects of silvicultural treatments in tropical rainforests, and then worked as an independent consultant contributing, among other activities, to the frequently cited study on the sustainability in the tropical forest mentioned above (Poore et al. 1989). Also joining the meeting were two colleagues from the Oxford Forestry Institute who had worked most of their professional careers in a forestry research institute in Malaysia. According to Thomas, all three of them knew nothing about certification, and in fact had not heard the word "accreditation," yet they had all worked in tropical forest management (interview, forester and consultant, 06/30/2011). Policy knowledge on forestry (in the shape of the scientists at the Oxford Forestry Institute) came together with politics knowledge (in the shape of FoE). FoE aimed to broaden its campaigning toolbox.

As a result of this meeting, Thomas drafted an outline of a study proposal addressed to the FoE activists two days later (Thomas 1988), which eventually resulted in a pre-project proposal to the ITTO. Others have elaborated on the political journey of the proposal from the meeting in Oxford, through the British Overseas Development Administration (ODA 1989) to the ITTO where it was rejected after a controversial discussion at the 7th session in Yokohama in November 1989 (Gale 1998, 159; Auld 2014, 74).

However, the proposals are an excellent means to examine how project proposals perform translational practices of enclosure/disclosure. On the one hand, they construct approved and sufficiently stabilized knowledge with regard to a certification system (enclosure); on the other, the authors outline what needs further research in a controlled setting (disclosure). Given their dialectical nature, the proposals can be analyzed by differentiating what the authors construct as certain or known, and what they deem to be uncertain.

The authors ascribe certainty to their assumption that the public and the market require sustainably produced timber (enclosure). While the first draft only speaks of "*enabling* consumers to select timber from approved sources" (Thomas 1988, 1, emphasis added), the rhetoric of the final draft is much stronger. It argues that "consumers *are expressing a preference* for sustainable timber since they believe that this *will encourage* both the conservation of the tropical rainforests and the long term economic and social benefit of producer countries" (Thomas, Ken, and Connor 1989, 2, emphasis added). The claim is substantiated by an intertextual reference to the chlorofluorocarbon case, which has become a major reference for successful policy change at the international level. The authors argue that "a parallel situation can be seen to be developing with Tropical Hardwoods in Europe, and the US" (Thomas, Ken, and Connor 1989, 2). Although the time period between the two documents is short, it already shows how the factuality of the "market or consumer demand" is constructed by slightly changing the modalities of the claims.

Having constructed what is known, the authors specify what is yet unknown requiring further attention (disclosure). A study would

> test the feasibility and describe the problems likely to be encountered in the design and implementation of a labeling system to identify and distinguish sustainably produced tropical hardwoods. (Thomas, Ken, and Connor 1989, 2)

In essence, a team of researchers would follow timber along the chain of custody and monitor and evaluate each step. The study already asked central questions with regard to a labeling system. Practices for identifying, marking, documenting, tracing, labeling, and monitoring tropical hardwood are mentioned, and said to be as yet uncertain. While the first draft selected the chain from Malaysia to the UK as the object of study owing to its wide range of land use and often criticized forestry practices (Thomas 1988, 2), the final draft avoids naming a producer country, presumably for political reasons (Thomas, Ken, and Connor 1989, 5). Also, the project proposal sought to provide a manual "of 'best practices and standards' describing systems and activities which yield timber in a manner which is considered sustainable" rather than to define sustainable practices in advance (Thomas, Ken, and Connor 1989, 5). The proposal was rejected for a variety of reasons and changed into a study in which the notion of labeling no longer appeared. Most sources name Malaysia and Indonesia as the main opponents to the proposal within the ITTO. Also, most representatives in the ITTO were timber traders who did not feel particularly strongly about environmental or indigenous concerns (interview, FoE activist, 08/12/2011). Certification was regarded with suspicion because it might restrict the export of timber.

Still, the six-page project proposal was nevertheless powerful because of the translation practices of disclosure/enclosure. The project proposal clearly laid out the questions that a labeling system would encounter. It envisioned such a system in its complexities without claiming certainty as to its future operation. Given the novelty of the idea and the problems involved, the study would produce further and more differentiated questions and create new objects of controversy rather than stable knowledge that could have been easily implemented.

Interestingly, the rejection of the study strengthened those voices who were lobbying for a private governance system. The emerging network of scientists, NGOs, and concerned timber traders once again experienced the unwillingness of the ITTO system and the involved governments to engage seriously with environmental and social concerns. As a result, NGOs such as FoE concluded that they had to lobby for regulatory systems beyond international institutions (interview, FoE activist, 08/12/2011; Gale 1998, chap. 10).

Displaying Paths Toward a Certification Process

In July 1990 Anthony, who had previously worked in community forestry projects in Bolivia, Ecuador, and Peru (with the Yanesha Cooperative), started to do research for a three-month study on behalf of the Homeland

Foundation (interview, forester and consultant, 06/28/2011).[9] The study, "Base Issues Document for the Development of a Sustainable Forest Products Certification Process," was based on 49 interviews with key stakeholders conducted in person or by telephone. It sets out various, often contradictory, paths toward a certification process. In contrast to the research proposal by FoE and Thomas discussed above, the study itself was far less ambitious in scope, and sought rather to gather opinions from a broad spectrum of groups and to stimulate discussion between these groups as to how a certification process could be initiated. As a document that assembles the views of a broad group of actors, one can examine what it constructs as certain (practices of enclosure) and uncertain (practices of disclosure) with regard to governance knowledge.

The introduction to the study states straight away that "a consensus exists that the best vehicle for effectively promoting sustainable forestry would be a certification process which could distinguish sustainably produced 'good wood' from other 'exploitative' non-sustainable sources" (Anthony 1990b). However, uncertainty exists with regard to the paths that will lead "to the establishment of a widely accepted and applicable certification process" (Anthony 1990b, 1). In other words, certification is constructed as *the consensual instrument* to promote sustainable forestry. The new study thereby overlooks the earlier controversy over and rejection of the research proposal on labeling by the ITTO in 1989. So, the framing of the new study indicates what the interviewees on the list were willing to support. It was tailored to the private sector and civil society organizations, leaving aside representatives of states or international organizations. It showed a survey of opinions of private actors regarding a certification process.[10] While Anthony provides some interpretation of the data, he also displays the anonymized answers that speak to politics, polity, and policy knowledge. Table 3 shows some aspects of the study, differentiating between the most important issues and the various perspectives on them.[11]

With regard to politics knowledge, different views are articulated on how to proceed in the development of a certification process. Essentially, tension exists between an *expert-driven approach* and a *representative approach*. The expert-driven approach argues in favor of a group of experts that develops and runs the governance arrangement. Experts either come from conservationist NGOs or are generally irreproachable. Their authority is derived from their expert knowledge that is "above reproach." In contrast, the representative approach attaches importance to the balance of different interest groups. A domination by one specific group is under-

TABLE 3. Selected Issues and Perspectives on the Development of a Sustainable Forest Products Certification Process

Issues	Perspectives
Participation in development of a certification process? (Politics Knowledge)	Conservationist groups, to avoid being co-opted by conventional industry and trade groups, support: 1. Groups and individuals with regional expertise, 2. Wood users, brokers, and marketers with a demonstrated commitment to sustainable practices, 3. Wood producers already utilizing sustainable practices. Actors with significant experience in sustainable forestry A team of experts
Definition of sustainability (Policy Knowledge)	Consider only technical and ecological factors Evaluate the system as a whole: social, political, and economic factors broken down into individual quantifiable bits with a value system Complexity of socioeconomic factors will make it very difficult to develop measurable criteria Has to evolve with new understandings of forest dynamics and the sophistication of technology
Scope (Policy Knowledge)	Tropical forests are the highest priority, and, to a lesser extent, temperate forests Emphasis on natural forests with certification considered only in certain plantation situations Certification of all forest' products; wood products would be first priority
Organizational structure (Polity Knowledge)	Certification performed by a US-based private monitoring body, which contracts technical assistance to evaluate individual wood sources, and develops its own set of standards and evaluation system Consortium formed among existing organizations and public groups that have significant experience or ongoing involvement with sustainable forestry issues. They would agree upon criteria for certification, perform evaluations and verifications. Certification programs developed and implemented by individual, well-recognized conservation organizations

Source: Data from Anthony 1990a.

stood as weakening the authority of the organization. Thus, there was no clear picture of how to develop a certification process in such a way that the antagonistic groups, namely environmental NGOs and business actors, would approve it and eventually participate in it.

Related to that, polity knowledge in terms of the organizational structure of the future governance arrangement was also multivocal. At one end of the spectrum a consortium was suggested made up of already existing organizations; at the other end, a private US-based monitoring body would develop standards and evaluation mechanisms. These two positions carried implicit assumptions about functionality and representation: a consortium would have to deal with the conflicts between the groups, whereas a US-based monitoring body would have to justify its authority.

Turning to policy knowledge, three notions of sustainable forest management can be detected in this document alone: a *minimal approach* focusing on technical and ecological factors, an *integrative approach* including social, economic, and ecological factors, and a *skeptical approach* questioning the possibility of finding criteria to measure the socioeconomic complexity. All three approaches might either focus only on tropical forests or broaden the view and consider temperate forests and plantations as well. Thus, the policy knowledge that was to form the basis of the governance arrangement was not at all consensual. Technical and ecological factors are easier to transform into standards and criteria and resonated with the practices of foresters in the 1980s (interview, forester and consultant, 06/30/2011). As outlined above, however, with the rise of new actors during the 1980s issues of social justice entered the discourse of sustainable forestry. Yet the question remained as to how indicators for issues such as social justice could be developed.[12]

So, what does this document *do*? By assembling the governance knowledge of key actors in one document it sets a discussion in motion. Rather than bringing the debate to a close the aim was to produce as many options as possible within a framework that prescribed certification as the best governance instrument for sustainable forestry. Yet, Anthony concluded, "not one group felt it had sufficient scope or the broad-based experience necessary to address all the pertinent issues" (Anthony 1990a, 12). As a consequence, a more collective effort and the inclusion of several groups seemed to be required.

To conclude, this section has outlined the emerging governance knowledge on sustainable forestry as well as some early attempts to design premodels of what later became a certification system. In various constellations actors worked on and experimented with new ways of engaging with a political problem. In some instances, these actors met, as happened when timber traders (the Ecological Trading Company) went to the Yanesha Forestry Cooperative to buy timber to ship to Europe. Yet what was missing was a collective and enduring process that would transform those insular activities into a system, and thus create a viable governance instrument.

The Team Begins Its Work

In established political systems the bureaucracy and civil servants—often in conjunction with other societal actors—work on the formulation of a policy. In this realm of state governance, a standing bureaucracy has provided and set up the rules for how such a process is to operate and is authorized to work on an issue. In the realm of private governance, an institutionalized structure does not exist nor do private actors have the formal authority to perform governance actions. For this reason, private actors have to build a quasi-institutional framework that iteratively translates conflicting positions, worldviews, or modi operandi—in short, governance knowledge. I will show how actors build a reiterative structure of meetings and documents that function as an institutional structure in the absence of one provided by a state. To begin such a process, a team needs to constitute itself, then be responsible for a series of meetings and documents that will perform the necessary translations.

An Initial Meeting: University of Massachusetts at Amherst, November 1990

In May 1989, Henry, a writer for *Fine Woodworking*, and Jackson, a partner at a California importer and purveyor of guitar parts, went in search of sustainably produced timber from the Yanesha Cooperative in Peru. Once back in the US, Henry and a number of like-minded woodworkers and ecologists founded the Wood Workers Alliance for Rainforest Protection (WARP) in New York City on September 8 of that same year (WARP 1993).

To fulfill their mission statement, to explore methods of sustainable timber harvest, they organized a conference at the University of Massachusetts at Amherst on November 16–18, 1990 (American Woodworker 1990). At this meeting, a group of 10–15 people representing the Rainforest Alliance, Ecological Trading Company, Homeland Foundation, Rainforest Action Network, Greenpeace, WARP, Luthier's Merch., the Sierra Club, and the WWF met and decided to found the Certification Working Group (Holly 1993a, 1). As a memorandum notes, they agreed on the following tasks:

> 1. to draw up a set of clear, observable, and verifiable criteria for sustainable forestry 2. to develop adequate mechanisms to monitor the production of timber from sustainable sources 3. to establish a system of certification which will identify all organizations involved in the production, trade, or manufacture of timber and timber products from approved sustained yield operations 4. to propose an organizational and operational structure for the agency [an international forest monitoring consortium]. (Kilian 1990)

These tasks built the agenda for the Certification Working Group that, from its inception in Amherst, Massachusetts, brought together, coordinated, and interpreted governance knowledges to create a governance arrangement. The organizations mentioned indicate that the early group consisted mostly of environmental organizations (Rainforest Alliance, Rainforest Action Network, Greenpeace, Sierra Club, WWF) that had a record of both campaigning successfully against corporations and working with them (especially WWF). The other actors in the working group represented ecologically minded companies and woodworkers who had an interest in obtaining timber from sustainable sources. Thus, the early members of the team were relatively homogenous and did not yet have to negotiate strongly antagonistic positions. Also, most actors already knew each other from other projects in which they had worked before or cooperated on. After this initial meeting, documents mediated between the otherwise dispersed actors.

In Between Meetings

Between meetings, documents such as letters, reports, or memos maintain connections between the members, creating a translational chain. Three of these connecting instances between the conference in Amherst and the first official meeting of the Certification Working Group in San Francisco can be analyzed: a memorandum written by Logan (WWF senior fellow and BOSCOSA[13] advisor) to the Certification Working Group dated December 2, 1990; a letter written by Kilian (Rainforest Alliance) to the Certification Working Group dated December 17, 1990; and a replying memorandum of December 22, 1990, by Anthony.

Three core issues run through these documents, all of which address facets of governance knowledge. First, the actors formulate different ideas about the pace at which a certification body should be established. A sense of urgency, "I think that if a certification program isn't functioning by the middle of next year (1991), we are 'missing the boat'" (Logan 1990), encounters some reluctance, "As for the creation of an international forest monitoring agency, I think it is an idea worthy of consideration, though I will need more time to digest it" (Kilian 1990). This leads to confusion and the rearticulation of the perceived common aims: "I am confused by the apparent hesitation on the part of RA [Rainforest Alliance] on the establishment of a monitoring consortium. . . . My understanding from the informal working group session Saturday evening at the WARP conference was that we had agreed to organize an international forest monitoring consortium" (Anthony 1990b).

Second, actors reflect self-referentially on their team identity by discussing issues of participation as well as renaming their project. For instance, Anthony demands in a letter "a need for a clearer understanding of *who*" they are, and to whom issue documents are distributed (Anthony 1990b, emphasis in the original). This indicates a discussion that was already visible in the study of the Homeland Foundation as to who should participate in the development of a certification process. It touches upon a number of questions regarding efforts to establish the group, to define protagonists and antagonists, to name it, and to outline the explicit tasks. Working titles include International Forest Stewardship Consortium or International Consortium for Sustainable Forestry (Anthony 1990b). While these names indicate the clearly global character of the project, its exact purpose in the broader certification process, especially in relation to already established certification organizations, remains vague.

Third, in these memos and letters actors refer back to existing instruments to envision and further develop the governance arrangement they are just beginning to name. Since Rainforest Alliance with their Smart Wood program had already certified a forest in Indonesia (Perum Perhutani), they circulated their criteria asking for comments and replies (Kilian 1990). This is how the new instrument first took shape—as criteria specifying what constitutes sustainable forestry on the basis of already established instruments.

So again, what do these documents *do*? They tie meetings together because they have the capacity to make knowledge mobile. That is, to express, describe, and envision an idea on the one hand, and to make connections and create a web of relations on the other. Documents mediate between dispersed actors and create an arena despite the physical absence of the people involved. They create an in-between, recontextualizing both the unity and differences between people. They keep the discussion going, that is, they ensure that issues move between the actors before they meet again to stage an event. In so doing, they begin to constitute an emerging group.

Inside a Meeting: San Francisco, April 20–21, 1991

The Certification Working Group met again in San Francisco at the Greenpeace office in April 1991. In total, 19 participants from environmental and social NGOs, certification organizations, foundations, and economic interest groups came together: four of them came from the UK, the others were all based in the US.[14] A couple of reports[15] documented the two-day event. They permit us to examine how the participants tried to engage in translational practices of disclosure/enclosure: the group began its work, and yet the products were "not policy for any group or any individual, but merely the initial workings and beginnings for procedures on certification" (Jennifer 1991, 1).

The group invited all participants to voice and write down their concerns and expectations, to display themes and potential controversies, and to find indications of what was yet unknown. With regard to the concerns, participants listed enabling and empowering local, forest people, as well as to engaging them in the entire certification process. Yet it was also noted that the marketing perspective should be represented. Actors wondered about the effectiveness of the tool, certification: Can a system of certification work? Will it go beyond the status quo of timber industry operations? Will it have a holistic approach, and what should be the areas of certification (tropical, or tropical/temperate/boreal forests)?

These concerns contrast with the expectations bought to the meeting. Participants wished for a definition of sustainable forestry and a clear articulation of the goals of a certification program from those present, and to leave the meeting with "something concrete—to get started now" (Jennifer 1991, 2). Among other things, some questions had to do with how the use of lesser-known wood species would affect the market and sustainable forest management. How could certification include educational aspects as well as the critical social issues? Also, self-referential questions appeared such as "Who are we, and who do we represent?" Or, "Are we more consumer-related than producer-related"? (Jennifer 1991, 2). This mapping exercise indicates a process of research. Participants had objectives in mind derived from past experiences but did not know how these objectives would be represented in the new governance arrangement.

To characterize some of the terms the team would stand for, they engaged in a general discussion on the concept of "sustainability" and on how to measure "equity/social/economic issues" (Jennifer 1991, 3) from a sustainability perspective. In fact, because of its ambiguity the team decided to avoid the term "sustainability" (Jennifer 1991, 3). Instead, it preferred to speak of *"forest stewardship* which subscribes to a long view / land ethic concept that more accurately identifies the holistic intent" of the project (Anthony 1991, 3, emphasis in the original). It was in this discussion that the name of the future organization started to take shape, the intention being to create a "clear, concise term for the public to hear"; a term that would distinguish itself from the notion of "sustained-yield" as used by the tropical timber industry (Jennifer 1991, 3).

With regard to social issues, the remaining traces of the discussion hint at an integrated view of sustainability; for instance, "social participation is actually needed for ecological sustainability" (Jennifer 1991, 3). However, one finds disagreement with regard to the problem of measuring social issues. Skeptics had reservations, noting that "social issues are hard to evaluate," or that the "best you can hope for is a certain indicator(s); the process itself is susceptible to change." Also, a certification organization had problems "with how to measure and assess the impact on social criteria" (Jennifer 1991, 3).

The group asked those who had constructed similar and yet different certification programs to introduce their prototypes to reflect which of the elements could be recontextualized for their own endeavor. The Ecological Trading Company presented a proposal for an International Forestry Monitoring Agency. Green Cross, the nonprofit wing of the for-profit organization Scientific Certification Systems (SCS), outlined its basic suggestions for a certification structure that was still in the developmental phase within their company. In contrast to Green Cross, Smart Wood, the certification program of the Rainforest Alliance, had already certified forests in Indonesia in the first third-party certification of forest management, and also spoke about their program (Donovan 1996). The participants questioned each presenter vigorously, criticizing unspecific criteria, lack of inclusion with regard to social NGOs, or absence of universal standards (Tom 1991, 3; Jennifer 1991, 4–6). The issue of exclusive commitment to the project of the Certification Working Group was also a theme in the discussion.

Having discussed some general terms (sustainability) and examined already existing instruments, they engaged in further translational practices. This (re)search process began with the participants temporarily agreeing on a common aim (practice of enclosure). They decided to create an "umbrella certification watchdog/standards organization, tentatively called the *Forest Stewardship Council (FSC)*. The heart of the council would be the *Forest Stewardship Charter*, a document that would allow participation by signatories (bioregional wood certification groups, foresters, forest peoples and other forest users/campaigners promoting the sustainable use of forest resources)" (Anthony 1991, 1, emphasis in the original). To further specify the two aims, the participants split the group in half to change the interaction order. One group discussed the content of the FSC, and the other the process of how it could evolve (Jennifer 1991, 8).

The notes still extant already map the objectives, the membership, the principles, and the further process of the emerging institutions. For instance, they outline broader categories for the Forest Stewardship Standards, namely "socio-economic, legal-political, silvicultural, and ecological" ones (Jennifer 1991, 8). Jennifer's report also reveals possible tensions since Green Cross stated that "they have a definite policy of non-disclosure with the company they are working to certify" (Jennifer 1991, 9). However, that was problematic in the view of others because "the whole point of certifying is to know exactly how forestry projects conduct their operations" (Jennifer 1991, 9). These are moments in which positions are incommensurable and not translatable into a new text. To solve this problem the Certification Working Group thought of seeking legal advice and advice from certification groups. The notes from the second group map in a similar fashion how the further process can be structured. Most importantly, it advised expanding the group to include more representatives from the Global South and to gain further input on a possible charter.

Before a meeting ends, people often try to agree on tasks that should be dealt with in-between meetings. It was key for the meeting in San Francisco to name Tom secretary of the Certification Working Group and specify his tasks during his three-month tenure. Among his duties was to coordinate the drafting of the charter including principles and Forest Stewardship Standards, as well as to identify additional members and facilitate communication between members (Anthony 1991, 3). In addition, meetings often close with a round of reflection. The participants encouraged each other, noting that "we need to keep spirit of cooperation going," or we are "happy to see a general consensus and the amount of energy put into [the] meeting" (Jennifer 1991, 11). Participants also raised some concerns with regard to future meetings. A representative from the Wood Workers Alliance for Rainforest Protection stressed that "certification should be based in the market perspective," whereas another actor demanded "participation of forest people throughout the entire process" and highlighted the lack of "Southern" representation (Jennifer 1991, 11).

To conclude, at this first official meeting of the Certification Working Group members agreed to tentatively call that what they were looking for the Forest Stewardship Council (FSC). Further, they sketched out some of the constitutive elements of the governance arrangement; it would have a governing body with "the general objective of overseeing and assuring the accountability of subscribing certificating groups," which meant that the FSC would not operate as a certifier itself (Anthony 1991, 2); and it would have a charter that explicated standards and criteria for forest stewardship. With regard to the team itself, it became clear that it needed to expand; Global South representation was needed for a truly global initiative to be legitimate. Tension appeared mostly between the dual aims of the emerging organization. Actors envisioned it as being centrally placed within the market and thus a viable business model; at the same time, it was intended to help local and indigenous communities to gain ownership of their land.

The Group Constructs Its Instruments: From Forest Stewardship Standards to Principles and Criteria

The Certification Working Group had the key task of creating standards or criteria that would work as measures for sustainable forestry. Taking into account the tentatively existing guidelines from FoE, the Green Cross, and the Rainforest Alliance, the aim was to compose a set of standards, globally applicable, that would incorporate and specify various concerns from social, economic, and ecological groups. Tom from the Ecological Trading Company, the interim secretary of the group, delivered the first draft of the Forest Stewardship Standards in July 1991. This first draft went through seven rounds (first draft to seventh draft) and a number of subrounds (drafts 7 a, b, c) before it gained preliminary approval from the Founding Assembly in Toronto in October 1993 (Thomas 2005, 17–19). In other words, elements of the document were deleted, added, and rewritten; the document changed its name from Forest Stewardship Standards to FSC Principles and Criteria; it grew and shrank in size. The participants again and again asked themselves whether a particular draft was ready to serve as standards for a certifier. Each round of revision made the fluid object more durable.

As a sample, I examine the first draft that was revised by Thomas in November and December 1991 (Thomas 1991), then compare this document at the end of this chapter with the Principles and Criteria that emerged from these Forest Stewardship Standards. The 18-page draft document of December 1991 consists of four subsections: (A) it provides a general introduction to the standards and their objectives; (B) it lays out aspects of forest management; (C) it presents the Forest Stewardship Standards, focusing on management objectives, technical and administrative elements, legal and political aspects, social and economic factors, and ecological end environmental factors; (D) it elaborates on the evaluation of forest management for the FSC.

In the introduction, the Forest Stewardship Standards states "that everyone involved in the long-term utilization or trade of forest products has a *common interest* in good forest stewardship, to ensure the continued existence of the forest" (Thomas 1991, 1, emphasis in the original). To stress the common interest of all sectors is to establish the emerging governance arrangement as a "political bridge" between the antagonist actors from environmental NGOs and the logging industry. The standards are referred to as "general, basic, but usable principles," as a "code of practice," and as "not immutable" but up for revision.

The Standards refer to the ITTO "Guidelines for the Sustainable Management of Natural Tropical Forests and Tropical Plantation Forests" published in May 1990 (ITTO 1990).[16] The FSC's standards are characterized as "complementing" the ITTO guidelines, and Principle 14 from these guidelines is cited later on (Thomas 1991, 2).

This indicates two things. First, it is fair to argue that there was international interest in finding some common criteria for how to manage forests sustainably. Nonstate actors were not satisfied with the norm-making within the ITTO due to powerful state interests. Although those who wrote the draft of the FSC standards incorporated parts of the ITTO guidelines, the consultation process involved civil society actors to a greater extent and was not politically influenced by governmental interests. Second, one has to keep in mind that the emerging FSC as well as other initiatives of that time were of a new kind. Klaus Dingwerth argues that the copying of standards from international institutions such as the ITTO was a way of claiming legitimacy for their own operations (Dingwerth 2017, 78).

In addition, the introduction highlights that the objectives of the Forest Stewardship Standards were to "set up internationally acceptable standards and principles of good forest management" (Thomas 1991, 2). While the focus lay on individual natural and seminatural forests in the tropics, the Forest Stewardship Standards also applied to temperate and plantation forests. Thus, the standards were global in scope, and had a fairly holistic understanding of forest management, since the text notes: "Different people have different perceptions of forests, influenced by their own needs, experience, education and beliefs. . . . These standards aim to blend these different perceptions into a common concept of forest management" (Thomas 1991, 4), which amounts to the notion of forest stewardship. Stewardship extends beyond the technical elements of forest management, since it "includes principles of social and environment responsibility as well as efficient enterprise management," so the authors argue (Thomas 1991, 4).

However, despite this commitment to a holistic understanding of forestry management, the FSC standards in the document are mostly concerned with specifying the technical and administrative elements. The legal and political aspects, the social and economic aspects, and the ecological and environmental factors are less characterized. This is because these aspects, which exceeded the pure management of the forest, were a step into uncharted territory. To characterize the implications of seriously moving beyond the notion of sustaining yield would have meant engaging with a broad range of actors—something that forestry science had so far been reluctant to do. Moreover, the Forest Stewardship Standards are not formulated as standards but appear in this early version rather as guidelines that describe and tentatively characterize elements of forest management although the title of the document claims the contrary. The standards were subject to further epistemic efforts at characterization up to the Founding Assembly and beyond, and I will outline their content at the end of this chapter. One of those instances of further negotiating the Forest Stewardship Standards was a meeting that took place in Washington, DC, in 1992.

Meeting and Controversy: The Expanded Certification Working Group Gathers in Washington, DC, in March 1992

A year after the San Francisco meeting, the Certification Working Group gathered for a second time in Washington, DC. The team had grown to 43 participants from 10 countries—six of which were tropical countries (Holly 1993b). Hence, the recurrent idea of including actors from the South had to a certain extent been realized. During the meeting the participants discussed the documents that had been produced since the previous meeting: the third draft of the FSC Charter by Logan, the fourth draft of the Forests Stewardship Standards, and the first draft of an Operations Manual for a Forest Management Evaluation and Certification System were presented (Thomas 2005, 14).

The participants elected an interim board consisting of Brian (WWF

International, UK/Switzerland), Adrian (WARP, A&M Wood Specialty, US), Nicholas (professor of forestry, Venezuela), Carlos (independent consultant, Proyecto Latifoliado, Honduras), Aaron (environmental coordinator, B&Q, UK), Stella (SCS, US), and Lisa (Cultural Survival, US) (Holly 1993b, 2). The composition of this interim board shows the development of the team. Whereas environmental NGOs dominated the group in the beginning, the composition of the interim board reflected some balancing with regard to sectoral and regional representation: two members were from South America, environmental (WWF) and social (Cultural Survival) NGOs were represented, economic interests from the North (A&M Wood Specialty, B&Q UK) and from the South (Proyecto Latifoliado) had seats, and expertise on certification (SCS, US) and on forestry (professor from Venezuela) was part of the interim board. The politics knowledge embedded in this composition hints at a representative approach that was very aware of the antagonistic forces the emerging FSC had to combine. The rationale was that the governance arrangement would only gain legitimacy with global audiences if the interim board represented some balance.

However, this view was also very much contested. In fact, a controversy emerged that essentially questioned the participation and the representation of actors on the interim board with an economic or commercial interest (such as Aaron from the British home improvement store B&Q). Also, the legitimacy of the interim board's decision-making power was contested. Both controversial elements could temporarily be settled but reemerged again at the Founding Assembly in Toronto a year later. With this in view, the initial purpose of the meeting was to gain consensus on the FSC Standards, but many participants "felt that the FSC could not establish itself as an accrediting organization until there was adequate participation from a wider diversity of people" (Holly 1993b, 1). To deal with this problem, the group decided to engage in a thorough regional consultative process around the world (see next section). They also agreed to set up six working groups that would focus on specific issues such as finances, the Principles and Criteria of forest stewardship, and the consultative process. The interim board hired an interim coordinator to facilitate communications and to coordinate the consultative process (Holly 1993b, 2).

To conclude, the Certification Working Group had started as a team of a dozen people mainly from the US and had evolved within two years into a transnational network with about 50 associates. Given the size of the group and the project, the emerging governance arrangement began to establish an interim governance structure. Yet the arrangement remained unstable and key aspects such as the representation of economic actors were highly contested. The decision to engage in a transnational consultation process indicates that the emerging governance arrangement lacked broad support. The antagonistic transnational civil society and business had not had enough opportunities to participate.

Strengthening participatory elements in the process was a risky endeavor. At the Washington meeting conflicts between the groups had already resulted in the contestation of the entire project. So, the group had to manage a difficult situation: it had to expand to give NGOs a voice in order to gain legitimacy. Reaching out to others meant in this case, however, also integrating deep-rooted conflicts that could prevent the emerging governance arrangements from becoming operational. Instead of meeting again transnationally, the interim board launched a test, a consultative process involving small-scale meetings across the globe to win, in a dramaturgical register, a "supporting cast" (Benford and Hunt 1992).

The FSC Consultative Process: Showcasing Governance Knowledge

Commissioned at the meeting in Washington, DC, in March 1992, the consultative process took a year and a half and temporarily came to a halt just before the Founding Assembly in October 1993. A working group (the Consultative Process Working Group) agreed on a general mailing to 5,000 targeted groups, enclosing current FSC documents as well as 11 in-depth country assessments (Ervin 1996, 18). Financial support came from the Homeland Foundation, the MacArthur Foundation, the Ford Foundation, and the Rockefeller Brothers Fund, among others.[17] The consultative process operated with a relatively small budget of approximately US$250,000 per year, and the Consultative Process Working Group was not paid (interview, FSC interim coordinator, 02/21/2012). I argue that the consultative process had intertwined political and epistemic dimensions. The political dimension was an attempt to legitimize the emerging governance arrangement through participatory practices. On that issue, the interim coordinator of the FSC noted:

> It is a process of engaging stakeholders in a creative and inclusive process. Therefore, the degree of success of a consultative process should be gauged by both the apparent, substantive results, as well as the less apparent, but equally important, increase in the participation and ownership of the process by a wider diversity of people. (Holly 1993b, 13)

The process was an exercise in making and testing governance knowledge as well as in developing further the participatory agenda of the FSC to recruit people from around the world for the new governance arrangement. Of course, groups responded differently to this invitation. In Ecuador, for instance, most of the timber industry was reluctant since they thought that the guidelines of the ITTO were sufficient. Whereas some social NGOs were surprised that for the first time someone recognized their concerns on a transnational level, others refused to participate because of the involvement of the timber industry (interview, Fundacion Natura activist, 08/05/2011). Thus, the political dimension of the consultative process in conjunction with the 5,000 disseminated information packages was to spread governance knowledge of the nascent governance instrument around the globe. The participatory elements that were constitutive of the emerging governance arrangements were partly followed and partly watched with a high degree of suspicion.

The epistemic dimension was to test the feasibility and applicability of the FSC documents that had been produced in the meetings and between meetings. Would the ideas produced by the working group also resonate in the world outside? Putting the tentative standards to a test, the working group selected the country assessments with a specific rationale in mind. The selected countries were to be a representative sample covering the following characteristics (Holly 1993b):

> type of forest management (community-based or industry-based)
> land tenure (publicly or privately owned)
> management type (primarily plantation or natural forest)
> type of product (timber, pulp, or non-timber)
> market (domestic or international)
> forest ecosystem (boreal, temperate, or tropical)

To reach a balance between the various factors, such as "type of management" or "type of forest product," the working group selected specific countries, and appointed consultants (see table 4).

The contracted consultants mostly had ties to environmental and social NGOs with expertise in the field (see also the next chapter). Although there was some "rumbling from the timber industry and the American Pulp and Paper Association" regarding the selection of the consultants, the process itself was not politicized (interview with FSC interim coordinator, 02/21/2012).[18] Together with the information package, each of the consultants received a manual that explained in detail the objectives, the suggested process (particular workshops), and the stakeholders

TABLE 4. FSC Country Assessment Consultants

Consultant	Affiliation	Country
Gabriel	Universidad de Sao Paulo, Escoloa Superior Agricultura	Brazil
Maria	Fundacion Natura	Ecuador
George		Ghana
Abel	Centro Mocovi, Lalek Lav'a	Indigenous Peoples (Argentina, Paraguay, Brazil)
Markku	WWF Malaysia	Malaysia
Frank	World Forest Institute	Pacific Northwest
Ramsy	Foundation of the Peoples of the South Pacific	Papua New Guinea
Santiago	Fundación Peruana para la Conservación de la Naturaleza	Peru
Mathias	Swedish University of Agricultural Sciences, Dept. of Wildlife Ecology; WWF Sweden	Sweden
Louis		Switzerland
Keith	WWF UK	United Kingdom

that might be included. In contrast to the first meetings, these "guidelines" as to how to conduct the meeting provided less opportunity to fundamentally challenge what had already been inscribed; the aim was mostly to receive feedback on the feasibility of a transnational certification organization from all concerned parties from the selected countries (Holly 1993b). The manual also laid out how the expected outcomes were to be structured, and what they should entail. Thus, the epistemic dimension of the process was a controlled testing of the emerging governance arrangement. The comments regarding the Principles and Criteria (former Forest Stewardship Standards) and the FSC Charter were incorporated throughout the year 1993 and finalized before the Founding Assembly in October.

Characterizing Documents: The Principles and Criteria
as of September 1993 and the FSC Charter

I have elaborated above on the Forest Stewardship Standards as they were in December 1991. Kilian and Logan (working for the conservation NGO Rainforest Alliance) reworked the Forest Stewardship Standards after the meeting in Washington, DC, in 1992, and turned them into the sixth draft of the Principles and Criteria that was sent out to 5,000 stakeholders worldwide and debated at the workshops set up for the consultative process. In late August 1993, the Principles and Criteria Working Group met in Burlington, Vermont to review comments and finalized the seventh draft of the Principles and Criteria, which was then presented at the Founding Assembly in October 1993 (cited as FSC 1993b).

The document changed considerably between the Forest Stewardship Standards and the Principles and Criteria: The one-page introduction constructs consumer demand as the driving force in the formation of the FSC that accredits certifying organizations in order to "guarantee the authenticity of their claims" (FSC 1993b). The Principles and Criteria are designed to complement, not supplant, existing laws. The purpose they serve is to be incorporated into the evaluation system of organizations that are accredited as certifiers by the FSC. Thus, the FSC is a certifier of certifiers. This introduction is followed by four pages setting out nine principles specified by the criteria, which the Principles and Criteria seventh draft lists as follows (see FSC 1993b):

Principle # 1: Compliance with Law and FSC Principles—Forest management operations shall respect all applicable laws of the country in which they occur and international treaties and agreements to which the country is signatory, and comply with all FSC Principles and Criteria.

Principle # 2: Tenure and Use Rights—Long-term tenure and use rights to the land and forest resources shall be clearly defined, documented, and legally established.

Principle # 3: Indigenous Peoples' Rights—The legal and/or customary rights of indigenous peoples to own, use, and manage their lands, territories, and resources shall be recognized and respected.

Principle # 4: Community Rights and Relations—Forest Management operations shall maintain or enhance the long-term social and economic well-being of forest workers and local communities.

Principle # 5: Optimizing Benefits from the Forest—Forest management operations shall encourage the optimal and efficient use of the forest's multiple products and services, in order to ensure economic viability and a wide range of environmental, social, and economic benefits.

Principle # 6: Environmental Impact—Forest management operations shall maintain the critical ecological functions of the forest and minimize adverse impacts on biological diversity, water resources, soils, non-timber resources, and unique and fragile ecosystems and landscapes.

Principle # 7: Management Plan—A management plan consistent with the FSC principles and appropriate to the scale of operations shall be written, implemented, and kept up to date, clearly stating the objectives of management, and the means of achieving them.

Principle # 8: Monitoring and Assessment—Regular monitoring should be conducted that assesses the condition of the forest yields of forest products, chain of custody, and management operations and their social and environmental impacts.

Principle # 9: Relations between Natural Forests and Plantations—Natural forests should not be replaced by tree plantations. Plantations should complement natural forests and reduce pressure on them.

Whereas the Forest Stewardship Standards had mainly specified the technical and administrative aspects, the Principles and Criteria in the seventh draft clearly emphasize the political and social aspects. This becomes particularly observable with regard to the rights of indigenous peoples. The Forest Stewardship Standards of 1991 had already elaborated at some length on the involvement of "local people," but spoke of adequate compensation and noted that "great care is needed to avoid either suppressing or exaggerating needs and rights" of local people (Thomas 1991, 15). These diminishing attributes are deleted in favor of more rights-based language that puts indigenous peoples in control of their lands. This change of language was also demanded in some of the country assessments. For instance, the report from Peru argues that indigenous peoples should also be seen as "executors of management and not as being affected" (Santiago 1993, 47). This issue of indigenous peoples also became an important issue at the Founding Assembly, as I will explain in the next chapter.

The second important document that received comments was the FSC Draft Charter. Tom from the Ecological Trading Company prepared the first draft in May 1991. This draft went through several rounds of consultation and revision. For instance, the interim board met in Burlington, Vermont in April 1993 with an environmental legal advisor (Holly 1993b, 9). The interim coordinator collated the comments and prepared the next draft in July 1993 (FSC 1993a).[19]

This FSC draft charter gives a short, one-page overview of the FSC's organizational philosophy, sketches the FSC's organizational structure on two pages, and ends by mentioning unresolved issues regarding the organizational structure. The memo and the FSC Charter already mention two important points: Holly notes that the charter "has not been written in legal language or with a particular legal system in mind" because the location of the FSC headquarters was at that time undecided, and the charter would be redrafted by a legal advisor in the nationally appropriate form (Holly 1993a). New international organizations are negotiated within legal frameworks provided by international law. Although this can also lead to confusion, intergovernmental negotiations provide a much clearer context than transnational politics where legal issues are more uncertain. Thus, despite the legal advisors the interim board consulted, the document does not contain the careful wording that is common in intergovernmental negotiations.

In addition, the memo points out that the FSC "seems to be moving towards becoming a foundation, which means that the charter that is agreed upon in Toronto will be changed only with great difficulty" (Holly 1993a). This is a central and contested issue. Following the legal advice it had received, the interim board opted at the beginning of 1993 for a governance structure that would be accountable to a board of *directors*, rather than a *membership*. The structure would then include a board of directors, an advisory board, a secretariat, various technical committees, and a number of regional representatives or national offices, or both (Holly 1993b, 11). An organigram in the FSC Draft Charter displays the proposed organizational structure, and thereby gives an element of the organization a visual representation (fig. 3). As the organigram shows, this governance structure for the FSC would have a managing board of directors at the international level, and would, in theory, "encourage the development of an FSC membership at a national level" (Holly 1993b, 11).

However, others proposed a membership organization instead at the international level, and therefore opted for an association with a membership base and not for a foundation. The International Federation of Organic Agricultural Movements, established in 1972, served as a powerful blueprint for a membership organization (Dingwerth and Pattberg 2009, 725). While the interim board preferred to set up the FSC as a foundation that would promise greater flexibility and efficiency, there was no consensus reached and the decision was left to the Founding Assembly (see next chapter).

The FSC Draft Charter also clearly points out that the FSC will be set up as an NGO, and that "it will remain independent from commercial timber interest and government control" (FSC 1993a, 1). At the same time,

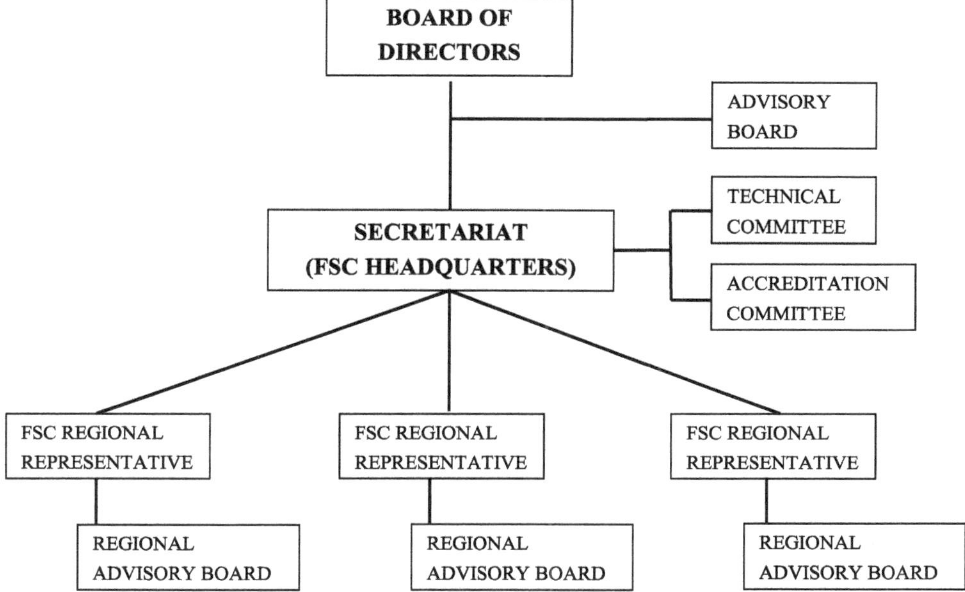

Fig. 3. The proposed organizational structure of an FSC as of July 1993 (adapted from FSC 1993b, 3).

it reiterates the sustainability discourse of balance, arguing for an "environmentally appropriate," "socially beneficial," and "economically viable forest management." This notion of balance can also be found in the proposed composition of the board of directors:

> There will be a total of seven Directors on the Board with at least two Directors from each of the following categories: social, environmental, and economic perspectives. In addition, the Board of Directors should reflect a geographical balance between temperate, tropical, and boreal regions, as well as possess a diversity of legal, organizational, management, and financial skills. No government representatives, or individuals who have any commercial interest in forest management or in the trade of forest products may serve on the Board (Economics representatives may include forest economics, retired business persons, academics, etc.). (FSC 1993a, 2)

The sequence indicates how the interim board carefully thought about orchestrating the composition of the board by, on the one hand, representing the perspectives of all main stakeholder groups and, on the other, keeping out those representatives or individuals who clearly had commercial interests. It was an attempt to link with all interested parties but, at the same time, to secure the FSC from being co-opted by powerful interests, whether governments or the forest industry.

These attempts to progressively characterize the governance structure of the arrangement remained vague. Many terms, such as "economic interest," lacked precise definition; the "unresolved issues" of the organizational structure point to questions regarding internal accountabilities within the organizations. However, this stepwise process was not only due to not knowing what a "viable and appropriate organizational structure" might look like (Holly 1993b, 11). The interim coordinator, Holly, notes in the memo to the draft that the FSC will remain in a "transitional phase" for several years at least, during which it will be difficult to predict how the FSC will change, "and even more difficult to try and direct that change by writing it into the Charter" (Holly 1993a). From her perspective, the FSC Draft Charter should therefore "1. Contain the minimum essential items which will ensure its integrity, 2. Focus only on what the Founding Group in Toronto needs to ratify, 3. Allow enough flexibility for future change and growth" (Holly 1993a). In other words, she performs translational practices of disclosure/enclosure: she suggests focusing on a few elements that will be stabilized through ratification by the Founding Assembly (enclosure) while leaving enough elements flexible, and thus unstable, to allow for as yet unforeseen events (disclosure).

Conclusions

Forest and forest governance were highly politicized issues throughout the 1980s and early 1990s. Social and ecological NGOs, with their different agendas, campaigned against the forest industry and the emerging international institutions that were dominated by those whose primary interest was in easily trading timber rather than accounting for environmental standards or social rights. It was against this background that concerned wood users and environmental and social NGOs searched for alternatives to deforestation and addressed social injustice. In this chapter, I have outlined islands of innovation and examined the governance knowledge that was produced in these contexts. The production of governance knowledge was required to constitute a team, which occurred at the first meeting in Amherst, Massachusetts. The Certification Working Group translated governance knowledge into a reiterative structure of meetings and documents, and further worked on and negotiated this knowledge in these meetings. The journey of the nascent FSC shows that actors had to be quite careful to add new members only gradually. The meeting in Washington, DC, in 1992 had grown in size, and thus the differences that came with new actors led to the unproductive breakdown of the meeting—the staged performance failed. At the same time, the attempts to interest not only a small group of people but to encourage broad participation from various sectors and various regions of the world were intended to legitimize the emerging arrangement. As a result, the strategy brought about the participative turn and win–win logic that have become a paradigm in governance beyond the state (Voß and Freeman 2016). I have shown how the consultative process of the FSC had not only an epistemic dimension (i.e., to produce governance knowledge) but also a political one (i.e., to make people realize that a certification system for forestry might solve the deadlocked conflict between the various antagonistic groups). The best governance arrangements do not help, however, if there is no supporting cast interested in buying into the logic of trusting a market mechanism to ensure conservation and social justice. Thus, the consultative process was a crucial element not only in furthering the construction of the arrangement but also in making the world ready for private authority. I explore the conflicts in the next chapters through a microanalysis of the FSC Founding Assembly.

4 | Paratext

The FSC's Founding Assembly

The FSC's Founding Assembly on October 1–3, 1993, was a meeting with a short history, loose institutional structures, and an ambitious agenda—to create a certification organization with a highly diverse membership. This chapter provides a paratext (Genette 1997), which frames the actual text, providing contextual information on the setting, characters, documents, issues, and dramaturgical structure of the Founding Assembly as well as rival theoretical accounts.

The Setting

The Westbury Hotel in Toronto served as the venue for the Founding Assembly.[1] The setup referred to a classical conference arrangement. At the front, there was a line of desks reserved for presenters, the facilitator, and the interim board of the FSC facing the other participants who sat at round tables in groups of 8 to 10 people. One microphone was placed at the front and one floor microphone was reserved for participants. The microphones not only served as transmitters of the event but also functioned as ordering devices for the event itself. Since there were interpreters located at the side, every participant had to speak into a microphone so that his or her statement could be translated. The microphone reflected the legitimate speaking position. Backstage conversations, chats over dinner, and caucus meetings were not recorded. In other words, the differentiation into backstage and front stage became a second spatial layer reinforced and made relevant by the actors themselves.

The Characters

The list of participants names 134 actors (see appendix). During the assembly, the facilitator enacted the list. According to him, the total number of representatives was 126. Forty-six percent came from the Global South and 44 percent came from the Global North; the other 10 percent consisted of participants who did not categorize themselves. Some scholars who attended the meeting were active in NGOs, others were not. The facilitator also gave a breakdown of the different sectors present. From the Global North, 38 percent of participants were categorized as belonging to environmental interests, while 42 percent came from economic interests (the forest industry) and 9 percent were representatives of social groups. From the Global South, 38 percent also came from environmental interests, 31 percent were from the forest industry, and 24 percent came from social groups. Again, there were also unknowns in these categories. The breakdown indicates that the roughly 130 participants were orchestrated by the interim board of the FSC with the rationale in mind of including a broad range of stakeholders while at the same time keeping a balance between North and South as well as the three sectors. The enactment of this balance discourse is one of the topics in the prologue.

However, the list of participants shows not only an attempt to find a balance but also reveals that, at the Founding Assembly, actors with strong antagonistic interests sat in one room. For instance, there were representatives from the Malaysian Timber Industry Development Council, which in the early 1990s financed a special task force in Europe to, in their own words, "repel falsehood and lies spread by evil-intended environmentalists" (cited in Human Rights Watch and Natural Resources Defense Council 1992, 51). On the other side of the spectrum, there were transnational and local NGOs in the room that had gained attention in Europe through boycotts and media campaigns. Indigenous organizations from Latin America and business representatives with a record of human rights violations spent a weekend together negotiating whether or not they should found an organization.

In addition, government representatives from Nigeria, Ghana, the United States, Sweden, the Netherlands, Malaysia, Canada, Ecuador, and a representative from the World Bank joined the meeting. These governmental actors, however, did not utter any speech acts (apart from the US representatives stating that they consider the FSC a private initiative). Thus, the list of participants shows that at the Founding Assembly it was not the case that only small-scale wood users with an interest in preserving the rainforest sat together with representatives from local community projects. Instead, participants reflected a broad spectrum of partly antagonistic interests.

Documents and Issues

By October 1993, the interim board, the Principles and Criteria Working Group, and the coordinator of the FSC had incorporated the comments received from the consultative process into the two documents that defined the nascent FSC, namely, the Principles and Criteria and the FSC Charter. Also, the FSC interim coordinator put together a 13-page document that summarized the FSC's history and background, the consultative process, the Principles and Criteria, and the FSC Charter as well as the development of these documents (Holly 1993b). Especially with regard to the development of the two essential documents (the Principles and Criteria and the Charter), the summary offers insights into the entire process. These were the working documents that the participants had received in advance and that were laid out at the assembly.

During the weekend in Toronto the participants negotiated a number of issues. They questioned the applicability and quality of the Principles and Criteria for sustainable forestry, the benefit of certification for indigenous peoples, the consultative process, the lack of procedural rules for the assembly, the participation of the economic sector, and the governance structure of the organization. These issues were often discussed in a rather unstructured way. Intertwined discussions of procedural and substantive issues caused confusion and led to the emergence of new speakers who presented themselves as experts on procedures; they enacted politics and polity knowledge. Despite the antagonistic forces, the participants had agreed on tentative procedural rules for the assembly and eventually opted for an association and not a foundation as the FSC governance structure. This decision implied that the assembly and not the board of directors would be the supreme authority in the organization. Consequently, the structure of the voting membership became a controversial issue. It was decided to create an economic caucus that had 25 percent of the vote, and an environmental and social caucus that had 75 percent of the vote. Both caucuses would have a North–South balance. A complicated voting mechanism was also created that would ensure a balance within the board of directors and would be enacted through the election of nine members to the first board of the FSC. Yet bringing closure to these issues and voting on them caused not only controversial discussions but also the withdrawal of some indigenous and environmental NGOs.

A Dramaturgical Structure

My discussion of the Founding Assembly follows a sequential order with a prologue, four acts, and an epilogue. The notion of acts refers to the script of the meeting that the participants reconstruct through their speech acts; they script the meeting and thereby determine speaker roles and cues for appropriate behavior. Most prominently, the interim board, in cooperation with the facilitator, engages in these communicative efforts to script the assembly in order to push their agenda. The participants add to these efforts and support or reject the attempts at scripting.

The participants in the Founding Assembly arrive on Friday evening. The *Prologue* opens chapter 4. The interim board of the nascent organization welcomes the audience. Two keynote speeches contextualize the meeting, introduce the participants to each other, and sketch the work ahead. On Saturday morning the *First Act* begins with further speeches and presentations on the organization. Ten country reports and the latest Principles and Criteria for sustainable forestry are presented. It is not until Saturday afternoon that the *Second Act* is opened when the assembly is invited to comment and have its say. Having been silent for quite some time the participants articulate in a vivid discussion that, in their view, certain issues deserve attention. The discussion runs on in smaller groups backstage until late at night. Early on Sunday morning participants are back in the assembly hall; it is the *Third Act*. The assembly moves toward voting on some of the issues. Then, a controversy breaks out. The meeting has its moment of drama. Dissident voices resign from the process, leaving the nascent organization. Chapter 5 commences when the dissident participants have vanished. The *Fourth Act* presents itself as a working session in which spokespersons articulate positions from their groups. In a series of translations the participants manage to manufacture consensus on the issues mentioned above. The act ends with the election of the first board of the FSC. The *Epilogue* honors all participants who have been involved in organizing the event. A round of applause celebrates what has been achieved in that short period of time.

Since there are basically no rules of procedure, the communicative situation is messy. Oftentimes the participants, even those who are trying to facilitate the meeting, are confused and remain puzzled about what they are actually debating. The dramaturgical approach does not streamline this complex situation but shows how the participants achieve order despite the high contingency and uncertainty regarding appropriate rules. A "chorus"—"a device to enable the audience to reach a more serene reflection of the hero: it is a glass through which our perspective is focused" (Goldhill 2013, 39)—will guide the reader through the three-day conference, reflecting on the mechanism of translation and its theoretical advantage against other rival explanations.

The Mechanism of Translation and Rival Explanations

The following acts continue to tell a story about the explanatory power of a microsociological account in general and the mechanism of translation in particular. The central claim is that we are able to observe the founding of the organization in its specific form only because practices of translation, with their constitutive effects, are present. In this sense, the mechanism of translation explains how antagonistic actors manufactured consensus in complex negotiations. In the absence of the translational mechanism, the FSC would have been constituted differently, or even not at all.

Especially in the context of negotiations, the predictions of two rival or alternative explanations must be considered—rationalist bargaining theory and deliberative approaches. Rationalist bargaining theory argues that the distribution of power across the negotiation parties explains the outcome. Power can be operationalized as power over material resources. Since we are in the field of markets, relative market size reflects companies' bargaining power (Steinberg 2002, 347). Market opening and market closure are the currency of negotiations (Krasner 1976).

Rationalist bargaining theory predicts that industry dominates process and outcome. If it decides to be part of an institution design exercise, it makes sure that it creates an institution with purely symbolic commitments. It has a clear preference for creating a decision-making body that can be controlled easily and shies away from a decision-making body with radical groups that might hold firms accountable (see Bartley 2007b, 305).[2] However, the actual outcome does not reflect these predictions. As I will show in more detail, industry accepts strong criteria for sustainable forestry as well as a minority position within the decision-making structure of a membership organization and not a foundation, an option which was also on the table. This outcome is somewhat puzzling for this type of bargaining theory and thus requires a different kind of explanation.

In a nutshell, I argue that only a process perspective can explain the outcome. Unpacking the process allows us to observe that industry is not a unitary actor nor are environmental groups homogeneous. Instead, it is possible to explore alliances and conflicts across and within the various subgroups. The specific decision-making structure does not reflect the distribution of power among the groups but rather the search for recognition. Participants anticipate the conditions under which a global audience would recognize the emerging organization as a private authority. For this reason, the negotiating parties successfully translate not only new knowledge about forestry and governance but also their own diversity into the emerging institution.

A second alternative explanation stems from theories of deliberation, conceptualized for IR by Thomas Risse (2000). This process-oriented account stresses the importance of communicative interaction (i.e., arguing and giving reasons) in coming to an integrative agreement. This strand of deliberative theory predicts that in situations of high uncertainty about interest or identities, the underlying rules of the game, as well as apparently irreconcilable differences, actors engage in arguing and give reasons (Risse 2000, 33). Following this line of thinking, one might assume that actors try to engage in trust building and establish common "rules of the game" (i.e., rules of procedure). However, the empirical story is more complex. I will show how participants try to find ways to build trust. They press for rules of procedure to legitimize the entire project. But these rules of the game are not the outcome of a deliberative process that tailors them to the needs of the group. Instead, participants mobilize already established politics knowledge and recontextualize this knowledge in the given situation. They rather take what is handy—established procedures that help them to manage the situation.

In addition, theories of deliberation predict that honest brokers can help to shift negotiations toward a problem-solving mode (Risse and Kleine 2010, 714). Again, the empirical story does not match this prediction. While deliberation-theory-based approaches are right in pointing to the importance of brokers, I will show that these brokers are neither "honest" nor always successful: a chair may be unable to perform the role properly because he or she clearly lacks politics knowledge. Brokers help the assembly to move forward, but their role as translators means choosing what and how to translate. Translation is an active choice. It leads to the exclusion of certain positions.

5 | Re-Presenting at the Assembly

This chapter examines participants' efforts to re-present at the assembly. The notion of re-presenting refers here both to the need to politically represent people, positions, and other forms of governance knowledge and to make present and perform in front of an audience. With Christian Bueger (2015, 7), I understand re-presenting as a translational practice of recontextualization since it is about making something "(con)textually visible and available" that "is absent and therefore needs to be introduced into the present situation." In what follows, the participants in the assembly engage in one way or the other in practices of re-presenting to determine or script the present situation. As the third act shows, this includes practices of excluding dissenters.

Prologue: Scripting the Founding Assembly

The Founding Assembly of the FSC began in the early evening of Friday, October 1, 1993 with an introduction by Adrian, an interim board member. Then Nicholas (also an interim board member) gave an overview of the history and purpose of the nascent FSC, and introduced the agenda for the two and a half days. His speech was followed by a keynote from Mark, a professional speaker and author.

In this *prologue*, the interim board scripts the event by determining (a) the characters, (b) the nature of the problem, and (c) the cues for appropriate behavior to address the problem. These efforts at scripting amount to a distinct storyline constructed to guide the participants through the two and a half days of negotiations. While such communicative practices are nothing unusual, I investigate how these efforts at scripting were used to overcome the controversies within the heterogeneous group of participants who had been engaged in deep conflicts for years. Scripting is a practice of *politics knowledge* that operates as a strategy to foster coopera-

TABLE 5. The Interim Board, Seated in the Front Row of the Assembly Hall

Lisa	Cultural Survival; US	Social NGO (North)
Adrian	Wood Workers Alliance for Rainforest Protection; A&M Wood Specialty; US	Economic Interests (North)
Stella	Scientific Certification System (SCS); US	Economic Interests (North)
Brian	World Wildlife Fund (WWF) international; UK/Switzerland	Environmental NGO (North)
Nicholas	Professor of Forestry: Venezuela	Science (South)
Carlos	Independent Consultant (Proyecto Latifoliado); Honduras	Economic Interests (South)
Aaron	Environmental Coordinator B&Q; UK	Economic Interests (North)

tion; it is in this sense a power tool. To empirically substantiate the argument, I lay out all three speeches (Adrian's, Nicholas's, and Mark's), and analyze how the speakers scripted the Founding Assembly.

The Narrator Welcomes the Audience and Introduces the Characters

Adrian, a member of the interim board, opens the event; he welcomes the participants to the Founding Assembly of the FSC. His speaker role this evening is that of a narrator: he announces the major characters at the conference and the agenda for the evening. The functions and duties of the characters provide a preliminary sketch of the speaker roles. He starts out by introducing the current interim board that is seated in the front row of the assembly hall (table 5).

The composition of the interim board already reflects a representational approach; each sector has a seat at the board and so has the Global South and the Global North. While the interim board has been in charge of the substantive work, the narrator also introduces a group of actors who have been, and will be, assigned to taking care of more procedural matters, such as the FSC coordinator and the facilitator for the Founding Assembly, Benjamin. All the characters are asked to stand, and the audience applauds each one as the narrator introduces them. The applause is a ritual honoring of already accomplished work and things that will be accomplished in the future. And yet the appreciation holds less for each individual than for the team engaged in a dramaturgical cooperation

(Goffman 1959, 88). The team has envisioned a dramaturgy with different types of knowledge input, and they will try to move the assembly forward when it runs into dead ends. The cooperation is by no means a fixed entity but is potentially open to others; I will show how in the third and fourth act, participants join the cooperative effort by developing specialized speaker roles.

Also, at the end of the assembly the participants will elect a new board that will operate as the team in the future. The narrator indicates this transition as he introduces the nominated candidates. He asks them to stand so that each of them becomes visible in the arena.[1] The nominees for the future board of directors consist mostly of people who have already been involved in the FSC process either from its inception or through the consultative process undertaken by the interim board.

By now, the characters of the play are more differentiated. A team with clear speaker roles seems to be overseeing the dramaturgical performance for the moment. The potential new members of the board will try to gain credits and choose words carefully to convince others they are the right individuals to belong to the board of directors. In addition, the narrator engages in more subtle, less obvious forms of scripting. For instance, he points to the translation devices for those who do not speak English, presents and leads the delegates through the agenda for the evening, introduces little "surprises to be won" (six tickets for an opera), and tries to fill the communicative gap as the assembly waits for the first keynote speaker. The audience responds to his announcements and his bridging attempts—"I am rapidly running out of things to say, and I don't sing very well"—laughter and applause follow (Adrian, Tape 1, Side 1). What these examples show is how the narrator (and in the further process the facilitator) and the audience reconstruct the interaction order and signal the kind of event participants can anticipate. This tacit agreement lifts the burden on the actors to constantly negotiate the situation. For the moment, the interaction order is fairly simple: the front stage is occupied by the team; the audience can applaud, cheer, and listen.

The First Keynote

In his keynote Nicholas, a member of the interim board, offers a second layer of scripting that not only constructs *(a)* the participants as the new governors of forestry (polity knowledge) but also *(b)* the nature of the problem (policy knowledge), and *(c)* the cues for appropriate behavior to address the problem (politics knowledge).

(a) Nicholas constructs a number of *different actor categories* (polity knowledge) that both further differentiate and unify the Founding Assembly at the same time. Here is a short passage from the speech:

> We have been able to bring to this room tonight a group of people which represent quite a variety of points of view [about] what forestry is all about—people from the South and people from the North, from developed and developing countries—and we made a specific effort to do so, to bring a balance of points of views from developing countries and developed countries. I think we have almost mathematically reached this balance. I think there are something like 68 people from the South and some 70 people from the North. We also made a very specific effort to reach another balance, which is about three major groups of stakeholders. Environmental groups, which are here probably the majority; people with economic interests, people that are related to industry or other forms of groups who benefit from forest operations economically; and people who are related mainly to social groups, indigenous organizations, or groups who work with social groups both in developing and developed countries. (Tape 1, Side 1)

Nicholas focuses on the audience, organizing the participants in accordance with an "invitation key" that differentiates the "audience" along two axes: a spatial axis of North and South equated with developing and developed countries, and a sectoral axis (ecological/economical/social). These classification efforts are not only developed in the welcoming speech but also exist as practice when participants register at the conference table, checking one or more of the above categories. The audience learns that these categories are *balanced* with and against each other, reaching "almost a mathematical" balance. The notion of balance is specified as a balance of "points of views [of] what forestry is all about"; it becomes reflexive in the sense that "'forestry'" is described as a product of diverging perspectives, perspectives that are still conflicting but which will be made consensual during the Founding Assembly.

These strategies construct and categorize the participants. Nicholas portrays *environmental groups* from the North and the South as demanding action to stop deforestation and degradation. They have campaigned for a sustainable management of forests all over the world and not just in the tropics. As he sees it, some of these groups find it problematic to work together with industry. He presents *industry* "as an important major group of stakeholders that works with forests" (Tape 1, Side 1). They view forests first and foremost as a product, a raw material that societies all over the world demand, and industry is the means by which forests are turned into consumable products. While industry has no interest in the disappearance of forests, current practice often leads directly to destruction and heavy degradation. Further, Nicholas describes *indigenous people* as living in the forests, and regarding forests as their homes. They may feel threatened by industry since "corporate rights seem to be stronger than human rights" (Tape 1, Side 1).

Nicholas connects these actor categories to the participants in the assembly: "The FSC is an organization which is trying to bring these people together" (Tape 1, Side 1). He categorizes the audience by sector and origin, distinguishes them by referring to their different interests, and eventually unifies them again by directly addressing them, "You are those people." This moment of unification is reinforced when Nicholas abandons claiming "responsibility" for the nascent organization in the name of the interim board, and assigns it to the participants of the assembly. He states that "this is the end of the responsibility that we as the board of directors assumed about a year and a half ago, and that takes a lot from us" (Nicholas, Tape 1, Side 1). To declare the end of the responsibility of the board is to declare the responsibility of the assembly. This notion of empowerment serves to call on the participants to engage productively in the process—a theme that will be repeated again and again.

(b) To outline *the nature of the problem* or policy knowledge, Nicholas embeds the Founding Assembly within the broader discourse on forestry and deforestation. He opens this passage with a common form of fact presentation:

> You are all aware that over the last years the issue of forest management has become one of the most controversial and most sensitive issues anywhere on earth. (Tape 1, Side 1)

Nicholas introduces the statement with a classical rhetorical figure ("You are all aware") that suggests that an argument is being presented that is beyond contestation. The speech act appeals to a presumably consensual belief held by the assembly, and in so doing it functions in two ways. Nicholas's description of the problem (forest management) will appear factual since to dissent from his claims would imply that one contests the consensual belief of the assembly. Hence, the words "you are all aware" act as a "we-construction." The factual description itself, however, does not operate on a level of content but rather as a structural description: forest management is labeled as one of the "most controversial," "most sensitive issues anywhere on earth."

To stabilize his rather hyperbolical depiction, he employs a number of intertextual references to international attempts to display and contain the problem.[2] His overview culminates in an examination of a recent crucial event, the Rio Summit in 1992, at which the international community again could not agree on binding rules. The rhetorical clue is to mirror the failed attempts of states to find an adequate response with the emerging institution, the FSC, in general, and the Founding Assembly in particular.

(c) In doing so, he suggests a solution to the constructed problem and eventually provides *cues for appropriate behavior* (politics knowledge). The following sequence is illuminating in this regard:

> The FSC is an organization which is trying to bring these people together to the same table and that is why you are here tonight, and that is why you were invited to this meeting. You are those people. You are the environmental groups, you are the industry, you are the social general public, scientists, academics, and other members of society and come to this meeting this weekend to overcome our personal limitations, or our personal concerns, or our national concerns, and see if we can find a common agreement, on what sustainable forestry is. (Tape 1, Side 1)

Nicholas establishes two groups of actors. On the one hand, the international community of states who have been unable or unwilling to address the problem of sustainable forestry. On the other hand, a variety of stakeholders who are driven by personal or national concerns that have prevented them, so far, from reaching a "common agreement." The FSC, then, is conceptualized as an institution that provides the spaces for the different stakeholders. By deploying the *pars pro toto*, "You are those people" and "that is why you are here tonight," Nicholas transfers the transnational situation to the local communicative arena. The numerous stakeholders find representation in "those people"; the numerous fora in which sustainable forestry had been discussed culminate in the weekend of the Founding Assembly. It is an intertextual mechanism to meet the challenge of scale and to suggest that in the local communicative arena transnational problems can be negotiated, and a "common agreement" may be reached.

Nicholas is explicit about the "*common agreement*," introducing four specific tasks: (1) the approval of the Principles and Criteria of sustainable forestry that have been generated through an extensive consultative process. Nicholas refers to them with the religious connotation of the nine commandments of forestry: "I wanted to have ten commandments, but I couldn't get that. So, nine commandments that would have to be respected anywhere on earth" (Tape 1, Side 1); (2) the legal structure of the nascent organization; (3) the election of the board; (4) and the question of whether economic interests should be represented on the board of directors. All four tasks are based on proposals that the "team" has prepared for the assembly. However, the epistemic status of the proposals is, according to Nicholas, sufficiently stabilized to work with, and yet at the same time imperfect:

> I would like to emphasize that all these proposals that you have on your tables are not perfect in any way. We don't pretend them to be perfect at all. Each of you can identify things that you disagree with. But at the same time, I ask you to consider that this has been created by talking to many constituencies. So, when you look at these proposals think about the possibility of accepting imperfect proposals that would allow this organization to go forward. (Tape 1, Side 1)

The notion of uncertainty and imperfection is important in this context. In their current status the proposals still attract disagreement despite the communicative work that went into them. Yet the Founding Assembly will be the arena in which they are at least temporarily brought to closure. This transformation process will not occur without further work. After all, actors with diverse backgrounds have assembled in the arena, actors who in the past had irreconcilable differences. Friction is likely to appear. According to Nicholas, the way to overcome these differences is by means of communication as a cue for appropriate behavior.

He conceptualizes the challenge to reach agreement as a communicative challenge to listen to each other and recognize a common interest:

> So, you can ask, how can we do something that governments have failed to do? I think it is precisely because governments tried to do it. Maybe we have a chance here, the civil society, to demonstrate that we try to understand each other. That we have at least the will to talk to each other, and that we have the will that we recognize that we have a common interest, as far as forest management is concerned. We all want good forest management. (Tape 1, Side 1)

Nicholas utilizes a strategy to construct an *out-group* (states) to strengthen the *in-group* (civil society). States failed to agree on binding international rules; civil society now has the opportunity to collaborate. Nicholas does not deny the internal differences within civil society but recognizes diversity as a resource ("I think it is healthy that we have different points of views") (Tape 1, Side 1). Yet he argues that civil society shares a common aim by deploying it as a fact beyond contestation ("We all want good forest management") (Tape 1, Side 1). The means to learn about that common aim is communication:

> I congratulate you for having in some cases the courage and in other cases the interest of coming to this assembly, talking to other people who have been in the past your enemies, or you have considered them to be your enemies. People that in the past you have not been able to understand. Discuss the issues with each other. (Tape 1, Side 1)

Nicholas operates with two binary constructions. First, failed attempts of states in the past are contrasted with civil society, which may succeed in the present. Second, the historical confrontation within civil society is replaced with the search for common agreement via means of communication. To strengthen his argument Nicholas presents a least likely case for the realization of sustainable forestry: he narrates his recent trip to Malaysia, Indonesia, and Brazil. To his own surprise, he says, he found the different stakeholders "working together in harmony. Recognizing the differences, recognizing the extremes in the positions but with the will to work together, and actually producing something that was worth looking at" (Tape 1, Side 1).

The Second Keynote

The narrator introduces the keynote speaker, Mark. The audience learns that he has written and talked on leadership and successful companies in Canada. In contrast to Nicholas, he is not a member of the interim board so that he can be considered as an external party. Yet, sitting at the front, he appears to be part of the "team," and thus engages in the dramaturgical performance of the event. The speech is less clearly structured than Nicholas's welcome note. Stories and anecdotes convey two themes: his keynote both substantiates Nicholas's speech with regard to the cues for appropriate behavior to address the problem (politics knowledge) and he defines the nature of the problem itself (policy knowledge). These two themes find reflection in the notion of a paradigm and in sustainable development as a learning process.

Mark organizes the first part of his speech around the notion of paradigm and paradigm shift as a distinct form of politics knowledge. The narration of each story follows a similar pattern. People act in accordance with a paradigm, for instance using a map to find a place. However, they run into difficulties when they realize that the paradigm they have relied on is wrong—the map actually depicts another city. Mark's underlying message appears again and again throughout his talk in different forms, as in this example:

> You see a paradigm determines our behavior and our attitude, all our thoughts and our actions through which we see the world. If you fundamentally wanna change something, change the way you see things. (Tape 1, Side 1)

Once he has established his notion of paradigm shift as a means of solving fundamental problems he applies the framework to the situation at the Founding Assembly.

His core argument is that the following sentences belong to a "wrong paradigm": "environmentalists and business cannot work together"; "all business is bad"; and economic and environmental aims contradict each other (Tape 1, Side 2). Instead of simply inverting each statement, he outlines success stories from Canadian companies. This part of the storyline is condensed in the following sequence:

> So, it was not only good for the environment; it was good for business. And we are not looking for a compromise situation. . . . And so, if I really want to develop a win–win situation, I have to begin by listening to the other party. . . . That requires us to be open. I have to listen to his concerns and his needs and he has to listen to mine in order to work this out. (Tape 1, Side 2)

The storyline incorporates the notion of a paradigm shift, that is, business interests and environmental concerns are reconcilable. And even further, the new paradigm is not a compromise, but a "win–win situation" that is realized through careful listening to each other's concerns; any notion of conflict vanishes; he conceptualizes political controversies as caused by a false paradigm and not by substantial differences.

The keynote speaker elaborates on the nature of the problem by summarizing sustainable development as a learning process (policy knowledge). Mark starts out by quoting professors at prestigious universities who "collectively tell us that if we don't significantly change the way we do business the whole world is gonna end in 100 years" (Tape 1, Side 2). This rather dark scenario is supported by statistical data to connect the speech act to a knowledge resource and established authorities.[3] Among others, he summarizes Thomas Berry's book *The Dream of the Earth* (1988), in which the author tells the story of environmental degradation in the Philippines. According to Mark, the degradation was done "to feed the people," which finally led to a situation in which the land was no longer fertile due to soil erosion (Tape 1, Side 2). Mark adds the metaphor of a goose that lays golden eggs until its owner becomes greedy and kills the goose to have all the eggs at once.

The metaphors are constructed to further enhance the power of the argument: the storyline draws on a discourse of sustainable development that describes sustainability in terms such as fixed limits, finiteness of resources, and responsible consumption. Mark refers on the one hand to a dark scenario of the "dying Earth" and the "limits to growth." The practices that normally follow from this discourse would fall into the category of less consumption and preserving and saving natural resources. Yet these are not the type of practice Mark advertises. Instead, his message speaks of a new form of governing: "we must move the market" (Tape 1, Side 2). Potential conflicts between both positions are due to "wrong paradigms," which can be overcome via communication and learning. To stress the notion of learning, Mark narrates little stories that end with catchy truisms such as "perfection is the killer of progress" and "true knowledge is gained through application, and not through study" (Tape 1, Side 2). This process-orientated notion of learning is finally linked back to the assembly: "And so, I challenge you all this weekend to have a bias for action in the pursuit that you have" (Tape 1, Side 2).

Chorus: Pushing a Script

The keynote ends, the audience applauds, the narrator announces some further organizational items, and then the tape stops. The two speeches skillfully use knowledge of governance and, specifically, politics knowledge of tactics for creating legitimacy. They introduce the notion of "balance"[4] to counter a natural system that is "out of balance."[5] Stories about paradigms provide cues for appropriate behavior, as the speakers argue for a paradigm shift from a paradigm of conflict, which was dominant in the 1980s, to a paradigm of cooperation, which is hoped to be realized with the creation of the FSC.[6]

In pushing this script, the speakers aim to establish shared knowledge with regard to the perception of the problem and the ways in which the problem should adequately be addressed. It is a first attempt at setting something as stable (practices of enclosure) so that the assembly can begin its work addressing what requires further deliberation (practices of disclosure).

Yet these translational practices will be contested. As the conference proceeds, an NGO representative from the Philippines will vehemently attack the grand narrative of degradation that occurred "to feed the people" as Mark argued when he outlined the nature of the problem. Instead of buying into the storyline of "the people" who have lived beyond their means, she will declare that, in fact, "the people of the Philippines" have been fighting for their land and forests against multinational companies. When she does this, power hierarchies, struggle, and controversies will find their way back into the assembly.

First Act: Enacting Governance Knowledge

On Saturday morning, October 2, 1993, the first working day of the Founding Assembly began. A facilitator outlined the agenda for the day, and from then onward through coffee and lunch breaks until roughly 4 p.m. in the afternoon, the participants listened to presentations on the consultative process and the status of the Principles and Criteria. A general overview of the consultative process and the history of the FSC preceded presentations on 11 case studies inquiring into the feasibility of an FSC in countries or regions all over the world. After a short question-and-answer interlude, a member of the Principles and Criteria Working Group outlined the history and status of the Principles and Criteria for sustainable forestry that would build the basis for certification.

In presenting the various documents, the consultants and interim board members enacted the emerging organization in all its tentativeness. Since translation is an active communicative process, the meaning of these reports is reconstructed through their enactment (Freeman 2009; Ringmar 2012). My analysis focuses on how the participants perform the various reports as well as how the performance of governance knowledge creates distinct roles.

Governing Through Devices

Whereas in the *prologue* a member of the interim board served as facilitator, in the *first act* this role was handed over to an external professional facilitator, Benjamin. Although claiming to be neutral, he is part of the team and responsible for orchestrating the Founding Assembly. In line with his role, the facilitator welcomes the participants, and encourages the presenters of the country reports to join the team at the front. He explains a number of "ground rules" that are closely involved with the microphones as a social-technical apparatus (Tape 2, Side 1). Microphones function as devices that contribute to ordering the event itself. There are two in total, one at the front and one in the audience, to signal legitimate speaking positions. Participants who want to speak have to go to the floor microphone located in the middle of the room, as one of the interviewees recalls.

This staging, which seems to be so embedded in the setting itself, is never uncontested. Throughout the conference the facilitator reinforces the legitimate speaking position (microphone) several times. If a controversy emerges in which participants violate the ordered form of deliberation by shouting their opinion, he will intervene, noting that the speaker is "out of order." To legitimatize his claim, he provides a justificatory argument that was already present in his introduction to the ground rules of the event:

> The other thing I would ask, and that I am sure you agree with, is to maintain an equality in participation. I would ask you that if you have points to make, that you please go to the microphone. We are working in simultaneous translation. (Tape 2, Side 1)

To introduce the floor microphone as a means of ensuring "equality in participation" legitimizes the asymmetrical allocation of speaking opportunities. It is hard to argue against "equality in participation" and the right to follow the discussion in one's preferred language. Although all participants are invited to speak, those who are sitting at the front desk have a greater chance to make a statement than those who are sitting in the audience. If anyone violates this interaction order he or she not only ignores the established procedure but also hinders the interpreters from translating from Spanish into English and vice versa. The facilitator introduces the apparatus of microphones and interpreters as a prerequisite to ensure equal participation at a large communicative event with diverse social actors.

The facilitator also anchors the presentation of the rules to notions of a "high level of cooperation, and, in fact a spirit of fairness and a spirit of democracy" that he apparently experienced in the meeting the night before (Tape 2, Side 1). Thus, he concludes:

> To a large degree the group will manage itself. My job should be fairly simple as we go forward. Because, quite frankly, I do sense that there is a momentum that has been built in this organization. (Tape 2, Side 1)

The reference to the storyline of the evening before with regard to cooperation aims to further stabilize the communicative rules of the assembly. At the same time, it suggests that the facilitator underestimates the conflicts and antagonistic forces that exist within the group. Besides introducing the ground rules, he also outlines the agenda for the day. A background talk on the history of the FSC and the consultative process will introduce the current state of the organization, which will be followed by case study reports. After a short question-and-answer session, the Principles and Criteria will be presented. For now, the interaction order remains simple. Uttering a speech act from the audience is restricted to the question-and-answer session. There is a clear divide between the team that gives input and the audience that receives knowledge.

Translating Policy and Polity Knowledge into the Meeting

To recall, one of the results of the FSC meeting in Washington, DC, in 1992 was a call for broader worldwide participation realized through a consultative process that is now to be presented at the Founding Assembly. The presentations last for several hours. Providing this wealth of knowledge is an attempt to legitimize the efforts of the interim board. Anyone who claims after these presentations that the interim board has failed to appropriately consult with concerned parties can then be asked, "Would you prefer to sit down even longer, and listen to even more country reports?" Stressing this performance element is important, since it makes a difference whether the interim board simply holds a folder of reports up in the air and claims, "Look, we have done everything we could in this short period of time to consult with all stakeholders," or consultants from the countries actually speak and perform the knowledge.

Since the FSC is designed as a transnational organization that seeks to operate globally, the challenge is to convince the participants in the assembly that the consultative process has taken locally varying sociopolitical characteristics into account, and that the Principles and Criteria are applicable around the world. Those who present specify how the nascent organization has conducted the transnational consultative process, and how the Principles and Criteria for sustainable forest management have been produced. It is a translational process that directs the inquiry to the ways in which policy and polity knowledge is enacted in the arena of the Founding Assembly.

Introducing the Consultative Process

The interim coordinator of the emerging FSC elaborates on its history and the consultative process that the team has undertaken to probe the feasibility of a transnational certification organization. Holly begins her speech with a quote from the anthropologist Margaret Mead: "Never doubt that a small group of dedicated individuals can change society; indeed, nothing else ever has" (Tape 2, Side 1). The quote serves as a reference to the few actors who began their work at the conference in Amherst, Massachusetts. Thereafter, she outlines the work of the Consultative Process Working Group. Central to her presentation are the working group's efforts to arrive at a representative sample of countries. She introduces the categories that have been used:

> One is the type of management—whether it is community-based or industry-based. Another is land tenure—whether the land is primarily owned publicly or privately. Another is forest type—whether the country has primarily plantation or natural forest. Another is the type of forest product—whether the primary product is timber, pulp, or nontimber forest products. The marketplace has been considered—whether there is a domestic or international market. And finally, they wanted to have a balance of forest ecosystems. They wanted to include boreal, temperate, and tropical forest systems. (Tape 2, Side 1)

Holly uses a reference to the speech by Nicholas from the evening before. Nicholas claimed in the *prologue* that the interim board had put a lot of effort into reaching a "mathematical balance" between the various stakeholder groups. The interim coordinator evokes a similar balance. It is a balance of "type of management," of "type of forest product," and of "forest ecosystems" that the team has invited to the Founding Assembly. She outlines this "invitation key" that is directed not at *political representation* but at the *representation of nature* in the Founding Assembly.

Political representation and representation of nature are intertwined. The generation of knowledge has also generated interest in the general project as Holly points out:

> But, more importantly, the objectives included starting a process within those countries of engaging a wide variety of people with a broader range of perspectives in dialogue and debate. And I think that is happening in a number of countries. In Brazil, for example, the process of dialogue and debate has led to a delegation of 16 Brazilians attending this assembly today. (Tape 2, Side 1)

By attending a small-scale workshop on forest management in a country, stakeholders have not only contributed to the production of knowledge on the feasibility of certification but have, in fact, became part of a so far loose collective that did not exist before. Holly underlines that agreement exists "that FSC is timely and appropriate. There is disagreement about how it will work and how it will overcome various obstacles" (Tape 2, Side 1). Consequently, the policy and polity knowledge produced remains partial, uncertain, and even contradictory at times.

Presenting the Country Reports

The FSC had commissioned case studies on the feasibility of an FSC with clear suggestions for the qualitative methods that should be used. Each of the consultants elaborates for 15–20 minutes on his or her country and, in doing so, enacts the knowledge he or she has generated. Although this exercise takes quite some time, the general content of these reports will not be questioned by the participants in the following acts. Yet the presentations shed light on the hopes and concerns regarding the new instrument as well as on the deep uncertainty of a multistakeholder certification program:

Abel notes on the indigenous consultation process:

> The indigenous peoples have suffered in the past, in the present, and maybe in the future from the permanent invasion of their countries by states and the timber industry. The latter never accepted our rights to the land. We consider the consultation process as a means to change this situation, and that is why Centro

> Mocovi welcomes the idea of an FSC and agreed to initiate a consultation process. (Tape 2, Side 2; translation A. E.)

According to Abel, colonial history continues due to the permanent invasion either by the state or the timber industry. Hence, the controversy on land rights remains; the FSC is envisioned as a means to secure the rights of indigenous peoples to their land.

By contrast, the country report on Ghana frames colonialization partly as a knowledge resource. The presenter thanks the former colonial power, the UK, for having introduced "scientific forestry" to Ghana. The colonial rules ensured, so he argues, that the local population did not destroy the forests. Furthermore, knowledge of forestry did not leave the country when Ghana gained independence but was further strengthened and institutionalized through universities that still cooperate with the Commonwealth and national ministries. These practices of appropriating knowledge on forestry through institutionalization allow Ghana now to be on a par with the former colonial power and the new transnational community.[7]

The presentations as a whole do not paint a clear picture. Rather, the summary of the UK report nicely holds true for the entire consultation process: the presenter notes that "drawing one line of conclusion is rather difficult with such a wealth of diverging opinion expressed, and [while] I think we certainly have many examples of misconceptions, the overall balance was, I think, positive" (Tape 2, Side 2). Thus, the governance knowledge enacted does not provide an unequivocal answer as to whether or not the FSC could operate globally.

Principles and Criteria for Sustainable Forestry

Logan, a member of the Principles and Criteria Working Group, discusses the document that the participants find in their conference package. The Principles and Criteria are a central element of the FSC, since they specify how and by what standards a certifier has to evaluate the management of a forest. While one might assume that Logan would start by presenting the Principles and Criteria, he instead emphasizes the process:

> It has been an enjoyable process. It is a very difficult process. The members—I will show an overhead with the members of the Principles and Criteria Working Group—there are a number of things

that I want to clarify from the beginning in terms of our way of working. First of all, the working group worked on a consensus basis in our meetings. We consider both the document and the process of equal importance. (Tape 3, Side 1)

Logan speaks slowly emphasizing certain terms such as "our way of working." To stress that the *document* (the Principles and Criteria) and the *working process* are considered as equally important is to invite people to open the black box of knowledge production; it is a promise of disclosure. He describes the process of working as dialectical, as both enjoyable and difficult. He displays the members of the working group and their various professional backgrounds—"some of them are consultants, some are from environmental groups, there is no one in the working group that is from large forest industry" (Tape 7, Side 1). He stresses that the group worked on a consensus basis—a claim that implies that conflict was resolved through fair deliberation.[8]

Logan attempts to describe the Principles and Criteria by making the audience familiar with the "philosophies guiding the Principles and Criteria" (Tape 3, Side 1). The first "philosophy" is centered on the notion of voluntarism. It is their "general spirit," as Logan highlights, that the Principles and Criteria function as a voluntary mechanism and do not turn into a "regulatory program" (Tape 3, Side 1). The Principles and Criteria should be generally global but applicable in any local context, incorporating a "balance" as Logan stresses. It is a balance between all the different systems of forest management, "across the different types of scale," and a balance between the Principles and Criteria, which will "be considered as a whole; this is a fundamental understanding of how we approach it" (Tape 3, Side 1). The Principles and Criteria are not hierarchically ranked since some elements may have a higher priority in some areas than others. Envisioned as applicable anywhere on earth, the process of localization requires translating the Principles and Criteria into regional standards, taking into account the specific economical, ecological, social, cultural, and political contexts. Or, as Logan notes:

So when you look at these P&Cs, these are marching orders for certification organizations; in other words, "show me as a certifier how you will address these P&Cs in your standards." . . . So, however different local standards might be, there must be some level of consistency—easier said than done. (Tape 3, Side 1)

Logan mentions a set of practices around the "chain of custody" such as forest auditing, tracking procedures, and tracking technologies. This more technical knowledge is necessary to ensure successful implementation. Logan's talk makes apparent that both the document itself and the practice of knowledge production are given a high level of attention; they are inseparably linked, and so is the process of further characterizing the Principles and Criteria:

> We would like to suggest that if this is put up for any kind of ratification or voting, or whatever happens, that these P&Cs are not be considered just by themselves but with a process suggested for subsequent follow-up. (Tape 3, Side 1)

The Principles and Criteria already entail elements but still lack operational details. Thus, the working group suggests a mixture of stabilizing practices while admitting openly that the Principles and Criteria are still in the making, and that only further epistemic work by all concerned will turn them into an instrument of transnational governance. As the spokesman for the working group, Logan suggests the following procedure:

1. ratification of the provisional Principles and Criteria by this assembly including a subsequent process
2. a first revision by this assembly within six months
3. within these six months further consultations should be carried out
4. a Principles and Criteria committee and the new board of directors are responsible for incorporating new knowledge
5. Principles and Criteria that result from this process will be submitted to a vote
6. the next revision will take place within one year
7. continuous input from various stakeholders is explicitly encouraged

In the further course of the assembly the notions of "ratification" and "continuous input" will be the subject of discussion. While "ratification" is a necessary closure practice for the Principles and Criteria to become operational, "continuous input" is potentially destabilizing since new input needs to be collated, consensualized, and incorporated. To call for both at the same time is to say "let's get started with certification, *and* let's collect more data before we utilize our manufactured instrument."

Chorus: The Performance of Governance Knowledge

It was early in the morning of October 2, 1993, that the facilitator called upon the various consultants to present the country reports to the Founding Assembly. Meanwhile, the participants have had a coffee break at about 10:30 a.m., lunch at about 12:30 a.m., and now they see the next coffee break approaching at 4 p.m.

Rationalist bargaining theories have difficulty in explaining why the negotiating parties spend several hours listening to reports. For these theories, negotiators have to establish "common knowledge" that entails information about the structure of the game and its underlying rules. Similarly, theories of deliberation would understand this situation as the attempts to construct a "common lifeworld" through narratives and so forth (Risse 2000, 16). Both theories assume that "common knowledge" or the "common lifeworld" are established through *interaction*.

In contrast to both rival accounts, the mechanism of translation is more sensible of practices of re-presenting, the making visible and available what is absent. Recall that at the Washington, DC, meeting in 1992 many critical voices demanded broad consultations across the globe. Responding to this call, the consultants engaged in a translational exercise that involved making visible the enormous work that went into the preparation for the Founding Assembly. They introduced into the present situation their knowledge about a new form of governance (polity knowledge) that was collected in local settings, transformed into reports, and now performed for the assembly. While the global applicability of a certification program remains ambiguous, presenters stress process and openness; further characterization during the assembly is required. Thus, the daylong performance of the process itself makes the difference. As a tactic of politics knowledge, the performance itself is even more important than the actual results as no conclusive answers can be given regarding the likelihood of success. In other words, the "common knowledge" or "common lifeworld" is less about an objective reality and more about attempts to construct the given situation in a particular manner. So far, the audience has had little opportunities to have its say; how will the participants respond to the performance of governance knowledge?

Second Act: The Audience Has Its Say

On Saturday afternoon, October 2, Logan ended his report, and the facilitator invited the participants to a question-and-answer session. What was planned as a short discussion with a subsequent vote on the Principles and Criteria turned into a controversial discussion. The recordings end at roughly 8 p.m., when the assembly adjourned for smaller meetings. The speech acts of the afternoon and evening constitute the *second act* in which the audience "has its say." The members of the audience support, contest, and question elements of the nascent organization, or reject the entire project. These negotiations are rather messy. Some of the speech acts refer to each other while others open up new issues. The agenda of the meeting is suspended, so that it remains unclear whether or not the assembly will actually found the FSC that weekend.

In this act, the participants have the chance to speak up, not only to respond to the presentations but to engage in the process of making present themselves. I examine how they articulate themselves, that is, present their character, and how they articulate issues that, in their view, deserve further attention. Three main issues are controversially discussed: the rights of indigenous peoples (policy knowledge); the organizational structure, especially with regard to the issue of representation of the economic interests (polity knowledge); and procedural issues of voting in the absence of procedural rules (polity knowledge). The articulation of the self and the articulation of issues are necessary steps toward manufacturing a consensus because they help to demarcate the lines of conflict in the first place. In so doing, participants engage in the translational practice of what is known or stabilized (practices of enclosure) and what, in their view, requires further work (practices of disclosure).

Articulating a Character

The participants of the Founding Assembly have been made present in the keynote speeches, yet they have not made themselves present: they have remained an audience, not active participants. Making themselves present is a crucial issue since the participants are often representatives of entire organizations or networks. It is their duty to voice positions and fight for specific wording. Thus, they have to articulate a character as representatives. The construction of a character is a performance that operates in relation to others. It is an attempt to position oneself in a communicative arena through articulation. In this context, I focus on the short introductions that actors deploy to display their dramaturgical selves on the one hand and support their claims on the other.

The first sequence is originally expressed in Brazilian Portuguese. Since there are no official interpreters for this language present, Gabriel (the presenter of the Brazilian country report) operates as interpreter. The president of the National Council of Rubber Tappers in Brazil, Amarildo, states his name, his institution, and makes his comment and Gabriel interprets.

> The reputation that they [the National Council of Rubber Tappers] have was the result of a very strong and hard historical process and many people have lost their lives in that process and he mentioned Arnoldo [?], Wilson Pinheiros, Chico Mendes, just to mention a few, and he [Amarildo] says they will continue their struggles and regardless of what people think here or anywhere else in the world because they care very much for their forest, the plants, the animals, and everything which is in the forest. (Tape 4, Side 1)

This sequence exemplifies how the introduction of the self exceeds a simple revelation of a personal identity. The speaker's name and that of the institution to which he or she is affiliated are not the only focal points. In fact, Amarildo situates himself within a social-political landscape. An uninformed participant learns that rubber tappers in Brazil are apparently involved in a struggle between different political and social forces. In the late 1980s and early 1990s, the social movement of rubber tappers in Acre, Brazil is frequently cited as an instance of a unity of environmental and social struggles (Keck 1995). Charismatic figures such as Wilson Pinheiros and later Chico Mendes, who were assassinated in that conflict, joined forces with international NGOs, and thus turned local practices of resistance into transnational politics.[9] Consequently, the movement transcended its local origin in the sense that it functioned as an intertextual device linking local politics to a transnational discourse on environmental and social struggles. When at the Founding Assembly in October 1993 Amarildo refers to this movement, he actualizes a transnational discourse seeking to enhance the power of his statement. In doing so, he does not necessarily reveal a personal identity, or a "true self," but, in fact, creates a character and makes himself a spokesperson for this discourse. I examine two further statements that operate very differently.

Lucas, a member of the forest industry, gives a typical account of his character. He states his name, and continues:

> The operation of Collins Pine which I represent is located in Northern California. We own, operate, and manage 92,000 hectares of

temperate forest; we also own and operate a sawmill that employs 200 people. The community where the sawmill is located in is called Chester. It has a population of 700 people, and we are the primary employer. . . . Collins Pine is the first industrial forest in the United States to have undergone an environmental certification. (Tape 5, Side 1)

There is a difference in the way the two speakers present their characters. Amarildo invokes a well-known political struggle, embedding his further claim in a broader political discourse. By contrast, Lucas presents the benchmark data of his company. The size of its landholding on the one hand, and the number of its employees on the other, are used to characterize the enterprise. The participants learn that Collins Pine was the first industrial forest company that already has been certified. That is to say, Lucas creates his character by outlining the economic strength and the environmental responsibility of his company. Interestingly, the structure of his (self-) presentation is akin to the way an international NGO introduces itself, as the following example shows.

My name is Oscar, I work with Greenpeace International. Greenpeace has offices in 25 countries and has 5 million supporters. I coordinate Greenpeace forests work; we have campaigns in 15 countries around the world. Greenpeace is involved in the FSC since its inception at the San Francisco meeting. We have been involved in writing comments to the FSC since that time. (Tape 5, Side 2)

Although the Collins Pine company and Greenpeace International are quite different in their daily working practices, their representatives deploy similar practices of self-description. To indicate the size of the operation, Lucas quantifies the amount of forest the company owns, while Oscar lists the number of offices Greenpeace operates and the campaigns it conducts; further, to indicate the weight of each enterprise, Lucas notes the number of his company's employees, and Oscar refers to the supporters Greenpeace has.

Creating a character is an attempt to strengthen one's own authority. When Oscar stresses that Greenpeace has five million supporters, or Lucas that his company employs 200 people in the region, they are essentially claiming, "It is not just me who is making this statement, in fact, I have a large number of allies who support me." Oscar, Lucas, and many other speakers seek to transcend the singularity of their own voice by referring to the people they represent; they recontextualize themselves into the communicative arena and make themselves spokespersons for a group of people.

Issues That Deserve Attention

The participants use the afternoon session to articulate issues that in their view deserve more attention (translational practice of disclosure). While some statements are directly addressed to the interim board inquiring into a specific topic, other participants challenge core elements of the nascent organization. Controversies emerge that severely threaten the storyline of finding win–win solutions that the team proclaimed the evening before. The issues indicate major conflicts mainly between NGOs and the economic interests consisting of individuals and groups who work in the forest industry. At the same time, the conflicts are articulated front stage where positions on issues are often articulated harshly in order to be heard and recognized by others. NGO representatives, for instance, may have to state the opinion of their network before they can engage in negotiations. In this section, I follow three main controversies: (a) the issue of indigenous people (policy knowledge); (b) the issue of organizational structure, especially with regard to the representation of economic interests (polity knowledge); and (c) the issue of procedural rules for the assembly (polity knowledge).

Indigenous Peoples' Rights

The issue of indigenous peoples' rights is expressed in Principle 3 of the Principles and Criteria. The principle itself reads as follows in October 1993:

> Principle #3: INDIGENOUS PEOPLES' RIGHTS—The legal and/ or customary rights of indigenous peoples to own, use, and manage their lands, territories, and resources shall be recognized and respected.
>
> 3.1 Indigenous peoples shall control forest management operations on their lands and territories unless they delegate control to other agencies with free and informed consent.
> 3.2 Forest management operations should not be carried out that threaten or diminish, either directly or indirectly, the tenure rights of indigenous peoples.

> 3.3 Sites of special cultural, religious, or economic significance to indigenous peoples shall be clearly identified and protected. (FSC 1993b, 2)

Whereas in the working draft version of July 1993, the rights of indigenous peoples were subsumed under a Principle 4 on "social rights" and a Principle 5 on "tenure rights" (FSC 1993a, 2), the language of indigenous peoples' rights gains more prominence in the draft presented at the Founding Assembly; it has been developed into a full principle. In addition, Principle 2 on tenure and use rights iterates:

> Local communities with legal and/or customary tenure or use rights shall control forest operations concerning their lands or resources unless they delegate control with free and informed consent to other agencies. (FSC 1993b, 2)

Considering Principles 2 and 3, the rights of indigenous peoples are an integral and prominent element of the Principles and Criteria (status in October, FSC 1993b). However, at the Founding Assembly the issue of indigenous peoples' rights remains unsettled. I examine some of the positions that express this theme.

The director of the Canadian Pulp and Paper Association is the first participant who addresses the issue, noting that "this business of indigenous rights is very complex and distressing" and that in his view the issue should be resolved "through a legal process" rather than by a forest-products company (Tape 4, Side 2). He further justifies his claim, arguing that

> I can foresee a situation in which a company can be caught in between these forces and be absolutely unable to defend itself against the Principle 2. . . . Because, if a forest company is caught in a situation where it is operating on land which is claimed by both the government of the country and by the indigenous peoples who live in the area, its main choice may be to operate immorally, if this is the correct word. . . . How do we get out of this problem? (Tape 4, Side 2)

The statement targets the Principle 2 cited above. Here, the conflict matter is clear and the interim board responds immediately, underling that, in this specific instance, the forest company has to engage in deliberation with the indigenous peoples or ultimately resign from the area. Along these lines, the interim board member Stella notes:

> And perhaps, the new paradigm would be one way to approach that which would be if you are in a situation in which you think that there is a conflict that you sit down with indigenous people who are in that area claiming that, and discuss with them how they want to proceed. (Tape 4, Side 2)

Stella refers back to the keynote speaker who introduced the notion of the "new paradigm" as an approach to solve conflicts by means of deliberation; it is not a compromise, but a "win–win situation" realized by carefully listening to each other's concerns. By evoking that storyline, Stella seeks to enclose the debate with an intertextual reference.

The controversy on the issue of indigenous rights continues, often without clear points of reference. For instance, a representative from the indigenous peoples' organization Cordillera Peoples Alliance in the Philippines, Cecilia, asks, "What will be the position of the FSC in a nation where the rights of the indigenous peoples to the ancestor land is denied?" And she continues, "We feel that giving certification to forest management is legitimizing again our government to give permits to the logging concession to continue to finish the forest that is left in my region" (Tape 4, Side 2). In contrast to the statement above, Cecilia does not so much question the principle as such, but doubts if the *instrument* of certification will have the intended political effect. Along these lines, a participant from Indonesia states, "the criticality of the FSC should be also, it is not technical, it should also be considered political" (Tape 4, Side 2). Similarly, Cecilia explains:

> The issue of the forest in my country is not only an economic or a cultural or a customary issue, it is a political issue, because the struggle of the people, the indigenous people in the Philippines, is their rights to their ancestor land and the right to self-determination and here we are just talking about the forest. (Tape 4, Side 2)

Both participants stress the notion of "the political," and contrast "the political" with the terms "technical" and "economic." In their view, the notion of certification seems to be an instrument that does not sufficiently address the political and social struggle since the participants "just talk about the forest"; the speakers stress that the political aspects of the controversy should be recognized in which the new instrument of sustainable forest management is envisioned as making a difference.

Other transnational NGOs also problematize the issue of indigenous peoples' rights. To give a brief example, Oscar from Greenpeace International notes:

> Unless the FSC can be independent we have to work in our own fashion. As the principles stand now, they are not acceptable for my organization. And this is a great problem for us. The principle for indigenous rights as it now reads could endorse the policy of the Canadian government and its treatment of the Indian nations of Canada, by noting that the legal rights of the indigenous peoples are upheld. (Tape 5, Side 1)

The statement clearly disapproves of the Principles and Criteria. Further participants suggest that indigenous peoples have not been adequately consulted. To weaken this argument a member of the Certification Working Group responds to the criticism:

> I do not understand how Principle 3 can be interpreted as undermining the rights of the Indians of Canada. What we are talking about is upholding the customary rights of the Indigenous peoples. That is something really unique, and I don't think you can find it in any other document like this. (Tape 5, Side 1)

The reply illustrates how a controversy loses a common point of reference. In such cases, any form of coming to an agreement becomes rather unlikely. Taken together, all the examples are very different in the way the issue of indigenous peoples' rights is negotiated in the communicative arena. Only the first speaker directs his claim at the Principles and Criteria. The other speakers either challenge the practicality of certification as an instrument in countries in which basic human rights are not assured or make accusations that lack a common point of reference. To conclude, the participants bring up the issue of indigenous peoples' rights as a central element of policy knowledge, and yet it remains unclear whether a common understanding of the problem actually exists that would make it worth negotiating further.

Organizational Issues and Representation of the Economic Sector

The second issue concerns the future structure of the organization and, more specifically, the representation of social actors who are classified as belonging to the economic interest group. The controversy boils down to the question of whether or not representatives from the industry (which were referred to throughout the Founding Assembly as the "economic interest") should have voting power in the decision-making organs of the organization. A number of social and environmental NGOs underline that they have great problems with the representatives of the economic sector having any form of voting power. To counter this claim, for instance, Michael from Trees for People argues:

> The notion of sustainability was developed by foresters, and it sounds funny to me that now there should be a motion in the room to exclude foresters from an organization that is to promote sustainability in forest management. And that is exactly what is going to happen if we follow the proposal not to have people with economic interests in forestry to vote. I am from Germany. In Germany and Switzerland basically, sustainable forestry was developed. And the notion of a culturally and socially defined sustainability far beyond the economic sustainability was developed by professionals in this area, by people with economic interests in forestry. (Tape 6, Side 1)

To strengthen his argument, Michael narrates the discourse of sustainability as a multifaceted concept that was developed in his country of origin, Germany. In fact, the idea that the notion of sustainability originated among foresters does not logically lead to the conclusion that the economic interests should be represented at all levels of decision making. The controversy continues with proponents and dissenters putting forward the following arguments, which can be displayed in a binary format (see table 6).

As table 6 shows, the participants support their positions with arguments that are sometimes a pure inversion of one another. This is especially true of the notion of "credibility" that either rises or falls with the representation of business in the FSC. In this act, some participants are already engaging in consensualization practices to dissolve the controversy. These moderate voices underline the importance of business but

TABLE 6. The Controversy over Representation of the Economic Sector

In favor of business representation because of . . .	*Against business representation because of . . .*
• credibility within the market • important knowledge of business • business is an integral stakeholder • otherwise, business will walk away from the process, and the FSC will be marginalized	• loss of credibility and independence if business participates • consumers will not trust the label • organization appears to be open to anybody, even to companies and governments with a bad reputation

call for an organizational mechanism that would hinder business from dominating the process.

Processes and Procedures

There is a general unease with the processes and procedures in the runup to the Founding Assembly and for the assembly itself. For instance, with regard to the specific practices and rules that are grouped around the notion of voting and coming to decisions: How does a motion come to the floor, what constitutes a majority, or how can transparency be assured? Alma from the Taiga Rescue Network notes:

> Many of the concerns that were raised concerning the structures was that it is still very unclear, no criteria for membership although the group is going for a membership organization. . . . The consultation prior to this meeting, although many organizations have received the documents there are also the majority of the organizations have not been part of the consultative process. . . . The document has to be thoroughly reworked, not just wording, and it has to go through a broader consultative process. (Tape 5, Side 1)

Others wonder, "What does ratification of the Principles and Criteria mean in terms of becoming operational? Are they to be applied by certification groups, or just polished within the next six months? Clarify, so that we know what the proposal is" (Tape 4, Side 8). The quotes exemplify on the one hand a deep skepticism with regard to the entire project of establishing an FSC. The issue of procedures for the Founding Assembly will become key in the fourth act. On the other, they indicate instances of articulating issues that can be further deliberated or voted upon.

While the statements articulated so far have been partly critical, in each case they were uttered by only one participant. However, after the assembly returns from a coffee break, a common paper from a group of 26 delegates is read out. Just before this speech act, the facilitator seeks to create a productive atmosphere:

> As an outsider and neutral party, I don't think you are debating the what. I think there is a consensus that I felt since last night and today that you need to proceed. What you are debating is the how, and hopefully you come to some positive conclusions on that. (Tape 5, Side 1)

Despite the controversial debates, the facilitator tries to establish an objective speaker position—"just as an outsider and neutral party"—evoking a consensus that at that point seems far away. Then, Connor from Friends of the Earth, who has been participating in the FSC project from its inception, reads out loud the critical statement by environmental and social NGOs:

> The statement arises out of very lengthy discussion amongst a number of the delegates here and represents the views of 26 organizations present at this conference covering local, national, and international environmental groups as well as organizations concerned with indigenous people's rights. The statement was addressed to the interim board in the first instance and the response to the interim board was to invite the statement to the full conference. The statement is as follows:

> We are at present lacking confidence in the FSC process as it has emerged at this founding assembly due to the following reasons.
>
> 1. There has been inadequate consultation prior to the Founding Assembly.
> 2. Voting will be by secret ballot, which causes an immediate loss of transparency to the FSC.
> 3. There is substantial representation on behalf of commercial forest-based industry interests at this meeting who appear to have voting rights.
> 4. The Principles and Criteria, which are at the core of the FSC, are still flawed and unacceptable despite efforts to date.

We therefore propose:

A. The voting procedure be open and transparent. For other than the election of Board members, voting should be by roll call and should be formally recorded.
B. Representatives at this meeting who have clear commercial forest-based industry interests together with government representatives should be welcomed to take part only as non-voting observers.
C. Voting on the current Principles and Criteria should be suspended at the Founding Assembly pending further consultation and revision through a broad in-country and/or bioregional process with a particular emphasis on environmental and social NGOs and indigenous communities.
D. Because the number of members of the Board is limited and will not be able to represent the diversity of regional concerns, an International Monitoring Committee, composed of regionally nominated NGOs, be established to provide oversight and assistance to the activities of the FSC. (Tape 5, Side 1)

There is a moment of pause; the statement does not only represent the opinion of one speaker, but expresses concerns from 26 organizations present at the meeting. Also, the statement aggregates a number of issues that have been voiced before but are now merged, ranked, and classified into a single text. The critical statement formulates issues of concern. The discussions continue in a rather chaotic manner, with some participants rejecting the entire project, while others try to find ways of moving forward.

Finding Ways of Moving Forward

During the afternoon, many critical voices from social and environmental NGOs raise concerns regarding the current state of the nascent organization. Since the FSC is a novel governance arrangement that brings together antagonistic groups, the skepticism is not surprising. At the same time, the question emerges of how to find ways of moving forward since there are no official procedures in place, and the situation is in itself uncertain. This task requires politics knowledge. In what follows, I show three typical ways in which actors argue in this situation.

Metaphorical Argumentation as a Translational Practice of Enclosure

The first communicative practice is a form of metaphorical argumentation in which actors tell short stories or provide metaphors. For instance, Gabriel (consultant of the Brazilian case study) introduces an Argentinian cartoon character called Mafalda:

> Mafalda looks at the world and feels very preoccupied about the world, and then she thinks of hunger, pollutions and wars, all sorts of problems. And then she walks away, nodding her head. And then at the last cartoon she looks back at the globe—there is the globe— and says, "Well, and you know what's worse? That we have too many problemologists and very few solutionologists" [*laughter*]. (Tape 6, Side 1)

The audience laughs: the invitation to the assembly to act as "solutionologists" is clear, that is, to manufacture a governance arrangement rather than to stress its potential shortcomings. The enclosure practice of storytelling allows one to step away from the concrete and to view a controversy in a simplified manner. Of course, the question arises as to whether the complexities of a controversy are just "simplified away," or adequately captured. Others perform emotion, or plead with the delegates to trust each other—like Anthony, who has been part of the FSC project since its inception. He says, "It is an imperative that this organization is created and that we start. And all I can tell you is that you are breaking my heart" (Tape 5, Side 1). Performing emotion is an attempt to build trust among the participants.

In addition, participants emphasize the current imperfections of the documents but argue in favor of moving forward despite these imperfections. This communicative practice continues the storyline of the first evening in which Nicholas argued that the organization should be founded despite the many uncertainties that still exist. Whereas the critical voices from many NGOs address the lack of consultation, or the insufficiency of the Principles and Criteria, these other participants argue that to become operational the Principles and Criteria do not have to be fully stabilized but in fact may change and stay blurry. For instance, Alonso, a professor from the Institute of Technology in Costa Rica, notes with regard to the Principles and Criteria:

> We can keep doing research on management of tropical forest for-
> ever and we will be spending 500 years doing that research and
> when we know everything about that forest we will come back and
> say, "Hey, where is the tropical forest?" It will be lost. I think we
> have to get the hands on with the best principles that we can. I have
> [been] trying to find something behind these principles, something
> that is not clear. I think it is a clear and an open position and that's
> why many people from different sources are here. And I think even
> the process for revision is open. It is the status that during the first
> six months there will be a revision of the Principles and Criteria. I
> think that we got to do something. They can change; they will prob-
> ably change, I do not know how many times. (Tape 5, Side 1)

In contrast to the widespread opinion that in a multistakeholder arena it is
always the scientist who demands further research, Alonso recognizes the
uncertainty within the principles. Yet he stresses the need for action. The
prerequisite for his demand is the integrated process of revision that will
allow the Principles and Criteria to become operational in a certification
organization, while at the same time their transformation and change is
assured. In a similar vein, Henry, a member of the interim board, points out:

> The great strength of the Constitution of the United States is that it
> is a living document. The foresight of the founders was to create a
> mechanism by which the Constitution could be changed, amended,
> could grow. I do not often find myself in any forum coming to the
> defense of the United States; having grown up there, come of age in
> the 1960s and '70s, I have been more often a critic. However, I think
> that the US Constitution is worth bearing in mind, and could be a
> possible metaphor for the efforts that we are trying to form here
> today. That is, if we look at this as a living document that can be
> amended, improved upon, and changed, the organization will not
> only survive but thrive. (Tape 6, Side 2)

As the speaker himself notes, he is deploying the US Constitution as a
metaphor to describe or, in fact, to prescribe the coming into being of an
institution, the FSC. However, his point is not to evoke the greatness of the
US but to refer to the Constitution in its capacity to stay a "living document" that accounts for change while at the same time preserving its inner
core. Both actors admit the document's imperfections but argue that, in

order to account for new knowledge, an institutionalized process of revision is more important than eradicating all problems.

Redefining a Controversy—the Translational Mechanism of Disclosure

A different attempt is to redefine the controversy, which will be a major communicative practice in the fourth act. For instance, James, a consulting forester from the US, argues:

> I believe the desire for resolution is suffering from a lack of precision as to what the real issue is. In my judgment it is not an issue of participation per se by various fractions but the question of whether or not inappropriate control of the council will result from that participation. (Tape 5, Side 1)

To note that so far the "real issue" has been obscured is a classic introduction to redefining a controversy in a particular direction. Shifting the conflict from a binary "yes or no option" regarding participation to the notion of "avoiding inappropriate control" by the economic sector is a way to open the space to negotiate the mechanisms by which inappropriate control may be avoided. That is to say, this translational practice of disclosure rearranges critical elements of a controversy. However, one should not underestimate the power effects of such a practice. To redefine the "real issue" is not an innocent practice, as I will show in the fourth act.

Changing the Communicative Arena—the Translational Practice
of Recontextualization

Translational practices of recontextualization become relevant with regard to the process of negotiation. A statement by Amarildo, the representative from the rubber tappers' movement in Brazil, is again interpreted from Brazilian Portuguese into English. In his interpretation, Gabriel notes:

> He [Amarildo] is saying that the assembly's hard work is a little messed up and we have to find an alternative to make it succeed. [Portuguese] He [Amarildo] is suggesting that we break up at this point and have different meetings, the NGOs, the business, and whatever group wants to adjourn, and then come back with specific proposals, and vote on them and decide on them. (Tape 5, Side 2)

To suggest changing the arena of deliberation is to engage in a practice of translation as consensus-making depends upon changing the context in which the issues are negotiated. Changing the context often changes the interaction order and may create trust, as a participant points out:

> Now, we have not talked enough. We have not known each other long enough so that we, at the moment, have difficulty in trusting each other: We need a little more rapport. I do not think that anyone will disagree with the contents, and the purpose and the ideology behind the FSC and its creation. But at the same time the process in which it is taking place, some of the processes, some of the elements of the process are missed, maybe because of so many consultations. Now, the group discussions and small group discussions, not within a large group, [but] in these special interest groups are essential so that we can come and present it in the plenary sessions so that consensus can be derived. (Tape 5, Side 2)

The speaker lays out the current situation that the participants find themselves in. Indeed, they have "not known each other long enough, so that" they have "difficulty in trusting each other." Therefore, he suggests assembling in smaller groups, to learn if they can or cannot create an institution together. Coming together in a large plenary session may be appropriate way of informing an audience, but this kind of communicative situation often does not work for trust building; meeting in smaller groups in which the individual is less exposed to a greater audience may allow people to engage in dialogue.

Chorus: Making Present

The audience has replied not with one, but with many voices. They have articulated a character that is not a presentation of an individual, authentic self but a representation of larger collectives and positions. Articulating a character makes these collectives and positions present in the arena; it is a way of creating a standpoint from which to speak and to connect to (or disconnect from) other participants in the assembly.

The first part of the act is largely in line with rationalist bargaining as well as deliberative theories. Both stress the importance of communication for learning about others' preferences, the perceived definitions of the situation, and their issues of concern (policy knowledge, indigenous rights; polity knowledge, organizational and membership issues; politics knowledge, win–win solutions).

However, it is the mechanism of translation that helps to understand how participants, once they have displayed their interests or identities, engage in further negotiations. They probe translational practices of enclosure (downplaying the imperfection of the documents), of disclosure (redefining issues), and finally agree to engage in recontextualization (retiring into smaller meeting rooms).

Probing a counterfactual trajectory, one could envision a meeting that would have skipped the second act so that participants would have gone straight into smaller meeting rooms. In such a scenario, the diversity of the group would not have become visible front stage in enacting the contestation of key issues such as indigenous rights or the representation of economic interests. In essence, it is a contestation of what is translated (i.e., made contextually available and thus negotiable) at the assembly. Thus, this second act was so enormously important because it allowed participants to put issues and positions on the table, and thus enroll them into further negotiations.

Third Act: Excluding Dissenters

The participants discussed controversial issues in smaller groups throughout the night. On Sunday morning, October 3, 1993, they returned to the assembly hall for the final day of the Founding Assembly, and the recording continues. In what follows, I examine a short but crucial part of the negotiations that was marked by tumult and shouting, and a number of NGOs resigned from the process.

Two aspects of translation become observable in this third act. First, participants begin to transform their general claims into positions. They work on these positions, switching back and forth. From the assembly hall participants move to smaller caucus meetings in which they negotiate their position on controversial issues and articulate this position once again in the assembly hall. In doing so, they further transform statements.

Second, this act shows how exclusion operates as an important aspect of translation. A successful translation requires recontextualization in another context; the context must resonate or connect with the translated claim. Yet a communicative context is not a given but something actively constructed. I will show how the facilitator and the interim board construct a context by defining this third act as a specific time in the negotiations: they only allow statements that further specify how the assembly could "move on," prohibiting other substantial claims since they would belong to another phase of the negotiations. As a result, dissenting voices are not so much excluded based on substantial arguments but because of the phase within the negotiations in which they practice disclosure. Thus, timing appears as a crucial dimension of politics knowledge.

Introduction to the Day

The facilitator welcomes everyone back for the final day of the conference, noting that the morning is to be dedicated to hearing the positions from the various groups that met overnight. Immediately Connor, a spokesperson from the environmental caucus, asks for an adjournment for a discussion among the environmental NGOs of a position from the economic caucus that has already been circulating. Others support his motion and advise further that, after the caucus meetings, the representatives from the groups should briefly meet as well. Consensus to adjourn seems to emerge. The facilitator recognizes the need to meet in the specific caucuses, but first invites the economic position to be articulated in the assembly hall.

Glenn, who chaired the economic caucus the previous night, presents its position. I will deal with questions of content later, but a central element is worth noting already:

> What we need to do is to create a system which addresses the fundamental issue of distrust; talking won't help. So, we are suggesting from the economic side, let's put forward a method here so that you are essentially assured that the economic side cannot control, that the economic side does not wanna control, has no interest in controlling. (Tape 6, Side 1)

The central issue of the position is to build an institutional mechanism that addresses the problem of distrust. The participants are about to adjourn, yet James submits a motion that everybody attending has the standing to vote on; some discussion takes place; the interim board suggests that each organization should have one vote. The participants leave the assembly hall.

Chorus: Making Positions Move

The participants assemble, probably tired and yet excited, in the main hall to carry out the translational practices of recontextualization: the articulation of a position and its movement. In contrast to the second act, participants no longer tell stories to engage in trust-building but seek to build an organization that accounts for differences, secures independence, and hinders control by a single actor group. Positions—units of semi-stabilized policy or polity knowledge—become the object of translation: to translate a position is to articulate it, to make it public, to take a stance, while, at the same time, it is an attempt to engage with one another, to find connections, overlaps, or disagreements.[10] Spokespeople perform the positions as a translational practice that involves moving from the written to the spoken, from the backstage to the front stage. Changes in meaning occurs in this process of translation. The spokespeople regularly check back with their groups that they have said what was agreed upon, or whether they may have missed anything. In fact, other members of the groups often add an aspect, or repeat what has already been said in different words to specify the position. In doing so, they engage in the communicative construction of a shared reality in the arena.

Leaving the Assembly

The participants return to the assembly hall after they have adjourned to discuss the position set out by the economic caucus. "I call the assembly to order! I apologize, we said 10 after 10, and now it is 10:25." The facilitator reopens the floor, noting that at least one group is not present. Nevertheless, he invites the economic caucus to start since time is running out. James appears as the spokesperson for the economic caucus and presents its position. He has just finished when the interaction order is challenged through shouting in the back.

FACILITATOR: Thank you.

[*Background shouting*]

> I am sorry you are out of order.

[*Background shouting*]

MALE WITHOUT MICROPHONE: Hi look, there was a very important caucus that not even heard the presentation. [*Background shouting*]
CONNOR: The point of order, Mr. Chairman, is that one of the caucus groups has just been excluded from this process by having part of the assembly being allowed to hear the proposal, but our caucus

was not being allowed to hear that proposal. And we consider unless the session can be restarted with our full presence in this meeting we will consider ourselves of being excluded from this assembly, and we will withdraw immediately. (Tape 6, Side 2)

For a moment the controversy seems to jeopardize the further process; the threat of withdrawal from the Founding Assembly that has been framed in terms of inclusiveness and participation has a high destabilization potential. Yet participants quickly appease one another; James reiterates the proposal from the economic caucus. Further presentations follow, and debate and discussion flourishes on positions as well as on voting procedures. Slowly but steadily the assembly moves toward voting.

But then there is hesitation and tumult again. Cecilia, a participant from an indigenous organization in the Philippines, makes the following statement:

> CECILIA: I have the feeling that it is expected that we participate in the vote. However, within the context of the national situation in the Philippines, I have decided that, on behalf of the Cordillera Peoples Alliance, that we do not participate in the Forest Stewardship Council though we appreciate it very much and we believe in its vision. But this is because we feel that it is impossible to do in a country where no democracy is still felt by the people. . . . The government has a law saying that it is the presidential decree 705. It says that [?] indigenous people have not any rights to participate in the management of the forest. And the implication of that also is that if the government gives a list to any logging concessions the indigenous does not have the right to say about it . . .
>
> FACILITATOR: I am sorry, could you kind of, we need to move on. And we wanna hear your statement, Ma'am, but at the same time, we need to proceed, could you please . . .
>
> CECILIA: And we have been really trying hard to preserve our forests and this time we are trying to preserve our forests going against mining companies. There are a lot of military employed in our region, which is making it very difficult . . .
>
> FACILITATOR: Ma'am, I am sorry would you please state what you want to state. There were speeches yesterday, there were presentations yesterday, and that's [when] we allocated that time. We are at a point, we are calling a vote and unless you have a comment about that vote I would ask that the assembly moves on. (Tape 7, Side 1)

The dialogue between Cecilia and the facilitator goes back and forth for another round until Cecilia finally announces that she is withdrawing in the name of her organization. Long applause honors her speech. However, her public announcement quickly finds imitators. An activist from the Sarawak Campaign Committee (based in Japan) also raises her voice since, in her view, the issue of overconsumption and the intimidation of people has not found adequate response in the FSC. Again, the facilitator clearly expresses the need to move on, cuts her speech off, and she withdraws.

Finally, there is a controversy between Gabriel and Connor. Gabriel, the consultant for the Brazilian case study, asks the facilitator if he can briefly share a position by a delegation of Brazilian NGOs.

> GABRIEL: We saw a very undemocratic mechanism controlled by some NGOs of northern-based countries to control this process. So, we felt very unhappy and distrustful of that representation. So, at that point yesterday we withdrew from the process. We felt that we could not decide democratically. There was a new colonial way of controlling decision-making. [*Loud applause.*] And people did not make clear what intent they have, and our understanding was that they felt FSC should not work, that was why they are blocking everything. . . . We changed our position because of the same spirit that brought us here. We have a positive attitude towards FSC. . . .
>
> FACILITATOR: Could you make your point, please.
>
> GABRIEL: I am done. Just another sentence. We are here to be positive, but I would just like everybody, especially the members of the board, not to call people from the northern countries to say, "Yes, is this person going to agree, is that group led by this person going to agree?" No, I think we should be more democratic. [*Long applause.*] (Tape 7, Side 1)

The statement contains key terms such as "new colonial way of control" and "undemocratic mechanism"; the controversy is picked up immediately. Connor, Friends of the Earth UK and spokesperson for an environmental caucus, demands the right to respond. The facilitator refuses, but Connor insists:

> CONNOR: He was given permission by yourself, Mr. Chair, to make this presentation to the full assembly. I feel that I have a right to respond to the full assembly. I can certainly make it brief.
>
> FACILITATOR: I was told that he was not mentioning your name, or

your organization's name directly. I am sorry, I get a sense that we
need to move on

CONNOR: In that . . . Mr. Chair [*background talk*]

BRIAN: Connor, I appreciate your concerns, but I do not believe that
your point of order was in order because there was no specific reference to you or your institution. I believe, if you want to talk about
that with Gabriel, obviously that is fine, but I do not think you were
singled out and there will be no record of you being spoken against
and therefore not being able to respond. [*long applause.*]

CONNOR: Well, in that case, Mr. Chair, I'd like to thank you for your
invitation for a formal withdrawal from the voting process to be
given to you in writing. And I just would like to use this opportunity now to say this with deep regret, having been involved in this
process for some three years or so and I believe having taken a very
constructive attitude towards it coming from an organization that
[was the] first anywhere in the world proposed independent certification of timber products in 1985. Being the first organization anywhere in the world to actually establish a certification program in
1987, proposing that the international community investigate timber labeling with a proposal for the ITTO in 1989. I take it as a deep
insult to hear that there are northern NGOs here who are opposed
to the idea of the FSC.[11] This is simply not the case. We are deeply
committed to the FSC. We have demonstrated our commitment to
the FSC. However, I cannot accept the basis on which the voting
procedure has been determined here, and will therefore withdraw
from any further voting. I would like to have this recorded as a full
abstention on the part of Friends of the Earth. I will continue to
participate, hopefully constructively, as observer. Thank you.
[*Applause.*] (Tape 7, Side 1)

The facilitator announces that he would like to go back to the theme of
voting procedures; the assembly resumes its work.

Chorus: Power as Constructing a Context

How do negotiating parties perform power? And who has power in this
specific situation? Rationalist bargaining theory suggests that powerful
actors dominate the process. Actors are powerful if they have a large relative market size. For NGOs this can be operationalized as having a large
constituency. While rationalist bargaining theory can explain to some
extent why smaller indigenous NGOs from the Philippines or an NGO

from Japan leave the assembly, it has trouble accounting for the fact that a large, global NGO like Friends of the Earth would abstain from voting.

Deliberative theories predict arguing and reason giving in situations of high uncertainty about interest or identities and the underlying rules of the game, as well as apparently irreconcilable differences (Risse 2000, 33). Interestingly, participating actors act in accordance with this prediction most of the time, but accept that the facilitator (with the backing of the interim board) can prohibit the exchange of arguments.

A sensitivity to translational practices will show that one way to perform power is to have the power to construct a context when this context defines the kind of utterances that are deemed legitimate. In essence, the interim board, in cooperation with the chair and not the participants of the assembly, decides what requires further characterization (translational practice of disclosure) and which elements are already adequately stabilized (translational practice of enclosure). Consequently, specific issues fail to be translated since they do not resonate with the constructed context of the act.[12]

To judge some controversies as worth deliberating on and others as insignificant is a performance of politics knowledge in a powerful practice of translation at a critical stage of the Founding Assembly. With Richard Freeman (2009, 434), we can understand translation as a conscious *choice*: "translators choose between alternatives." The storyline set out in the prologue whereby equal participation and listening to each other are tools to construct win–win solutions finds only partial reflection in the practice of the assembly. In the absence of general rules of procedure (polity knowledge) that would grant dissenters the right to articulate their positions, the interim board chooses to move forward, aiming to constitute a new political entity.

This clear act of exclusion invites one to think of an FSC that would have considered more carefully how certification might operate under authoritarian regimes. Cecilia explicitly expresses concern that certification could turn into a "double blade," as she puts it. From her point of view, political struggles including military involvement create problems for the very idea of certification. This is an interesting assessment as until today the real impact of certification remains hard to measure (Arts 2021; Van der Ven and Cashore 2018). However, studies point to severe problems with certification in authoritarian settings (Bartley 2018). In excluding voices such as Cecilia's (the representative of the Cordillera Peoples Alliance) the interim board missed the opportunity to create more policy knowledge within the FSC about the problems of certifications.

6 | Constituting the FSC

After the tumult and withdrawals during early Sunday morning on October 3, 1993, the participants continued to negotiate over the nascent organization throughout the day. By late afternoon, they had managed to solve contested issues and to vote in the first board of the FSC. How did this become possible? The assembly faced problems. It lacked clear rules of procedure, which threatened the democratic principle of equal participation. Thus, the participants experienced what might be termed the paradox of a constitutional moment. Since there were no pregivens, no transnational rules for doing governance democratically, each act of founding a new governance arrangement necessarily operated beyond democratically legitimized rules; it revolved around a void of contested, often implicit assumptions and scripts concerning knowledge about governance. This chapter shows how the mechanism of translation can explain the stepwise process of linking positions and people with each other.

Fourth Act: Manufacturing Consensus

Participants continued to articulate proposals on contested issues that they had worked on throughout the night in smaller caucus meetings. Whereas some of these groups can be related back to categorizations introduced in the prologue such as the economic interest, other groups were spontaneous assemblages of participants or subgroups. Thus, who was speaking for and representing which interest often remained opaque. These two problems, lack of procedure and lack of representation, led to a rather diffuse situation. The interim board, the facilitator, and various participants developed speaker roles as "experts in procedures," and navigated the assembly through this situation. My analysis focuses on how those actors, despite the complex situation, managed to come to decisions regarding the future organization.

Three main issues were negotiated. First, the *question of procedure*—that is, who was allowed to vote on that particular day, how voting would take place, and how motions would come to the floor—was contested and required specification. Second, while the assembly had opted for an association as the organizational form for the FSC, the participants had to agree on the *voting structure of the membership* of the organization. The question at issue was how an institutional mechanism could be designed that would prevent domination by the economic interests. Third, the *composition and election of the future board* of the FSC turned out to be not a simple process of voting; instead, the participants constructed a complex institutional key that ensured the representation of the various groups on the FSC board of directors.

Examining the manufacturing of consensus in this act sheds light on the microprocesses of making positions equivalent, forging alliances, and performing power—in other words, of doing *translation*. The main argument is that consensus is manufactured by translational practices of recontextualization: displacing positions or elements of positions as well as re-presenting them in different contexts. There is movement between the backstage and the front stage, between different forms of (visual) representation, and between speaker roles. Also, there are practices of disclosure/enclosure: participants use provisional, ad-hoc solutions (practices of enclosure) and lay out what exactly would require further negotiation (practices of disclosure). I specify this argument empirically when I discuss each of these issues.

Presenting All Positions

On Sunday morning the participants assembled again in the main hall to articulate their positions.

Displaying Difference—the First Round of Presentations

In the morning, spokespeople from the various caucus meetings in a first round presented the groups' positions on a number of issues that seemed salient to them. A total of six positions were read out loud by an economic group, a social group (read in Spanish), an environmental group I, an environmental group II, a nonalliance group that rejected the categorizations, and, finally, the interim board. The positions addressed only issues to do with the governance structure of the nascent organization, but they focused partly on different aspects. Some referred to the controversial issues regarding voting, the composition of the board, and criteria for membership, or suggested additional committees. The main controversy running through all the positions was the voting power of the economic interest. To map the differences and overlaps with regard to content, the positions are summarized in table 7, and I comment further on the contested issues below.

Chorus: Keeping Economic Interests In, Keeping Economic Interests Out

The table displays a variety of issues that were discussed in caucus meetings on Saturday night and presented on Sunday morning. It was within this first round of presentations that some disturbances occurred, and participants decided to withdraw; I discussed this in the third act.

The positions do not address the pertinent issues in an easily comparable way, and they are underspecified, often only hinting at a solution for a problem. For instance, the notion of the "economic interest" and the term "organization" lack clarity, which leaves room for interpretation and will lead to further contestation. Also, the positions embody controversies since the spokespeople for the groups are disputed as exemplified by Gabriel's comment quoted in the third act on "being more democratic."

Beyond these overarching points, the positions show essentially that there was a division between the social group and environmental group II on the one hand, and the other four groups on the other. The first positions suggest ways of keeping the economic interests away from the organization's decision-making bodies. This entailed calling for an advisory committee on which the economic interests would be represented but denying it a seat on the new board.

By contrast, the other positions grant the economic interests rights in the decision-making bodies of the organization. The positions here suggest ways of controlling the influence of the economic interests by allocating one-third or less of the membership's voting power to it, along with one to two seats on the board. Interestingly, the division of positions cuts across environmental groups I and II. The spokesperson for the first group is from the WWF, which has a history of cooperation with economic interests. The spokesperson for the second environmental group is from Friends of the Earth, an NGO that became known for its campaigns and boycotts of tropical timber. Before the participants can consensualize this contested issue, the working procedure of the assembly turns into an issue itself.

TABLE 7. First Round of Positions

On Voting	
Economic Group (James)	1 vote per organization
Social Group (Spanish)	1 vote per organization
Environmental Group I (Bentley)	1 vote per organization
Environmental Group II (Connor)	No voting for industry. Mandate board to elaborate a proposal for voting procedures and structures
Nonalliance Group (Michael)	1 vote per organization
Interim Board FSC Charter (Brian)	1 vote per organization

On the Composition of the Board	
Economic Group (James)	7 member board; 2 of them representing economic interests
Social Group (Spanish)	No economic interests
Environmental Group I (Bentley)	7 member board; 1 representing economic interests. Indigenous people on board
Environmental Group II (Connor)	*(no position stated)*
Nonalliance Group (Michael)	9 member board; 2 economic interests; 2 positions that can be co-opted; skills more important than balance
Interim Board FSC Charter (Brian)	*(no position stated)*

On Nomination for the Board	
Economic Group (James)	Each chamber (economic, environmental, social) puts forward 4 nominees. Entire body votes
Social Group (Spanish)	*(no position stated)*
Environmental Group I (Bentley)	*(no position stated)*
Environmental Group II (Connor)	*(no position stated)*
Nonalliance Group (Michael)	*(no position stated)*
Interim Board FSC Charter (Brian)	*(no position stated)*

On Criteria for Membership	
Economic Group (James)	Mandate board to elaborate criteria for membership within 6 months; highest priority
Social Group (Spanish)	*(no position stated)*
Environmental Group I (Bentley)	Fundamental issue; needs to be resolved, everything falls into place
Environmental Group II (Connor)	Mandate board to elaborate criteria for membership within 6 months
Nonalliance Group (Michael)	Establishment of a credentials committee; for the moment, declare adherence to the principles of FSC
Interim Board FSC Charter (Brian)	Mandate board to elaborate criteria for membership within 6 months

On Additional Committees

Economic Group (James)	Establish a membership committee: elected by the body; or appointed by the board → 2 reps. from economic interests
Social Group (Spanish)	Economic sector should be member in a separate committee
Environmental Group I (Bentley)	Convene a committee that looks into membership
Environmental Group II (Connor)	Advisory Committee [economic interests]; Grievances Committee to (a) ensure accountability of board (b) challenge certification decisions
Nonalliance Group (Michael)	Against advisory committee with industry → better to involve directly
Interim Board FSC Charter (Brian)	*(no position stated)*

On Balance and Representation

Economic Group (James)	*(no position stated)*
Social Group (Spanish)	*(no position stated)*
Environmental Group I (Bentley)	Strive for regional balance and geographical representation
Environmental Group II (Connor)	*(no position stated)*
Nonalliance Group (Michael)	*(no position stated)*
Interim Board FSC Charter (Brian)	Chamber system: representation North/South and sector

On Membership Voting

Economic Group (James)	*(no position stated)*
Social Group (Spanish)	*(no position stated)*
Environmental Group I (Bentley)	25% industry vote with the membership operating under 2/3 majority
Environmental Group II (Connor)	Mandate board to elaborate a proposal for membership-structure within 6 months
Nonalliance Group (Michael)	*(no position stated)*
Interim Board FSC Charter (Brian)	Within chambers northern/southern reps. have equal numbers of votes

Solving the Issue of Procedure

I reenter the scene after all positions have been articulated in a first round, and the dissident voices have resigned from the process (the topic of the third act). As spokesperson for the interim board, Brian just has elaborated on the advantages and disadvantages of the two organizational structures, namely association and foundation. He recommends organizing the FSC as an association. Also, the team has tried to call a vote on their proposal, but the participants need to be clearer about procedures. I will show how the translational practices of disclosure and enclosure allow the assembly to move forward.

The Interim Board Presents a Motion

Once again, the facilitator calls for a vote on the *type* of organization brought forward by the interim board; does the assembly favor an association or a foundation? "All those in favor of an association please stand," he asks. All voting members stand, the vote is unanimous, no one is opposed. Applause and cheering, congratulations and laughter follow. The speaker for the interim board, Brian, moves forward, reading out loud the second motion of the interim board (as also displayed in table 6 in chapter 5).

> The General Assembly of the FSC is the supreme authority of the organization. It elects board members and may also dismisses them. The members of the FSC are divided into three chambers: social; environmental; economic.
>
> Each chamber has one-third of the votes in a general assembly irrespective of the number of members in each chamber. Within chambers northern and southern members have equal numbers of votes irrespective of the number of northern or southern representatives.
>
> Allocations of members to chambers and classification as northern or southern is the responsibility of the board. All decisions taken by the General Assembly require a two-thirds majority vote. General Assemblies are held every two years, and may be convened by postal ballot. That is the proposal.
>
> I just would like to add an explanation that the board's understanding is, if this is adopted, the future board has to come back within a period of something like six months with more detailed criteria for membership. (Tape 8, Side 1)

Chorus: Trying to Enclose a Controversy

Brian reads the proposal slowly and clearly with a hint of a British accent. It is, however, not only his voice that sounds convincing; the wording of the proposal is familiar. The interim board asks people essentially to vote in favor of the invitation key introduced in the prologue. Differentiating along the axis of sectors (environmental, social, economic) and of region

(North/South), the invitation key constructs and categorizes the participants of the assembly. Viewed through these categories a nearly perfect balance of different regions and different sectors appears. To reinvoke the invitation key of the prologue is to connect an already known categorization to a decision that is at stake. What is known is integrated into what is at stake so that the proposal appears convincing. Yet the question arises as to whether there are any controversies hiding behind the convincing construction of this motion.

The interim board's proposal does not mention explicitly the critical issue of the representation of the economic interests. It neither addresses the issues debated beforehand, nor engages in any consensus-making efforts. It is an attempt to enclose the critical issue by providing wording that obscures the actual controversy. The interim board, in cooperation with the facilitator, is clearly pushing its agenda: the proposal by the interim board is the last of five that have been presented. While all other proposals have simply been presented without taking a vote, the facilitator immediately calls for a vote in favor of the interim board's proposal. Hence, the facilitator appears as by no means the "neutral party" or "outsider" he has suggested he is. Instead, he is part of the team in a dramaturgical cooperation trying to push for a vote. Will this strategy work?

Contesting Content and Procedures

> FACILITATOR: Calling to a vote [*background*: "no, no"]. Oh, I am sorry. You are right: discussion!
>
> BORIS: My reading of this particular motion gives me the impression that its approval would establish the percentage of votes by chambers or sectors. This morning . . . we have heard that certain sectors should have no votes at all; that some sectors should have 25 percent of votes, or that they should have 33 percent. I think we should note very clearly if people vote on this, it has direct implications for that, and may I ask the board to clarify deeply and clearly exactly what the intent is because I think there is a variety of interests here.
>
> BRIAN: That it is quite clearly that the board has heard a variety of proposals on this and many subjects you might care to think of, as a matter of fact. And this is the board's proposal. . . .
>
> BRIAN: I just think that we should not get into a long discussion about all the options here, because there are many and multiple. I repeat, you are giving general guidance to the board. Now that this organization, if we get through the day successfully, will be an association,

> there will be unlimited opportunities to come back to the board
> with all sorts of proposals. . . .
> MALE (UNKNOWN): I just wanted to state my view that fundamentally
> the divisions—whatever divisions the board or assembly come up
> with—are artificial.
> CAMILA: In the interest of procedure, could you just outline what are
> decision-making procedures, how motions are going to come to the
> floor, how questions will be raised? What are the decision-making
> structures here? So that we all understand how we are working,
> please. (Tape 8, Side 1)

These short statements were uttered over a total time period of 17 minutes, reflecting some major points of the discussion. Brian, speaking for the interim board, and the facilitator both pushed toward a ballot. Not without an ironic undertone, Brian notes that the board has "heard a variety of proposals" on "many subjects you might care to think of." By framing the vote as only giving "general guidance" to the board with "unlimited opportunities" to change the organizational structures again, he downplays the importance of the specific vote.

By contrast, the other statements challenge the proposal by the interim board on the level of *content* and the level of *procedure*. On the level of content, the implications of the proposal are revealed and reconnected to the diverging views on the participation of the economic interests brought forward in the morning. Also, the notion of a chamber system is labeled as artificial. In other words, a simple institutionalization of the "invitation key" seems unlikely at this point. On the level of procedure, the participants ask to clarify how the assembly is operating.

Chorus: Disclosure of Content and Procedures

The suggested script creates friction. Participants disclose both the interim board's position and the script under which the assembly operates. To indicate that the current process is governed by unclear and obscure procedures is to challenge the legitimation of the process and of those who act as the facilitator and board. Negotiating the rules under which decisions are taken has not been given a separate space on the agenda of the Founding Assembly. Neither the facilitator nor the interim board nor the participants have demanded that the issue of how to proceed in the absence of institutionally given rules should be separately discussed. In fact, the early comment by the facilitator, "to a large degree the group will manage itself;

my job should be fairly simple as we go forward," suggests that potential controversies around decision-making procedures have been sidestepped (Tape 2, Side 1). Deliberative theories label speaker roles such as the facilitator's "honest brokers" because they can help to shift negotiations toward a problem-solving mode (Risse and Kleine 2010, 714). Yet the sequence shows that an empirical analysis that simply checks whether a facilitator is present is not sufficient. One has to examine the performance of such brokers to judge their enactment of politics and the polity knowledge that is required for such a role. The lack of established procedures creates a controversy as soon as the creation of the FSC assumes further shape, as the following sequence highlights.

An Ad-Hoc Solution for the Procedural Void

> MALE AMERICAN: I am sorry to ask this, but another point of order, are we using simple majority or two-thirds?
> FACILITATOR: This is simple majority.
> CAMILA: Whose decision was that, the interim board's or this group's?
> STELLA: It was the interim board's decision.

[*Background talk*]

> BENTLEY: I think the assumption is that we are operating under two-thirds majority because that was the voting procedure put forth on an earlier motion, which had an overwhelming majority. So, I think the majority of the people in this room make the implicit assumption that everything we do from now on here is on a two-thirds majority. [*Applause.*] And, if not, we need to discuss this issue before we proceed.
> FACILITATOR: In order to clarify that, it is suggested to put that question to the assembly. And the question would be whether you want to proceed on a two-thirds majority, or a simple majority. And again, we are voting on procedures today. We will do a straw poll to start, and maybe that resolves the question.
> All those in favor proceeding under a two-thirds majority, or in essence 66 percent, please stand.
> All those in favor of a simple majority, 51 percent, please stand.
> My sense, without going on a roll call on this, is that it is two-thirds. (Tape 8, Side 1)

The sequence begins with "another point of order." While the assembly is in the middle of trying to vote on a motion, it becomes apparent that there is no consensus on the decision-making procedures. In line with his speaker role, the facilitator provides an answer—"the assembly operates under simple majority." Yet his authority is immediately challenged by Camila from the Institute for Sustainable Forestry: "Whose decision was that?" Stella, an interim board member, supports the facilitator by backing up his claim: "It was the interim board's decision." That is to say, she takes advantage of her authority as an interim board member to strengthen the statement.

The justification is debated; there is only some mumbling on the audio files. Then, Bentley (World Resource Institute) speaks up, dissenting from the board's decision. Whereas the team has derived its authority from their speaker roles, Bentley claims to be giving voice to the "majority of the people in the room" and their "implicit assumptions" about voting. His statement receives applause and, most importantly, a positive vote: the assembly decides in favor of a two-thirds majority. Camila makes a further request: "Could you just outline what are the decision-making procedures, how motions are going to come to the floor, how questions will be raised?" The "you" in her statement could potentially be addressing the assembly as a whole; it could equally be interpreted as an invitation to each participant to ponder on appropriate and inclusive structures. Yet her call is answered by Brian, a member of the interim board, who gives a first account. But his answer seems too vague, and therefore, she asks again:

> CAMILA: Just a clarification, we are using *Robert's Rules of Order* then in terms of how we are making that decision? When motions [are] brought forward. Can you clarify that?
>
> BRIAN: I am not familiar with *Robert's Rules of Order*.
>
> BENTLEY: I'd like to help you on that one if I can. Just for sake of moving this forward. You would have a motion brought to the floor that then would be seconded. After it is seconded, it would be discussed, reappear for discussion and then discussion would be brought to a close and then it goes to a straw vote, and if the straw vote dictates a roll call then it goes to a roll call, and then if that does not work then you take motions for counterproposals from the floor and then it goes through the same procedure. [*Applause.*] (Tape 8, Side 1)

The default American framework, *Robert's Rules of Order*, based on the rules and practices used in the US Congress, is put forward for enactment.

As the statement by Brian shows, this framework is by no means universally known or accepted. However, in the absence of clear procedural rules, Bentley offers knowledge that comes in a recognizable package from *Robert's Rules*. Once introduced, however, the decision-making structure is not always followed; Bentley comes back a few minutes later, "I plea that we respect procedure because if we lose procedure this whole thing quickly falls into anarchy" (Tape 8, Side 1). Throughout the negotiation, Camila continues developing the role of a discloser of decision-making practices that are either unclear or not consensual. Similarly, Bentley establishes himself as spokesperson for procedural practices. Although the two actors play this role differently, each role requires the existence of the other.

Chorus: The Productivity of Enclosure and Disclosure

This crucial episode showcases the importance of translational practices of disclosure/enclosure. The participants have different backgrounds and bring their own assumptions about decision-making procedures to the assembly (polity knowledge). In this situation of "institutional void" (Hajer 2009)—the presence of conflicting ideas and practices regarding how to organize the institution-making process—new speaker roles emerge. They either disclose the operating procedures as insufficient or enclose the process by giving guidance in the absence of procedures. Thus, the assembly deals with this situation productively, as the new speakers mediate between audience and team.

The power of the mechanism can be judged by its potential absence. If the two participants (Camila and Bentley) had not performed their emerging roles, the assembly would most likely have collapsed due to the lack of stabilized polity knowledge of procedural rules. To create a multistakeholder organization, participants have to operate under procedural rules that enjoy at least some legitimacy. *Robert's Rules* did this job. An alternative pathway might have been the disintegration of the assembly because the team underestimated the institutional void in which the assembly was negotiating.

While deliberation approaches are right in pointing to the importance of "honest brokers," the above sequence illustrates that their "honesty" requires empirical exploration. The honest brokers introduce the polity knowledge of *Robert's Rules of Order*, which in itself is performative insofar as it creates a very specific negotiation situation. *Robert's Rules* are not tailored to the needs of the assembly. Rather, something is taken that is handy—a problematic framework that perhaps few know, but many will now follow. In fact, it has been criticized for excluding stakeholders who are not familiar with its rules (Susskind, McKearnan, and Thomas-Larmer 1999). It is in these moments of applying polity knowledge that power asymmetries in knowledge systems become apparent. Those who declare themselves to be procedural experts are all from the United States and simply apply what they are accustomed to. A representative from an indigenous organization notes that the indigenous system of coming to a decision takes much longer, because they deliberate until a consensus emerges.

The Structure of the Membership

The issue of membership structure appears alongside the discussion on voting procedures. Thus the participants are challenged to establish issues, find positions, produce motions, and finally vote on a motion. Participants engage in translational practices of recontextualization. They single out issues, merge positions, and substitute aspects under a new claim. In doing so, they recontextualize the various proposals into a new motion.

Presenting the Second Round of Positions Focusing on
Membership Structure

Participants remain uneasy about the current process. The oral presentations are hard to compare. Some of the procedural experts suggest hearing the proposals once again, and then writing them down on transparencies and discussing them over lunch. The facilitator agrees and suggests focusing on the *structure of the membership* in the quick round of proposals before lunch. In this second round four proposals are presented, again orally without any visualization.

> LOGAN: The proposal I would like to make is that the economic group—and I think we have to be more specific about who they are—have 25 percent of the voting membership, the vote—that those people self-identify themselves to vote for the block for that chamber and that the other groups will select or vote as including social, environmental, indigenous, and others will vote as the other chamber with the remaining percentage of vote. I am not talking about board representation; it is membership.
>
> RAIMUNDO: I have another proposal on membership. I like to propose: 20 percent business; 40 percent social; 40 percent environmental.

In this case in the 40 percent we have 20 percent from North and 20 percent from South, the same for social, 20 percent for North, 20 percent for South, and business 10 percent each.

FACILITATOR: Thank you, next.

CAMILA: This is a proposal that was dated on October 1st from concerned NGOs and certifiers. The assembly should mandate the board to elaborate proposals for membership structure within the next six months. These proposals must include inter alia clear criteria, procedures for the selection of members, voting procedures and structures, block voting options, election procedures, mechanism to achieve transparency, i.e., distribution of minutes, newsletters, and accounts, and a grievance and recourse procedure and a challenge committee, to ensure (a) that the board of directors is accountable and (b) that a mechanism exists to challenge certification decisions, guidelines from the accreditation of certifiers.

FACILITATOR: Thank you, next.

BENTLEY: I would like now speak in my other capacity as spokesperson for the caucus with which I was asked to articulate their views and that particular caucus had put forth a motion that a task force should be constructed to resolve this issue. And I think the particular caucus I was with would endorse what we just heard and that those issues be charged to a group to look at those and the results should be put back to the general assembly for approval and ratification. So that what we adopt right here is provisional, contingent upon the results of that and its ratification. (Tape 8, Side 1)

After this second round of proposals the assembly adjourned for lunch.

Chorus: Singling Out Issues

Between the first and second round of presentations, dissident voices abstained from voting and the assembly decided on some working procedures. In the sequence above, the facilitator singles out one of the contested issues. He asks the presenters to remove an issue from its context within the position it is embedded in and to present it to the assembly.

Focusing just on the presenters, the second round of presentations has either brought new spokespeople into the arena or the spokespeople have shifted. The empirical data cannot offer a decisive answer. In any case, one can observe that those participants who were very articulate in the discussion on decision-making procedures reappear prominently. This change of speaker roles is enacted most explicitly by Bentley who states that he is now speaking "in his other capacity as spokesperson for a caucus."

In terms of content, two different decision-making strategies are implicitly suggested by the presenters. On the one hand, there is a differentiation of conflict, and on the other the conflicts are resolved by delegating it to a third party or expert committee. The proposals that offer a differentiation of conflict have two important elements: (1) a two-chamber system in which the economic interests have a 25 percent vote, and all other groups 75 percent, and (2) the Brazilian proposal reformulates the interim board's proposal by differentiating along sector (business, social, environmental) and region (North/South) lines. The balance, however, is not a "balance in equilibrium" but one that reduces the influence of the economic sector to 20 percent and includes a North/South balance in all chambers.

The type of knowledge that becomes important here is a mixture of polity and politics knowledge. It is polity knowledge inasmuch as the actors seek to create an organizational structure for a heterogeneous group. The participants do not come with ready-made models or refer in their presentations to other organizations that work similarly. Instead, a stepwise process of creation is to be observed. It is also a form of politics knowledge because those who come up with options for a differentiated organizational structure realize that, in order to consensualize the antagonistic groups, their demands and concerns have to be reflected in the organization itself: it is a demand for participation and a concern about domination.

Displaying the Third Round of Presentations

The participants had left the front stage for lunch, while in the backstage negotiations continued, leading to some degree of synthesis. Yet differences remain that make a two-thirds majority for any single position unlikely. Bentley, switching speaker roles again, gives a "procedural recommendation" for the third round of presentations: "More interestingly, you should also talk a little bit about the negotiations that happened between caucuses not so much the position of a particular caucus, but focus on the commonalities, because that is where you're gonna find the two-thirds majority" (Tape 8, Side 2).

In contrast to the rounds before, the proposals have slightly changed their format since the oral presentations are now supported by handwrit-

TABLE 8. Third Round of Presentation

Issues	Position 1 Synthesis between parts of the economic and environmental groups (Jason)	Position 2 Economic interests (male voice)	Position 3 Nonalliance group (Michael)	Position 4 Oceania (male voice)	Position 5 NGOs and Certifiers (Camila)
Membership: voting	25% economic; 75% other	25% economic; 75% other	Nonchamber system; individual voting	25% economic; 75% other	
Industry means	Certifiers; work for profit companies incl. industry associations and consultants				
Membership: criteria	Membership committee that reports back within 6 months → should develop an application procedure including criteria	Members should be selected by a credentials committee	Credentials committee develops criteria for membership; board of directors decides upon membership applications every 6 months		Membership committee that reports back within 6 months → should develop an application procedure including criteria
Representation	Toward regional representation	Equal weighting within each chamber of North and South	North and South should be represented but as long as 2/3 no problem	Toward regional representation	
Other Committees	Independent monitoring committee	Independent monitoring committee; credentials committee (allocation of members to chambers)	Credentials committee (allocation of members to chambers)		

ten slides displayed with an overhead projector. The assembly listens to five positions in total. Yet it is only partially clear whether the same groups have changed their positions or if new groups have emerged. The positions come from (1) a group that has synthesized the old economic and environmental positions, (2) a group that represents economic interests, (3) a nonalliance group, (4) an Oceania group, and (5) a group that consists of NGOs and certifiers.

Chorus: Merging Positions

Judging from the presentations, the displayed positions have merged on some issues: proposal 1 is a joint synthesis developed by some environmental NGOs and parts of the economic interests that are very close to the second proposal by the economic interests. Since proposal 5 does not mention the question of membership voting the only proposal left that argues for a competing formula is by the "nonalliance group" that sees all divisions between groups as artificial, and is thus in favor of a nonchamber voting system. However, the efforts to recontextualize continue. Since the assembly does not break again to meet in special caucus groups the speech acts that transform and reshape the multiplicity of voices can be traced back.

Interlude on the Front Stage

After the five proposals have been presented, the facilitator suggests changing the communication format: "Again, I don't want to avoid your parliamentary procedures or your democratic process, but I think there are some similarities, at least that I have seen that are maybe worth building on" (Tape 8, Side 2). Instead of following *Robert's Rules of Order* as agreed earlier, the assembly engages in a different type of consensus-building practice to create motions that can be voted upon. To do so, different elements of positions are negotiated on the front stage to get an indication of what the issue exactly is—as the following sequence exemplifies:

> THOMAS: Can I clarify one other point? We are talking here specifically about voting in any assembly, not about membership of the association. Is that the right understanding? Are we talking about membership or voting?

FACILITATOR: Membership.

[*Background talk*]

FACILITATOR: It's the voting membership.
JAMES: No, I would respectfully disagree with that. I believe that it is
the weight of a vote taken. But the membership can differ from that,
In the event that, for instance, the economic exceeds 25 percent,
their weight of the vote is scaled back to 25 percent. [*Loud applause.*]
(Tape 8. Side 2)

Although all positions focus broadly on the question of voting, a precise
definition or even an agreement on what exactly the object in question is
seems to have remained opaque. Yet the definition "the weight of a vote
taken" enjoys overwhelming support as the loud but anonymous applause
signals.

These forms of clarification continue in different ways. The spokesperson of the Brazilian proposal, Raimundo, declares that he will withdraw
his statement and agrees to the 25 percent for business and 75 percent for
all other groups. A number of environmental NGOs pull out of the process, and abstain from voting; their "voices" disappear completely from
the final text. In addition, actors try to substitute utterances under a new
claim. Consider, for instance, this short statement by Bentley:

I just would like to offer some commentary that might help us to
move along. Looking at all those proposals I did not see anything
that was mutually exclusive. . . . So what you can do and if you
accept that 25 percent is the limit, the only chamber that you need
is an economic chamber, when things come to a vote to ensure that
it does not go over 25 percent. That is the only time you need a
chamber. (Tape 8, Side 2)

Yet the attempt to substitute all claims under one assertion is challenged
by the spokesperson of the economic interests. He stresses that the concept of "adequate distribution of representation between the Northern
and Southern Hemispheres" would be diminished or even deleted by having a chamber only for the economic interests.

In a further attempt at substitution Bentley reformulates concerns
raised by participants as "needs." He concludes that the following "needs"
require further attention:

> There is a need for some more regional balance, there is a need to control a particular interest group, and that needs a certain percentage if it comes to a vote, and we need some type of independent monitoring, and we need a process by which those who feel uncomfortable can come back into. So you have four needs. Come up with something that addressed those four needs, and I think you got it done. (Tape 8, Side 2)

Chorus: Substituting

Bentley continues to enact his speaker role as a trusting, consensus-orientated translator of the different voices of the assembly. In his commentaries, he essentially reviews the existing proposals and substitutes their claims with new ones. In doing so, he displaces existing elements and recontextualizes them into a new framework utilizing vocabularies of need: (1) a need for regional balance; (2) a need to control the interest groups; (3) a need for an independent monitoring system; and (4) a need to integrate all the voices in the assembly. Through this translational practice of recontextualization the controversy has been made visible differently.

Presenting the Fourth Round of Positions

The fourth round of presentations deviates from those mentioned above inasmuch as they are staged now by the facilitators as straw polls to test their potential for achieving a broad consensus. They are now motions, not positions. Participants are asked to indicate by a hand signal whether they agree or disagree with the content of the motion. In total four motions are presented to the assembly: Motion 1 comes from a group combining the economic interests and moderate environmental NGOs; Motion 2 is from NGOs and certifiers; Motion 3 comes from the nonalliance group; Motion 3a is a variation of Motion 3 from the social NGOs; and the final motion is the consensualized product of all previous positions. Table 9 displays all motions that were presented one after another with speech acts in between that challenged them.

The efforts to abstract an element from one position to relocate it in a motion leads to friction as this participant from the economic sector demonstrates:

> I am indeed surprised, in fact shocked, by the presentations. Board membership needs to be addressed. It was, and remains, the request,

TABLE 9. Presentation of Motions

Issues	Motion 1 Econ. and Env. (Jason)	Motion 2 NGOs and Certifiers (Camila)	Motion 3 Nonalliance group (Michael)	Motion 3a Variation social NGOs (Gabriel)	Consensualized Motion (Camila, Jason, and 'team')
Voting: Membership	Weight of voting: 25% economic; 75% other; with a North/South balance	Weight of voting: 25% economic; 75% other; North/South and essentially toward regional representation	Nonchamber system, voting by individuals (it implies that individuals are members); but economic not more than 25% of the vote	Most important change: organizational representatives, not individuals, are members	- 25% voting weight for economic interests that represent both individuals and organizations with a North/South regional balance - 75% social, environmental, indigenous peoples—organizations only
Industry/ economic means	Certifiers; work for profit companies incl. industry associations and consultants		Consultants do not equal economic interests		A membership committee to report within 6 months. Its goal is to evolve regional balance within the organization and clear membership criteria and selection procedures, and to define the following: 1. voting procedures 2. election procedures 3. transparency including the independent monitoring committee 4. a grievance committee All 4 items to be determined by the board and proposed by postal ballots within 6 months.
Membership criteria		Membership criteria, with regional and North/South balance; a member selection process, clear voting procedures, election procedures → determined by the board and put to members by postal vote	Credentials committee develops criteria for membership; board of directors decides upon membership application every 6 months → that is put to the General Assembly		
Representation		Toward regional representation	North/South; but as long as 2/3 majority unproblematic		
Other Committees		Independent monitoring committee (transparency); grievance and challenges procedure → determined by the board and put to members by postal vote	Credentials committee (allocation of members to chambers); North/South and regional representative is recommended		Independent monitoring committee
Vote	Straw Poll: It would carry	Straw Poll: It would carry	Straw Poll: It would fail	Straw Poll: It would fail	Formal vote: Carried

> the respectful request of the economic interest group that they have two designated members of the board. (Tape 8, Side 2)

The facilitator is quick to remind him that "from a procedural standpoint" it would be more coherent to handle *voting* membership first, and then engage with *board* membership. Although his concern is obviously unjustified since board membership will be a topic in the further process, it signals an unease on the part of the "economic interest" that its voice may not be fully acknowledged.

Other practices that advance the amalgam of similar, yet slightly distinct, motions can be identified. For instance, Camila complements Motion 2 with the elements of "regional balance" and an "international monitoring committee," with both components having been requested by the Oceania group and other participants.

While Motions 1 and 2 pass almost without debate, Motion 3 triggers greater controversy. Two elements provoke objection, namely, the notion of "individuals being members," and the question of "consultants being part of the 75 percent caucus." Both issues are initially raised by members of the social caucus, a voice that seemed to have been silenced in the process of consensualization. The spokesperson for the caucus speaks in Spanish and, as he notes, only in the name of the social groups. Voting members have to be representatives of organizations or NGOs, he argues. Otherwise, one might find oneself in situations in which the voice of a person speaking in his or her own name only is equivalent to a person speaking in the name of 50 indigenous organizations. Similarly, an NGO representative from Brazil claims:

> Sorry, I'd like to say, we had a similar question in Brazil when we were at a Brazilian NGO forum. And the consultants, it is a very big problem for us because we understand that in the 75 percent that you want to put in the membership, we need organizations, people who represent people. Consultants do not represent people. (Tape 9, Side 1)

"People who represent people," so the argument goes, have a greater right to vote than consultants, or individuals more generally. The issue is obviously salient for the participants; it calls into question, in addition, Motions 1 and 2, which have already been passed by a straw vote.

Gabriel writes up his statement motion and hands it over to the facilitator. Yet both motions—Motion 3, which suggests individual membership, and Motion 3a, which talks of non-individual membership—fail to gather a two-thirds majority. Finally, the spokespeople for Motions 3 and 3a announce a literal marriage between the two motions, break up again, then join all the presenters on the front stage to draft the consensualized motion. They leave the front stage, agree bilaterally on a motion, and put the final motion to the assembly for a formal vote. The assembly approves, and the motion is carried.

Chorus: Recontextualizing

The translational practice of recontextualizing allows for consensus-making on the issue of the voting membership structure. Elements of former positions are singled out and put into new motions.[1] The final motion recontextualizes the positions of the four caucus groups. The membership structure consists of an institutional design with two chambers: an economic chamber (25 percent of the vote) and a broad chamber of social and environmental NGOs (75 percent of the vote). Further controversial issues are delegated to expert committees. An independent monitoring committee will provide feedback to the FSC. These design choices settle the controversies around representation.

Due to their active role as translators, the presenters of the various motions have changed their speaking roles in the assembly. Now, they occupy a distinct position between the "audience" and the "team." This new position becomes spatially significant because the speakers join the team on the front stage, which is where the final motion is drafted and then put to a vote.

Composition and Election of the Board

Having agreed on the *structure of the membership*, Brian, who had established himself as the spokesperson for the interim board, took over more and more the role of the facilitator who guided the assembly through its remaining hours. He noted:

> The next issue we have in front of us is this very difficult issue—which is obviously contentious and challenging—of industry representation on the board. (Tape 9, Side 2)

In what follows, I discuss how the assembly managed to find agreement on the issue of industry representation on the board, and how they subsequently elected the first board of the nascent organization. Industry or economic representation had been a major controversy throughout the entire making of the FSC. Should the industry become part of joint efforts to protect social and environmental rights? Was there truly a win–win opportunity, or did representation of the economic interests weaken networks and initiatives fighting for environmental and social ways of doing forestry? These issues were debated by inventing a decision tree that put the positions of the various groups into a new context.

Inventing a Decision Tree

The team created a decision tree to structure the discussion. The keynote speaker from the first evening, Mark, appeared now as part of the "team" sketching and initiating the first version of this instrument. The tree suggests four controversial questions with binary options for answers: (A) Should the economic interests be part of the board at all? (B) Should the economic interests have voting power? (C) Should the economic interests have one or two representatives? (D) Should the board have seven or nine members?

Procedural experts as well as spokespeople immediately challenged the structure of the tree:

> OSCAR: I'd like to change your decision tree so that voting "yes" to representatives with economic interests on the board still includes the option that they may not be voting members, thank you.

> [*Background talk*]

> CAMILA: Mark, perhaps under C you could just put a third choice. Two nonvoting reps. No, no under C, Number 3, two nonvoting.

> [*Background talk*]

> CAMILA: Now take out your little box from the side there.

> [*Background talk*]

> MARK: In this decision tree we have two choices:
> Either yes to voting or, no. OK, let's clarify this. This is voting representation!

Yes or no to voting representation for economic interests.

Do you want economic interests to vote on the board? Yes or No. That is a simple decision. If it is No, "Do they have nonvoting inclusion on the board." If it is "Yes," we end up coming down here to option number C. And we decide the number after we have decided the size of the board, and, finally, we look at two specific proposals that have been presented to us. (Tape 9, Side 2)

Chorus: A Translational Object

Visualization involves translation.[2] The decision tree recontextualized the various proposals staged before into specific questions that were put to the assembly. A translational object converts antagonistic positions into binary choices.[3] Yet this device itself became an object of communicative work. Utterances from the floor were translated into the decision tree so that each speaker would ask him- or herself, "Is that a fair visualization of what I just said?" Constant communicative work transformed the first into a second, and a third, version.

Focusing on the Decision Tree to Eliminate Controversies

Once the decision tree had been introduced, working on it became intertwined with questions that remained controversial, leading to situations in which substantial comments were not recontextualized into choices for the assembly to vote upon. For instance, the Brazilian spokesperson for the social caucus, Raimundo, requested Gabriel to interpret from Portuguese into English to avoid any misunderstandings. In essence, Raimundo's proposal laid out an option for the private sector to participate on the board "under certain circumstances."[4] A few seconds later the facilitator displayed a revised version of the decision tree in which the element suggested by the Brazilian spokesperson was obviously missing; objections followed immediately:

> RAIMUNDO: No, no we made a proposal that in some conditions we might vote yes. We can vote no if you don't know if you put in some conditions. Yes or no.
>
> FACILITATOR: That discussion came up, sir, and I felt that there was no consensus here. (Tape 9, Side 2)

A short discussion followed in which Stella, an interim board member, finally asked Gabriel, "I wonder if you could [*pause*] the proposal was not clear to the assembly here" (Tape 9, Side 2). Gabriel elaborated at some length on the proposal, stressing that "if we go for yes, these people should not be employees as has been suggested but also should be either certified or show a long-term commitment with the principles of the FSC" (Tape 9, Side 2).

Chorus: The Power of Translators

Translational practices of recontextualization are not an automatic process. The sequence shows that statements have to be (a) transformed in a way that resonates with the context, and (b) articulated by someone holding the role of a translator. How does this work? On transformation, Raimundo expressed himself in English earlier but now feels the need to be interpreted. Gabriel serves in this capacity. Yet the proposal does not find entry into the decision tree. The Brazilian spokesperson, Raimundo, insists on his modification, but it immediately fails to pass the facilitator, who says: "I felt there was no consensus here." Raimundo's proposal provokes attention but does not become recontextualized into the decision tree. By contrast, Gabriel transforms the statement by using the notion of "conditionality" with respect to the economic interests, and that of "long-term commitment with the principles of the FSC." Although he is still struggling to define the notion of *economic interest* conclusively, his framing ties in with the vocabulary deployed by other actors before resonating with the context.

Equally importantly, he holds a translator role. This point becomes particularly visible since the interim board, that is, Stella, does not ask Raimundo to repeat or clarify his proposal but, in fact, requests to elaborate on the salient issues. Thus, the statement is recontextualized from one speaking position into another—from an "audience speaking position" to a "translator speaking position." Politics is involved. The sequence shows how the team moves away from a participatory approach in which all voices are taken into account toward a more restricted form of constituting the organization. Statements have to pass translators to become recontextualized in the final document that is then presented for a vote.

Defining Economic Interest

Although the participants constantly deploy the notion of "economic interest" it is far from clear how this category is defined. Thus, Brian invites the assembly to work collectively on a definition of who would and who would not be eligible to become a member of the board. The basis for discussion is the definition in the Draft Charter of the FSC, which Brian reads out loud:

> No government representatives or individuals who have any commercial invested interest in forest management or in the trade of forest products may serve on the board. [*Applause.*]
>
> Employees or representatives of forest products companies, certifiers, industry associations (whether for profit or not for profit or any other organization with direct financial interest are considered to have a conflict of interest), economic representatives may include forest economists, retired businesspersons, academics, etc. (Tape 10, Side 1)

Again, Mark sketches this definition on the overhead to display it for further negotiation. Two clusters of speech acts can be observed. First, a couple of actors continue to comment on the general issue of economic interest. Here, the full spectrum of the controversy is presented. To illustrate, Abel, a spokesperson for indigenous organizations, stresses in Spanish that any form of business participation on the board would diminish the credibility of the FSC. On the contrary, a business representative argues, "What we want though is involvement and participation and to share the responsibility of this thing" (Tape 10, Side 1). These general arguments reflect some of the views held in the assembly room, yet they do not directly feed into the decision tree.

In contrast to these general arguments, three participants—Bentley, Camila, and Gabriel—deploy their "translator roles" and devise categorical distinctions, suggesting framings and visual representations on the overhead. Especially, Gabriel reverts to the Brazilian delegation's claim and recontextualizes it into the text. The wording that is finally approved by the assembly is summarized in table 10.

Once a definition is crafted, the facilitator proceeds to a straw vote: "All those who do not agree, please stand," he asks. A short pause ensues on the audio files, and then he notes, "The straw vote indicates a general agreement" (Tape 10, Side 1). Loud applause suggests consensus. In a similar fashion, the facilitator seeks to continue to take straw votes on the entire decision tree.

TABLE 10. Criteria for Board Members

	NO	YES
FSC Draft Charter	Government; commercial interests; employees of business, associations with direct interest	Academics, retirees
Gabriel		Certified; have shown long-term commitment to the principles
Straw vote: (carried)	Governments, commercial interests not committed to the FSC, employees of noncommitted companies and associations	Academics, consultants, retirees, FSC certified and those organizations who have shown long-term commitment to the principles

Chorus: Failing to Recontextualize Opposition Against Economic Interests

The new version of the decision tree presented a major change that apparently appeared unnoticed: as shown in table 6 (see chapter 5), the initial position taken by the social groups was to have no economic interests on the board of directors. Abel (spokesperson for the indigenous organizations) repeated this position minutes before the assembly took a straw vote. However, this position never found its way into the decision tree. No translator appears to have ensured that the position was recontextualized into the motion. For this reason, the assembly did not even have the chance to count the votes against representation of the economic interests. Although the empirical evidence is not definite, the politics behind this choice seem clear. The team opted for a constellation in which the economic interests had some form of representation on the new board of directors. The team thus elegantly avoided a binary (yes/no) vote on the question of economic representation. Such a vote could have provoked an outburst from the economic groups that had, in part, been involved in the project since its inception. The assembly was only able to *specify* the conditions of representation of the economic interests; its representation as such was not up for a vote even though many groups had advocated this option (see the second act).

Initiating Rotation and Balance

I reenter the scene when the facilitator is just about to take a straw vote on all the decisions displayed on the decision tree. It is already Sunday afternoon, the participants have only a few hours left to vote for the first board of the FSC, and yet there is still disagreement on the current version of the decision tree and its implications for the future board.

Spokespeople for the social groups demand a balance of four members from the South and three from the North including regional representation as well as a differentiation between the social interest and the environmental interest.[5] Again, nobody picks up the claim. The discussion continues to focus on other topics. Yet, after a couple of minutes Gabriel makes the following statement:

> I would like to make a proposal to take into consideration the indigenous peoples' claim here and have the same rotation there. Social groups have four, and environmental groups have three in the first term and then rotate again. I think this would make the social movements more comfortable by giving them an assigned slot. I see Thomas's comment, and I think it would be interesting to have it free to the individuals but I feel that there are some social movements that are concerned that they could be wiped out. Because they have a tradition of being wiped out within decision-making processes. So, anyways, the suggestion is to have four and three rotating in the same way as North and South. (Tape 10, Side 1)

No critical voices regarding this proposal are heard until a woman notes, "One comment: It does not have to be up on the board, but [should] we strive for gender balance as well? As we had about 50 male speakers in a row" (Tape 10, Side 1). Suddenly, skepticism emerges: instead of recognizing "all this balance," a male speaker wants to remind voters that there is "a mixture of skills needed" (Tape 10, Side 1).[6] Another contrasts attempts to ensure North–South and gender balance with certain qualities board members should feature, namely "intelligence, passionate commitment, and foresight" (Tape 10, Side 1).[7]

Chorus: Representation and Gender Trouble

Two views on representation compete for recognition: an affirmative action approach argues that particular actor categories (North/South, regional, sectoral, gender) should be recontextualized into the future board structure of the FSC. Those who demand this approach inhabit a classical marginalized actor category within world politics. Mostly, they are activists from the Global South working on issues of social equality who have, as Gabriel notes, "a tradition of being wiped out within decision-making processes" (Tape 10, Side 1). The other view on representation blindfolds itself to these social categories. Triggered by the call for gender balance, proponents construct "skills" vs. "gender" and "region of origin" vs. "passionate commitment" as binary oppositions in which one side embodies the negation of the other. In doing so, they suggest that the balance approach would *not* account for "skills," "intelligence," "passionate commitment," and "foresight." However, the politics knowledge of "balance," introduced in the first act, clearly favors the affirmative action approach and assures marginalized groups a voice on the board of directors.

A Decision Tree Does Its Work

Despite competing views on the notion of balance the facilitator calls for a straw vote following the path laid out by the decision tree. The result is a motion that is extracted from "decision tree 3." It entails the following aspects:

(a) Economic interests on the board have the right to vote. Those who do not qualify as board members are governments, commercial enterprises not committed to the FSC, employees of non-committed companies and associations; those who qualify as board members are academics, consultants, retirees, the FSC-certified, and those organizations that have shown long-term commitment to the principles.
(b) The Board will have nine members in total.
(c) Of these nine members, two will be representatives of the economic interest. The seven remaining members are to be subdivided by region (North/South), and by sector (environment/social). The motion also notes an intention to strive informally for regional and gender balance. The motion is carried with 63 yes-votes, 0 no-votes, and 9 abstentions.

Of the 22[8] candidates for the board the nine board members are obviously not chosen freely but have to be elected according to their sector and regional origin (North/South).[9] Each candidate introduces him or herself to the assembly. Even now disagreement remains as to, for instance, the participation of certifiers on the board. Yet the team is quick to bring this controversy to closure. The assembly votes, some time passes, and then,

TABLE 11. The Board of the FSC as Elected at the
Founding Assembly in Toronto in 1993

South / Economic	Alonso
South / Environment	Maria
South / Social	Arcadio
South / Social	Norberto
South / Social	Pablo
North / Economic	Russell
North / Environment	Brian
North / Environment	Bentley
North / Social	Lisa

the facilitator announces that 84 ballots have been cast in total, of which
four have been annulled. In the applause and cheering the facilitator
requests the new board to join the old board at the front.

Chorus: Consensus Manufactured

The first board of directors was voted into office. The participants accomplished this task by performing two sets of translational practices. First,
new speakers emerged who disclosed the lack of procedural rules as well
as providing polity knowledge of the established procedures enclosing the
controversy on negotiation rules. Disclosure and enclosure operated
together, creating a situation in which the participants could move forward in constituting the organization.

The second set of translational practices bundled a series of recontex-
tualizations. The participants had the enormous task of turning conflicting positions into motions. They singled out issues, merged positions, or
substituted aspects under a new claim. These practices allowed for deleting, adding, rearranging, and so forth. In so doing, they crafted the voting
structure for the FSC membership. For negotiating the composition of the
board, participants invented a peculiar object, a decision tree that represented the various positions as choices for the assembly to vote on. Translators played an important role in forming this device for reaching agreement. While the notion of the translator or mediator might suggest a
neutral position, they, in fact, executed power by structuring the way the
positions were presented and put to a vote. As the analysis has shown,
positions that would have denied the economic interests a seat at the
board were not recontextualized into the decision tree and thus did not
appear as voting options.

Things could have been otherwise. The fourth act makes it clear that an FSC without economic interests on the board of directors was an option in the room and even on the negotiating table, but it did not mature into a motion. Social and indigenous groups struggled to enact their politics knowledge of forming a strong alliance against the economic interests on the board of directors. If they had managed to occupy one of the translator roles, they could have mobilized broader support for their position and enacted translational practices of recontextualization, changing the course of events. As shown in the second act, there were many groups who argued against a strong presence by the economic interests in the institutional design of the FSC. Over the course of the assembly and especially in its constitutive phase (the fourth act), these participants could have created the momentum for an FSC free of an economic interest at least on its board of directors.

It is hard to tell whether the economic interest would have accepted an institutional design in which it had no voice on the board of directors. Like Tim Bartley (2007b), one can think of the emergence of private institutions as the outcome of political contestation. Thus, proponents of an alternative institutional design would have needed to convince the economic interests that a certification organization would only be perceived as legitimate if its board had no economic ties. As table 6 shows (see chapter 5), the arguments for such an alternative design were known and articulated during the assembly. Yet these arguments were not recontextualized skillfully in existing contexts such as the notion of balance of all interested parties.

Epilogue: Until We Meet Again

The new board of directors joined the interim board on the podium as one of the most visible achievements of the conference. But the old board still felt that it was within its duties to bring the meeting to an end. Adrian, who had opened the Founding Assembly two days earlier, took the microphone again for a round of appreciations. His thank you notes went first to the less visible participants in the play. He thanked the organizational team, those who took notes, the volunteers, the "audio man," and the interpreters; he added a further thank you to the facilitator, the FSC coordination team, the keynote speakers, and explicitly to those who operated in a translator role:

> And I think there are some other people here who intervened when we needed intervention. Gabriel [*applause*], Logan [*applause*], and

Bruce, where is Bruce? You know, when you made that statement about process and procedure, I understand completely how you can get fixated about that. (Tape 10, Side 2)

And then he referred back to the keynote speeches on Friday evening that had evoked the notion of a change of patterns:

And this weekend we are looking at new patterns, we are looking at new ways of doing things, and I think it applies to all groups here. I am personally saddened by the fact that there are groups that are leaving. I think that they have something very valuable to contribute; all of us are taking risks, and I think that if we don't take those risks those things won't happen. (Tape 10, Side 2)

The meeting could have ended here, but there were more people who wanted to say a few words. In "a final act of acknowledgment" Logan devoted a personal thank you to each member of the interim board for the work they had done (Tape 10, Side 2). Another reflection came from Henry, founder of WARP, who thought back to a meeting in a hallway at a conference in Amherst, Massachusetts three years before; they never would have thought "that this would have been the outcome." But he also turned toward the future and reminded the assembly that "the success, the strength of this organization will remain with us, with the assembly. We have to work to enlarge it. Act as critics, supporters in whatever ways we can to bring the message of the FSC to our constituencies, and to the rest of the world" (Tape 10, Side 2). The very last words that appear on the audio files come again from Adrian who declares the end of the conference, and notes, "Thank you very, very much. I hope you enjoyed your short visit to Toronto, and until we meet again!" (Tape 10, Side 2).

Chorus: What Have We Learnt?

The Founding Assembly ended with a proposal to meet again and with a glance into history, referring to the very first meetings of the emerging organization. Participants constructed a trajectory of many meetings within which the meeting in Toronto would become the founding moment of the organization.

The most important decision taken at the assembly was to set up the organization as a membership organization and not as a foundation; this ensured that the assembly was the supreme authority of the organization. The politics behind this decision was driven by the vivid and controversial negotiations in which NGOs resigned from the process. With the call for a membership organization, it was easier for the team to argue that any decision taken by the assembly could be undone again. This argument tied into the storyline of moving forward despite the imperfection of the documents that were presented. Thus, the team played out its politics knowledge.

Yet the decision in favor of a membership organization intensified the controversy surrounding industry representation that was prominent throughout the negotiations toward an FSC. The mechanism of translation can explain how participants managed to move forward despite this delicate situation. First, translation is a mechanism of exclusion as it is about the powerful choice to recontextualize something in another context (Freeman 2009). There were several instances in which the interim board managed to define the context of the assembly in a way that would not allow for dissenting voices to be articulated. This was done, for instance, with reference to time: the content of the claim was not dismissed, but its moment in the course of the assembly was rejected (see the third act). This enabled the team to continue to narrate its storyline about equal participation while de facto excluding several participants.

Second, translation is a mechanism with constitutive effects due to the moving of entities from one context to another. In deliberative theory this constitutive effect is a result of actors' willingness to be persuaded by rational arguments (Risse 2000). It situates the driving force of consensus-making in subjects' minds. Detecting the change of interest or identity is methodologically extremely complex or even impossible (Risse and Kleine 2010). By contrast, the mechanism of translation does not stem from theoretical deduction but from empirical investigations in negotiation situations—not actors' minds, but their practical doing forms the interest of research. Following from this, the mechanism of translation suggests that change occurs because positions are constantly recontextualized (into a new negotiation situation, a new document, a decision tree, and so forth). Positions change because actors constantly adapt them to new situations and contexts. As a result, representation of the economic interests could be incorporated into the institutional design of the FSC.

One might ask why the economic interests accepted a minority position within the institutional design of the organization (25 percent voting membership and two board members out of nine). Rationalist bargaining theory would predict that the economic interests would have little interest in creating a decision-making body in which economic interests have such a minority position. It is tempting to relax assumptions about the distribution of power as well as preexisting interest, and then argue that the economic interests simply read the room and decided that *a* deal is better than *no* deal.

This theoretical shortcut misses both the heterogeneity of the groups as well as the dynamics of process. On heterogeneity, recall that the majority of those who spoke for the economic caucus were concerned wood users who were searching for timber from sustainable sources. They had been working in community forestry projects or had sustainability posts in their companies. While they were interested in participating in votes, they also distrusted those economic participants who had a record of human rights violations and unsustainable forestry practices. Untrustworthy attempts to certify timber emerged for instance in Indonesia at that time (Tape 5, Side 1). Thus, a vocal part of the economic interests wanted to clearly distance itself from those actors. It aimed for an organization that a global audience would recognize as a private authority.

The dynamics of process point to the fact that there was no preorganized economic caucus as such with clearly defined preexisting interests partly because the assembly operated without clear rules of procedure. Instead, various subgroups were formed and changed during the negotiations. These dynamics led to the emergence of (more or less) honest brokers: they created the complex organizational structure, cutting off extreme positions on both ends of the spectrum. The economic interests became a minority position within the institutional design, and the option to vote against having the "economic interest" on the board was not even put to a vote.

In sum, the founding of the FSC was an instance of political novelty created in a situation of high uncertainty about the interests and identities of participating groups, the underlying rules of the game, and the political effects. Neither power and preexisting interests, nor the power of the better argument, can explain the dynamics and outcome of this event. What triumphs is the artful performance of a fusion of different kinds of knowledge, borne by translation mechanisms.

7 | After All

The Politics of Beginning

How to begin? The problem of beginning is familiar to everyone who writes. It is rare for writers to face a blank sheet of paper; often the sheet of paper is already inscribed with aphorisms, stories, catchy titles, but also with misleading metaphors or tautologies. Thus, the problem of beginning requires one to make choices, conscious choices, in order to translate the messiness of thoughts into an arrangement that allows something novel to develop. To begin is to engage in performances of ordering. I have examined this problem of beginning by inquiring how political activists, concerned wood users, firms, and scientists engaged in negotiating a new model of governance. They founded the Forest Stewardship Council, a transnational certification organization that nowadays is paradigmatic for private authority.

In this chapter, I revisit the argument that the making of the FSC can be viewed as a constitutional moment for private authority by reflecting on the FSC's trajectory in time. Then, I summarize the main findings and outline the major implications with regard to three major themes in world politics—the emergence of authority, expertise, and negotiations. With respect to authority, I present the mechanism of translation and outline the social role of meetings and documents in creating private authority. In so doing, I show how dramaturgical methodology contributes to recent debates on how authority emerges (Sending 2015, 2017; Zürn 2018; Krisch 2017). With respect to expertise, the chapter explains why environmental knowledge must be viewed as political practice that represents some voices and neglects others. It examines how knowledge making is a practice by which actors seek to promote their own authority. As far as negotiations are concerned, this chapter shows how the book's approach extends existing accounts that view negotiations through the lens of a logic of consequences, appropriateness, or arguing (Risse and Kleine 2010). It offers a framework of how negotiators in practice manufacture a consensus, including by silencing certain voices.

A Constitutional Moment in Governing the Earth

As a microstudy in global governance, this book has examined a "constitutional moment" in governing the Earth, a brief period in which basic rules of political practice were rewritten (see Jasanoff 2011).[1] Scholars in Science and Technology Studies (STS) have stressed that such "constitutional changes necessarily involve renegotiating the manner in which states and other authoritative institutions employ the power of expertise" (Jasanoff 2011, 624). In line with this argument, this book has paid particular attention to the ways in which nonstate actors generated new knowledge not only about forestry but also about governing as such (Voß and Freeman 2016). "A clear organizational model for making transnational rules did not yet exist" when the FSC emerged (Dingwerth and Pattberg 2009, 17). For this reason, founding members had to experiment and gain expertise in how to conduct governance without the involvement of states. Part of this governance knowledge has sedimented in the institutional structures of organizations such as the FSC and formed their course over time (Hanrieder 2015).

The Trajectory of the FSC

In the trajectory of the FSC, its Founding Assembly still constitutes a point of reference. At the 6th FSC General Assembly in Kota Kinabalu, Malaysia in July 2011, those who had taken part in the Founding Assembly were asked to gather for a picture.[2] A group of eight or ten people assembled, cheering, laughing, and smiling for the camera.

Beyond this ritual dimension, many decisions taken at the Founding Assembly continue to structure the FSC. For instance, the board of directors still reflects the economic, social, and environmental sectors as well as the Global North and South. Likewise, the controversies around industry membership articulated by Friends of the Earth, Greenpeace, and many other groups have impacted the discussion on the FSC's credibility ever since (Cadman 2011; Auld 2014; Bartley 2018, 260; Elliott 2000, 21). In 2018 Greenpeace International did not renew its FSC membership partly because of the influence of the economic interests in the organization.[3]

The Founding Assembly created a chamber structure giving 75 percent of the voting rights to a collective environmental and social chamber and restricting the voting rights of the industry chamber to 25 percent. However, in the course of its consolidation, the FSC's organizational structure changed in 1996 to a three-chamber format with environmental, social, and economic chambers (Elliott 2000, 19). Today, all chambers have 33.3 percent voting rights.

Other defining elements of the Founding Assembly have drastically changed. I have examined in detail the ad-hoc creation of rules of procedure. The negotiations reflect that participants came with conflicting ideas and practices of how to organize the institution-making process. While such situations are increasingly common (see Hajer 2009), the FSC itself has over the years not only developed procedural rules but also information packages that are handed out to participants at its assemblies. They provide detailed explanations of how the General Assembly operates. Facilitators organizing discussion sessions are nowadays better equipped to deal with conflicts that arise in a multistakeholder organization (Cadman 2011, 49) than the facilitator of the Founding Assembly who had assumed that "to a large degree the group will manage itself; my job should be fairly simple as we go forward" (Tape 1, Side 3).

An Alternative FSC

The FSC grew out of a biotope of initiatives advocating certification as a solution for various and perhaps conflicting problems such as a bad press, deforestation, and social injustice (Auld 2014; Bartley 2007b; Green 2014). The consultative process in 1992 was a means to generate interest in this specific instrument globally. Only days after the FSC's Founding Assembly, the "Canadian Pulp and Paper Association (CPPA), announced it would work to create a domestic certification program" (Auld 2014, 87). Other domestic programs followed including discussions within the International Organization for Standardization about using the FSC's standards for forest certification. The FSC's model was even adopted in other sectors. For instance, the Marine Stewardship Council, a standard-setting organization for fisheries, is modeled on the stewardship idea of the FSC (Dingwerth 2017). Thus, the FSC has heavily shaped what Dingwerth and Pattberg (2009) call the organizational field of "transnational sustainability governance."

However, the FSC in this specific configuration was the product of distinct translational practices. Things could have been otherwise (see Clarke et al. 2015). Founding members could have chosen alternative pathways; an alternative FSC could have been possible. In the late 1980s, there was a wide spectrum of initiatives that experimented with new techniques of governing, creating islands of innovations (see chapter 3). These initiatives ranged from fair trade models, as in the coffee sector (Auld 2014), to extractive reserves that had very little in common with a certification organization (Anderson 1990; Colchester and Lohmann 1993; Counsell and Rice 1992b). I sketch three competing trajectories.

First, the negotiations could have failed. The microanalysis of the Founding Assembly has shed light on the serious conflicts between the participants. Negotiating sensitive issues in the face of competing practices of how to organize the institution-making process could have easily jeopardized the entire project.[4] If skillful translators had not provided polity knowledge that ended the controversy (translational practices of enclosure), a collapse of the negotiations would have been likely. The participants needed to perceive the process as based on "'democratic' or 'democracy-like' foundations" because the FSC was pioneering private authority (Dingwerth 2017, 81). After the Washington, DC, meeting a year before produced no conclusive results, the interim board could have dismissed the ambitious project. A momentum would not have been set up and then seized. In that case, forest certification would have played only a marginal role in the governance of the global forest (Arts 2021). After having reviewed the initiatives in the 1990s, Brian concluded that "without FSC, certification would probably still be a concept that had been tested in a few cases, rather than a reality" (Elliott 2000, 20).

Second, an FSC could have been constituted with less participation by social and environmental NGOs. In the early discussions about an FSC, participants recognized the relative lack of social groups, especially from the Global South (see chapter 3). Responding to this call, the interim board managed to create a nearly perfect balance between the various groups (see chapter 4). However, during the Founding Assembly the interim board once again excluded some of the social and environmental groups because they continued to voice their concerns. Also, some of their positions—such as allowing no economic interest on the board of directors—were not recontextualized into a motion. If a translator (Gabriel) had not ensured that other central concerns were included in the institutional design, it is likely that social groups from the Global South and more radical environmental groups would have declined membership. The recent resignation of Greenpeace from the FSC points in that direction. For the economic interest and the forest industry a certification program with less rigorous standards and less critical NGO involvement might have been attractive. The launch of the Pan-European Forest Certification Scheme in June 1999 is indicative in this regard (Gulbrandsen 2010, 59). Forest landowners in six European countries created this certification project as an alternative to the FSC. So there was potential for a certification project with less involvement by social and critical environmental groups. In the end, this type of FSC would have granted these groups greater autonomy in advocating for their causes outside and not within economic networks such as the FSC (Jacques 2016).

Finally, there was an FSC looming with considerably more emphasis on social and environmental issues and their representation in the organization. In general, the literature views the FSC as a strong case for participatory norms and equality (Dingwerth 2017; Quack and Malets 2014). At the same time, Klaus Dingwerth (2007, 49) concludes that struggles over meaning-making "deserve a more solid empirical analysis." In focusing on these struggles, the mechanism of translation can explain when and how participatory norms were ignored so that social and environmental NGOs resigned from the process (see chapter 5, third act). Issues of overconsumption, certification in authoritarian settings, and the strong influence exerted by the economic interest are concerns preoccupying critical scholarship and activism today (Bartley 2018; Kill 2016). Yet these issues were already present during the assembly. NGOs circulated critical memos before the assembly and articulated their views at the conference. While some of these groups may never have intended to become part of the FSC, others had participated in the negotiations for many years. Connor (Friends of the Earth) was such a case, as FoE had already experimented with certification in the mid-1980s (see chapter 3). Connor read aloud the critical declaration signed by 26 groups present at the Founding Assembly (chapter 5, second act). A central concern of the statement was the representation of the economic interest in the design of the organization. If translated otherwise, the economic interest might have been (a) excluded from voting membership, or (b) denied a seat on the board of directors, or both. As argued in chapter 6 (the fourth act), proponents of such design choices would have needed to convince the economic interest that a certification organization would only be perceived as legitimate if its board had no economic members. They would have needed to provide a convincing legitimation narrative (politics knowledge).

Most likely, participants would not have constituted this alternative FSC in October 1993. Radical NGOs would have needed to continue their naming and shaming campaigns, while simultaneously integrating the economic interest into the discussion. In that case, more social and environmental NGOs might have supported the project, launching an FSC a year later. This alternative FSC would have reflected to a greater extent core concerns such as deforestation and social injustice. Yet it is unclear whether this project could have turned into a viable business option (another core concern of the early team). It probably would have not grown as quickly, being less successful in terms of hectares of certified forest (Arts 2021).

Private Authority in the Making

Scholarship on authority has suggested that the social processes should be examined by which authority becomes stabilized rather than focusing solely on formal delegation (Sending 2015; Krisch 2017). In responding to this call, this book has provided the mechanism of translation, studied in a dramaturgical register. Belonging to the greater "family" of practice theory accounts (Bueger and Gadinger 2015), a dramaturgical methodology pays attention to "what actors do in a particular situation" and how "political realities might be different because of it" (Hajer 2009, 54). It allows scholars to investigate how nonstate actors actively produce knowledge and order beyond state governance. FSC founding members "sought to create new rules" (Dingwerth 2017, 78), thus embodying what Jessica Green has termed "entrepreneurial" private authority, defined as instances in which nonstate actors "make rules or set standards that other actors in world politics adopt" (Green 2014, 6). In so doing, nonstate actors along with governments and international organizations engage in ordering practices from which the order of world politics emerges (Adler 2019). This book has implications for the study of the emergence of private authority in two respects. First, I have developed the mechanism of translation that accounts for the stepwise making of a new organization preparing to claim authority. Second, meetings and documents appear in the analysis as having a social role that contributes to the emergence of private authority.

The Mechanism of Translation

A key finding of this book concerns the mechanism of translation. IR scholarship has mobilized theories of translation to account for the change in norms and standards as they travel and are implemented elsewhere

(Berger 2017; Graz 2021; Risse 2017a; Zimmermann 2017). When norms are transported, they are transformed and they change their local contexts. Borrowing from Actor-Network Theory in particular (Callon 1986; Latour 1999), I have added the *constitutive effect* of translation. In translations, different parts or elements are associated with one another. This book has shown how the constitutive effect of translation accounts for private authority emergence.

More specifically, nonstate actors engage in two performances of translational ordering. One operation is concerned with fixing and stabilizing (*enclosure*); actors hold constant what seems to work, relying on proxies and sticking to working assumptions. Countering messy, contested realities with different perspectives, they suggest seemingly consensual knowledge. The other operation is concerned with "opening up" (Stirling 2008), or *disclosure*; it is an operation that liquefies political order, problematizes what seems given, keeps options open, and faces uncertainty. Each operation presupposes the other. The "magic" happens in the dialectical space constituted by both operations; it is here, in the in-between, that innovation in governance becomes possible.

The empirical chapters have investigated various facets of these translational performances. For instance, in 1989 a founding member of the FSC prepared a pre-project proposal for a labeling system for the International Timber Trading Organization. It states that "consumers are expressing a preference for sustainable timber" (Thomas, Ken, and Connor 1989). As I showed in chapter 3, earlier drafts of this proposal framed the notion of consumer preference much more cautiously. Thus, the document is an instance of fixing an assumption even though there is no conclusive evidence to warrant it. At the same time, the proposal suggests several items that are to be researched, such as how to follow timber through the chain of custody. The example indicates that differentiating between the given and the to-be-researched is an active construction process that renders some elements as known, agreed upon, and technical and others as unknown and up for discussion and research.

In performing these operations, nonstate actors inevitably reframe, silence, and suppress competing forms of knowledge. In his study of the Mexican forest Andrew Matthews (2011, 236) reminds us that silencing "is not a scandal but an inescapable result of the ways that knowledge is built and sustained." This argument is not an invitation to employ undemocratic practices and systems of repression. There exists a politics of translation that organizes which knowledges and voices find representation in performances of negotiating a document as well as in the fragmented architecture of global environmental politics (Campbell et al. 2014). Dramaturgy makes these politics explicit by examining how actors perform specific roles, engage in scripting and counterscripting, and stage events for a global audience. The analysis of the Founding Assembly has shown exactly this—exclusion is an active process even in meetings that are framed as fair and participatory.

The Social Role of Meetings and Documents

This study has paid particular attention to the social role of meetings and documents. They appeared in the analysis for their capability of eliciting action. This view of meetings and documents as artifacts in the emergence of private authority asks what documents and meetings *do* and *what is done with them* (Asdal and Reinertsen 2022). Meetings and documents form a reiterative structure, a chain of meetings generate documents, which generate meetings, and so forth; they are "crucial parts of systems for organizing" (Hilgartner 2000, 19). As the politics of beginning cannot draw on an institutional infrastructure, meetings and documents link globally dispersed actors in a common project. In so doing, this structure creates an emerging group membership through a suggested shared vocabulary. Like established international institutions (Haas and Haas 2002), they create a setting where nonstate actors can negotiate reiteratively and arrive at problem definitions and response options.

Documents generate and bundle knowledge on phenomena such as deforestation and make this knowledge available for meetings. As Christian Bueger (2015, 10) explains for the case of piracy, "violence in the maritime world is represented in a single artifact, the IMO [International Maritime Organization] reports. This document can then be easily circulated across distance and reach sites such as the UNSC [UN Security Council]." For this reason, the production of documents as well as the ways in which a document presents different voices is highly relevant. Preparative documents frame topics for meetings and outline what requires further negotiation. As such, this book has shown how they are a site or setting to be studied.

Documents play their role in preparing a claim to authority. This argument can best be illustrated with the FSC consultative process. Before the FSC was founded, the FSC working group sent around their working documents in which FSC standards as well as a possible organizational structure were outlined. In addition, consultants across the globe organized meetings with stakeholders to discuss the working documents. This process centered the discussions on possible forms of certification, generated interest in the instruments of certification, and led to a high participation rate in the FSC Founding Assembly by nonstate actors, especially from Latin America. Thus, documents are an important device to prepare the ground for claiming private authority. They are a means to "compete for authority" (Sending 2015).

Expert Knowledge in Private Authority

The existing literature on private authority has theorized expert knowledge as an important aspect of its emergence (Hall and Biersteker 2002a; Cutler, Haufler, and Porter 1999a; Djelic and Quack 2010). Jessica Green in particular develops a theory in her book that argues that private authority emerges when private actors have "existing expertise and can provide benefits that other actors cannot" (Green 2014, 16).[5] While not questioning Green's theory, I have argued that the notion of "existing expertise" deserves closer consideration. Based on the empirical analysis, there are three major arguments for this claim.

Expertise and the Claim to Authority

As the FSC was negotiated in a constitutional moment, there was no simple blueprint in the form of existing knowledge for this specific type of organization. In such a situation, gaining expertise is often a first step to claiming authority (Quack 2016, 364). This book has provided the mechanism of translation to explain how the process of generating expert knowledge operates; this knowledge can be analytically distinguished as policy, polity, or politics knowledge.

The previous chapters have shown that, as far as the "policy knowledge" of forestry is concerned, there is more than one vison of what "sustainable forestry" or "forest stewardship" might mean (Mathews 2011). For a long time, tropical forests were seen as unmanageable because they are complex ecosystems. The rights of indigenous people living in the forest were regarded by some as a political issue that governments ought to be responsible for, while others suggested that these rights needed to be secured by any forest operation.

As regards "polity knowledge," the FSC represents a shift not only in ways of doing governance but also in knowledge of governance. "Polity knowledge" of governance did not exist when the founding members of the FSC negotiated a certification system. The FSC itself was to become a model for others to adopt (Dingwerth and Pattberg 2009), but its founders definitely had to create something new, copying and translating from other experiences. They had to convince bystanders and a global audience that a new instrument now existed for forest management.[6]

With the rise of private authority, the "politics knowledge" covering how to conduct private governance had to be developed. Part and parcel of this new knowledge was a narrative that "all relevant stakeholders had been included in transparent and open decision-making processes" (Dingwerth 2017, 76). The dramaturgical analysis has shown how notions of "balance" and "new paradigms of deliberation" were introduced and structured the founding of the FSC. These three forms of knowledge, while analytically distinct, are often intertwined and condition one another. The point is, though, that this governance knowledge had to be *created* and did not preexist as the basis for claiming private authority.

Institutionalizing Diverse Forms of Knowledge

A further argument for attending to the construction of expert knowledge concerns the different types of knowledge on which private governance arrangements are built and inevitably raises the question of whose knowledge has been translated into mechanisms for governing. Scholars in STS have been particularly vocal in asserting that "expertise does not simply lie in specific exercises of knowledge-making" but also in "the institutional dynamics in which knowledge is rendered authoritative" (Beck et al. 2017, 1069). Institutional designs and their enactment define the power relations between participants and bring about specific knowledge products (Montana 2019).

Much of the existing literature on the FSC comes to the conclusion that the organization is based on a pluralistic set of actors with diverse types of knowledge (Quack and Malets 2014; Dingwerth 2017). The empirical material presented here suggests two refinements to the integration of diverse forms of knowledge. First, the inclusion of nonstate actors from the Global South, especially social and indigenous NGOs, was the product of continuous pressure from these groups. They demanded broader consultation and explicit recognition of their rights. As I have shown by tracing the development of the FSC's Principles and Criteria, the rights of indigenous peoples developed only over time into a separate, full principle on its own (Principle #3).

Second, the microanalysis of the Founding Assembly shows that a number of social and indigenous groups had massive problems integrating their voices into the emerging procedural structure of the assembly. This has to do with the provisional voting procedure taken over from *Robert's Rules of Order* as well as substantive and procedural comments. The facilitator and interim board actively denied deliberation. Only when already established speakers reiterated claims from some groups did the claims become a voting option.

These findings have implications for the ways in which we theorize private authority. This study suggests that scholarship has to examine negotiating practices to evaluate whether private organizations live up to their participatory ideals. Mechanisms of inclusion and exclusion determine what kind of knowledge becomes translated into institutional design and rules for governing. Less powerful actors either have to constantly lobby for their voices to be heard or have to rely on skillful translators (Doerr 2018).

Implications for the Study of Expert Knowledge

Important contributions in IR have theorized the power of expert knowledge for the creation of political order. For Peter Haas (1992, 2017), epistemic communities—networks of scientific experts within a specific policy area—may change states' interests because of their authoritative claim to consensual, policy-relevant knowledge. Jessica Green, as elaborated above, theorizes preexisting, often technical knowledge as the basis for private authority emergence. These accounts have in common that expert knowledge appears as the *explanans* (that which explains). In contrast, the perspective advanced in this book focuses on the construction of expert knowledge so that expertise turns into the *explanandum* (that which is to be explained).

The theoretical background for this approach to knowledge and order can be found in STS (Beck, Forsyth, and Mahony 2024; Jasanoff 2004; Latour 1999). Here, the study of expert knowledge is "about how the making of knowledge is organized; who participates, in what ways, and at what points in the process; who has rights and responsibilities to speak authoritatively about knowledge; and the norms and rules for both making and applying knowledge to important societal decisions" (Miller 2017, 912).

The reason for confronting IR with this set of questions about knowledge is rooted in the assumed co-production of knowledge and order (Jasanoff 2004). Instead of distinguishing the making of knowledge and the making of order, scholarship stresses that they are mutually constitutive. Or, in the famous words of Sheila Jasanoff (2004, 2), "the ways in which we know and represent the world (both nature and society) are inseparable from the ways we choose to live in it."

In IR Bentley Allan has mobilized the idiom of co-production to investigate how the climate came to take on a geophysical rather than a bioecological form in global governance. As others do, he points to the close linkage between geophysical scientists and state institutions (Miller and Edwards 2001; Beck, Forsyth, and Mahony 2024). Had other actors been involved, the conception could have been different. Thus, co-productionist accounts draw our attention to the "competing, contested representations of the climate in the scientific literature and a variety of ways to translate them into governance arrangements" such as the Intergovernmental Panel on Climate Change or the United Nations Framework Convention on Climate Change (Allan 2017, 131). While not denying human-made climate change, there are diverse voices within the natural and human sciences who "disagree about climate change," about possible response options and forms of governing the climate (Hulme 2010). The same holds true for knowledge about the forest and conservation politics more broadly.

This book contributes to a literature in IR that extends the epistemic community framework, recognizing that the analysis needs to begin earlier. Constituting consensual knowledge is itself a contested process that favors particular assumptions, voices, and representations over others (Esguerra 2024; Littoz-Monnet 2024; Pantzerhielm 2023). The coexistence of multiple, partly competing forms of knowledge is the rule rather than the exception. As Sigrid Quack (2016, 362) points out, "We often find different actor groups competing and struggling over knowledge-based claims for authority within and across transnational governance fields."

While this book has focused on the emergence of private authority, similar questions arise in cases of international authority more generally. Expert knowledge is not a neutral or technical description of a given reality but frames the problems and solutions. It is closely linked to the institutional design and form of governing. A good example is REDD+, a voluntary mechanism under the United Nations Framework Convention on Climate Change that provides compensation to Global South actors to conserve or restore their forests.[7] Esther Turnhout, among others, has pointed to the ways in which such mechanisms classify, standardize, categorize, and measure biodiversity (Turnhout and Lynch 2024). She concludes, "When electing to represent the environment in a specific way, science produces objects that are amenable to certain specific governance logics and which attract and privilege certain groups of actors" (Turnhout

2018, 366). Her argument also holds for governing arrangements that claim private authority. For this reason, the legitimizing force of expert knowledge always needs critical reflection when examining private authority.

Performing Negotiations: Structure, Materiality, and the Manufacturing of Consensus

Meetings are the "engine room of world politics" from which macrophenomena of order emerge (Pouliot 2016, 2). That is why students of global environmental politics participate in Conferences of the Parties or in smaller expert committees trying to make sense of how politics unfolds in action (O'Neill and Haas 2019; Campbell et al. 2014; Hughes and Vadrot 2023). Those who study meetings in action have come to realize that metaphors of theater can explain why and how actors engage in performing meetings on a world stage (Aykut et al. 2022; Death 2011).

In line with this type of research, I have provided a fine-grained analysis of the birth of private authority. I have examined the Founding Assembly of the FSC in 1993 in terms of drama. I have found the following: (1) Meetings are distinctively structured and yet socially emergent—actors bring about this inbuilt order for a meeting by performing specialized roles. (2) Embodied performances and materiality play a greater role in the accomplishment of a meeting than most students of meetings would suggest. (3) Consensus does not magically emerge from communicative rationality but requires active communicative work.

Distinctively Structured and Yet Socially Emergent

Attending to the "politics of performance" (Campbell et al. 2014) requires a nuanced concept of the meeting as a distinct communicative form or institution (Knoblauch 2020). Meetings are distinctively structured in the sense that I have observed a variety of roles (keynote speaker, facilitator, experts of various sorts) and of communicative practices (introducing the meeting, presenting expertise, articulating positions, expressing discontent, manufacturing consensus) that structure the event. The staging, the seating arrangements, and the acting out of particular roles seem to follow an order: participants almost invariably know how to perform (Freeman 2008).

Meetings are in themselves, in fact, the major "building blocks" for the construction of global environmental politics; they assemble actors, rules, knowledges, and artifacts of various kinds; they serve as a means of producing order and orienting action at different scales toward varied goals. Anna Holzscheiter has termed this inbuilt order a "funnel," "a process of narrowing down the possibility of articulation" (Holzscheiter 2010, 65). She has developed this model in a case of intergovernmental negotiation with specific governmental rules and states securing their interests. This study has taken the funnel model a step further by focusing on negotiations in transnational governance. It has introduced the theatrical notion of acts that further divide the funnel into specific parts. Each act has a function and a corresponding order; actors actively create this order at a meeting. They not only engage in the process of narrowing down the possibilities of articulation, they also open up and create room for contestation. As mentioned at the beginning of this chapter, established organizations such as the FSC today operate with much more explicit rules regarding how to negotiate. While not adhering to the formality of intergovernmental negotiations the order of meetings in transnational governance has been professionalized. Often actors with specialized roles such as the facilitator are instrumental in enforcing order at a meeting. Their role suggests that they act in a disinterested, neutral manner, committed to fostering the process not individual positions. Performing these roles requires a distinct type of knowledge of process and politics, of tactics and techniques.

At the same time, many contingencies shape the struggle over the order of meetings. Meetings are socially emergent in the sense that role expectations are not met; participants invent ad hoc rules of procedure, silence dissenting voices openly, or gain authority in matters which are only vaguely defined. It is perhaps an awareness of this messiness in negotiations and an interest in situational accomplishments and the creativity of actors that I bring to conventional accounts of constructivist work on negotiations, norms, and appropriate behavior (Risse 2016).

In meetings much more is going on than simply norm internalization, rule following, or arguing. Evoking concepts of theater and performance, I have shown how expert knowledge is carefully staged to make an impression on the audience. Erik Ringmar rightly observed that in "early modern Europe, the first rulers who called themselves sovereign all faced the problem of how to gain legitimacy for their rule, and they all responded by means of theatrical displays through which they came to appear before their subjects" (Ringmar 2016, 116). If the birth of the sovereign nation-state required credible performances, then it is likely that the same holds true for the making of private authority.

Ruling has become more complex than a dualism of those who rule and those who are ruled (Hajer 2009). As this book has shown, often the audience is competent; it speaks back loudly and vehemently. Actors appropriate the front stage in their performances and claim that their voices must be heard. It is here, at the front, where rules of procedure matter most since they create legitimacy. Success or failure—especially for emerging institutions—can depend on the credible performance of those who ask for power and support. Thus, it is crucial not to misread the metaphor of drama. The conceptual repertoire of scripts, roles, and acts emphasizes the structural and stable elements; but the theatrical metaphor also accounts for the fact that scripting involves counterscripting, existing roles can be challenged, and the structure of acts is only maintained through power. It is absolutely *not* the case that the metaphor of theater suggests an uncontested repetition of already known subject matter and roles. Instead, concepts of theater provide an instrument for inquiring into the staged performance of politics, which is prone to mistakes; it alerts us to analyze carefully how speech acts are staged.

Embodied Performances

Speech on stage is world politics' primary mode of action. This insight has produced groundbreaking studies on the power of words and discourse in IR while failing to account for the material and embodied dimension of speech acts (Risse 2000, 2017b; Holzscheiter 2017). Performing a speech act requires a physical body (Ringmar 2018). It begins with breathing in, perhaps holding that breath for a moment, and then performing a statement in front of an audience, in front of other bodies. It is the body that "features in all communicative actions. Be it the articulation of a sound, the writing of a letter, the pressing of a button or a glimpse, it is the body which incorporates action" (Knoblauch 2013, 303). Talking, then, is embodied communication of voice and gesture. Actors perform emotions of enthusiasm or skepticism, and they raise their finger to emphasize a warning.

The stage of world politics assembles more materiality than bodies that speak. Our bodies engage with many physical objects; indeed, we live in a material world (Pinch 2008). Scholars of international negotiations have begun to examine the infrastructures of conference settings. In this book, I suggest that the microphone constitutes an excellent example of the involvement of material objects in negotiations because it turns a micro speech act into a macro statement. In the moment of enactment, microphones serve as complex social-technical arrangements that are an indispensable component of creating legitimacy on the front stage.[8]

Interpreters transform speech into other languages so that all participants have the chance to listen and even vote or agree on what has been suggested. The microphone is part of an apparatus that may include interpreters, recording instruments, headphones, and rules of procedure. Agreements have to go through this apparatus to become binding decisions. Emerging organizations especially, be they state or nonstate, are marked by an ongoing politics of legitimation in which category-making and rules of procedure are contested (Esguerra, Beck, and Lidskog 2017; Geis, Nullmeier, and Daase 2012). It is here at the front stage where rules of procedure create legitimacy for the process.

Beyond Logics of Action: A Microfoundation of Consensus-Making

I have proposed a microfoundation for consensus-making. Instead of investigating the prevalence of a logic of action—whether bargaining or arguing—I suggest that a process perspective (Adler-Nissen 2015; Pouliot 2016) should be adopted to engage with their embodied performances (Ringmar 2012). The central question then becomes, What does it take to manufacture consensus? This question resonates with calls to examine the institutional scope conditions of negotiations (Holzscheiter 2017; Risse and Kleine 2010; Deitelhoff 2009); yet it is much more open to the various knowledges, practices, actors, procedures, and so forth that the researcher finds in the negotiation situation. In other words, not only the somewhat stable institutional conditions but the material components (microphones, screens, computers, word processing programs), communicative practices (introducing, presenting reports), knowledges (governance knowledge of content, polity, and process), institutional rules (the doings of diplomacy, procedural rules), and participating actors (members, nonmembers, technical support staff, observers, and so forth) become part of the analysis.

More precisely, my concern has been the involvement of these different objects in the making of consensus. It is through the concept of translation that I have come to view consensus-making as establishing relationships of equivalence between positions, voices, knowledges, and materials that are otherwise different (Best and Walters 2013). For establishing these relationships, the concept of translation points to the travel and transformation by means of which neither the context nor the object that is moved stays the same. What I have found is that the participants use translation as a communicative practice to manufacture consensus step by step.

To come to an agreement, participants constantly seek to change the communicative context; they change discussion fora, park contested issues for later debates, or create visualizations of possible options. Different contexts co-construct a position anew. Positions and identities change when they are represented in a new organization, and it is through translational acts that formerly antagonistic actors founded a transnational organization. I have uncovered the politics of translation and pointed to the crucial role of various translators within negotiations. Often translators have seemingly neutral, functional roles such as facilitators and experts on thematic or procedural matters. They constantly structure the communicative situation in which the negotiations unfold, make conflicting positions equivalent, and find compromises but also silence actors and positions. The politics of translation are not necessarily willful acts by strategic actors. Again, the aim has not been to investigate logics of actions but to explain the creation of a temporary stabilization, the institutionalization of a distinct form of governance knowledge.

Opening Up, Not Closing Down

While some participants in the Founding Assembly either left or were actively excluded from the negotiations, the majority of those invited made the promise to create an FSC. But why create such innovations if their influence remains vague? Perhaps because innovating environmental governance is necessarily ongoing and messy; there is no silver bullet that will simply solve the environmental crisis we are facing today. The constitutive feature of global environmental politics is complexity. Scholars and activists have forcefully argued in favor of moving away from an easy binary of nature and people, and of understanding how environmental problems are intertwined with social issues of justice. Environmental concerns are necessarily entangled with postcolonial histories of exploitation and silencing, of eco-racism and injustice.

In this book I have investigated how unexpected collaborations become possible, how new beginnings are situated and try to grow so as to make a difference in times in which politicians and business interests neglect environmental degradation. Experimenting with modes of living that are less harmful to the earth and its habitants, opening up to new visions of democracy, and organizing the commons have just begun; it is from these spaces that futures of global environmental politics will emerge.

Appendix

Overview of Primary Sources

Interviews

Interview, FSC interim coordinator, 02/21/2012
Interview, FoE activist, 08/12/2011
Interview, Fundacion Natura activist, 08/05/2011
Interview, forester and auditor, 06/25/2011
Interview, forester and consultant, 06/30/2011
Interview, World Rainforest Movement activist, 06/29/2011
Interview, forester and consultant, 06/28/2011
Interview, WWF US activist, 06/25/2011

Audio Files and Documents

July 1988	Thomas [pseud.]. 1988. "Letter Outlining a Study Proposal for the Promotion of Sustainably Produced Tropical Timber." Copy with the author.
May 1989	ODA. 1989. "Letter from the Minister of the Overseas Development Administration to Ken [pseud.] (FoE), 19 May 1989." Copy with the author.
August 1989	Thomas [pseud.], Ken [pseud.], and Connor [pseud.]. 1989. "Pre-Project Proposal to the ITTO: Labelling Systems for the Promotion of Sustainably Produced Tropical Timber." Copy with the author.
September 1990	Anthony [pseud.]. 1990a. "Base Issues Document for the Development of a Sustainable Forest Products Certification Process. Homeland Foundation No. 2-90-27." Copy with the author.
November 1990	Kilian [pseud.]. 1990. "Memorandum to the Certification Working Group." Copy with the author.

December 1990   Logan [pseud.]. 1990. "Letter to Anthony and others. Memorandum, Forest Products Certification Ideas, Dec. 2nd." Copy with the author.

December 1990   Kilian [pseud.]. 1990. "Memorandum to the Certification Working Group." Copy with the author.

December 1990   Anthony [pseud.]. Letter. 1990b. "Memorandum, Ref. Ken's [pseud.] (Rainforest Alliance) Letter of Dec. 17. 1990, Letter to the Certification Working Group, Dec. 22. 1990." Copy with author.

April 1991   Jennifer [pseud.]. 1991. "Certification Working Group Meeting Notes—April 20th-21st 1991." Copy with the author.

April 1991   Anthony [pseud.]. 1991. "A Report on the Certification Working Group Meeting. Prepared for the Homeland Foundation. San Francisco, April 20th and 21st 1991." Copy with author.

April 1991   Tom [pseud.]. 1991. "Report on the Meeting of the Certification Working Group, Held in April 20–21, 1991 at Greenpeace Office, San Francisco." Copy with author.

December 1991   Thomas [pseud.]. 1991. "Forest Stewardship Standards: Draft for Comments. First Draft by Tom, July 1991. Revised by Thomas, November 1991. This Draft Revised in Yokohama, December 1991." Copy with the author.

July 1993   Holly [pseud.]. 1993a. "Memo to All Charter and Statutes Working Group Members and Advisors." Copy with the author.

July 1993   FSC 1993a. "Working Draft of the Principles and Criteria (Draft 7A, July 1993)." Copy with the author.

August 1993   Executive Summary UK, Forest Stewardship Council Consultative Process. Copy with the author.

August 1993   Executive Summary Switzerland, Forest Stewardship Council Consultative Process. Copy with the author.

August 1993   Executive Summary and Report Sweden, Forest Stewardship Council Consultative Process. Copy with the author.

August 1993   Executive Summary and Report Peru, Forest Stewardship Council Consultative Process. Copy with the author.

August 1993   Executive Summary and Report Papua New Guinea, Forest Stewardship Council Consultative Process. Copy with the author.

August 1993   Executive Summary and Report Oregon Washington as well as Report British Columbia, Forest Stewardship Council Consultative Process. Copy with the author.

August 1993   Executive Summary and Report Malaysia, Forest Stewardship Council Consultative Process. Copy with the author.

August 1993   Executive Summary and Report Ghana, Forest Stewardship Council Consultative Process. Copy with the author.

August 1993   Executive Summary and Report Ecuador, Forest Stewardship Council Consultative Process.

August 10, 1993   Executive Summary and Report Brazil, Forest Stewardship Council Consultative Process. Copy with the author.

September 1993   Letter to Holly with FSC Principles & Criteria 7b. Copy with the author.

September 1993   FSC 1993b. "Forest Stewardship Council Principles and Criteria as of September 1993. After the Blue Moon Meeting." Copy with the author.

October 1993   Holly [pseud.]. 1993b. "Summary of the Forest Stewardship Council Consultative Process." Copy with the author.

October 1–3, 1993   Audio files of the Founding Assembly, 16 hours, transcribed.

List of Participants at the FSC Founding Assembly in Toronto, October 1993

Organization	Country	Sector	Hemisphere
Asociación Interétnica de Desarrollo	Peru	n/a	South
A&M Wood Specialty/WARP	Canada	Economic	North
Abracruz Int'l Ltd.	Brazil	Economic	North
Accion Ecologica	Ecuador	Environment	South
Aracruz Celulose	Brazil	Economic	South
Aracruz Celulose	Brazil	Economic	South
Aracruz Celulose	Brazil	Economic	South
Arbor Nova Ltd.	Ghana	Economic	South
B&Q	UK	Economic	North
Brazilian National Assn. of Pulp and Paper	Brazil	Economic	South
Brazilian National Assn. of Pulp and Paper	Brazil	Economic	South
Brazilian Silviculture Society	Brazil	n/a	South
Brazilian Silviculture Society	Brazil	n/a	South
Camara Nacional Forestal	Peru	Economic	South
Canadian Forest Service, Natural Resources Canada	Canada	Economic	North
Canadian Institute for Forestry	Canada	Economic	North
Canadian International Development Agency	Canada	Government	North
Canadian Pulp and Paper Association	Canada	Economic	North
Centro Mocovi	Argentina	Social	South
COICA-Oxfam Research Project	Peru	Social	South
Collins Pine Company	US	Economic	North
Collins Pine Company	US	Economic	North
Colonial Craft	US	Economic	North
Colonial Craft	US	Economic	North
Concejo Civil Mexicano Para la Silvic Sostenible	Mexico	Environment	South
Concejo Civil Mexicano Para la Silvic Sostenible	Mexico	Environment	South
Conselho Nacional dos Seringueiros (CNS)	Brazil	Social	South

Conservation International	US	Environment	North
Consultant	Germany	Economic	North
Consultant	Mexico/UK	Economic	North
Consultant Forester	Malaysia	Economic	South
Cordillera Peoples Alliance, Philippines	Philippines	Environment	South
Costa Rican Timber Industrialist Chamber	Costa Rica	Economic	South
Cultural Survival (Bay Area office)	US	Environment	North
DOMÄN AB	Sweden	Government	North
Earthlands/North Quabbin Farm	US	Economic	South
Ecoforestry Institute Society	Canada	Environment	North
Ecological Trading Company	UK	Economic	North
EcoTimber International, Inc.	US	Economic	North
Environmental (EARTH)	Philippines	Environment	South
Experience International	US	Economic	North
Fauna & Flora Preservation Society	UK	Environment	North
Federação de Órgãos para Assistência Social e Educacional—FASE	Brazil	Social	South
Forest Industry Association	US	Economic	North
Forest Management Foundation	UK	n/a	North
Forest Mgmt., Evaluation and Coordination Unit, Federal Department of Forestry	Ibadan, Nigeria	Government	South
Forest Partnership	US	Economic	North
Forest Research Institute of Malaysia	Malaysia	Academic	South
Forestry Department	Ghana	Government	South
Forestry Department, Sarawak	Malaysia/ Sarawak	Government	South
Foundation of the Peoples of the South Pacific	Papua New Guinea	Social	South
Foundation of the Peoples of the South Pacific	Papua New Guinea	Social	South
Foundation of the Peoples of the South Pacific	Papua New Guinea	Social	South
Friends of the Earth	England, Wales and Northern Ireland	Environment	North
Friends of the Siberian Forest, Pacific Environment & Resources Centre	US	Environment	North
FSC, Administrative Assistant	US	FSC	North
FSC, Assembly Co-coordinator	Canada		North
FSC, Coordinator	US	FSC	North
FSC, Volunteer Coordinator	US	FSC	North
Fundacion Natura	Peru	Social	South
Fundacion Natura	Colombia	Environment	South
Fundacion Natura Ecuador	Ecuador	Environment	South

Global Forest Policy Project	US	Environment	North
Greenpeace	Netherlands	Environment	North
Greenpeace Canada	Canada	Environment	North
Grupo Trabalho de Amazônico (GTA)	Brazil	Social / Environment	South
IKEA Engineering AB	Sweden	Economic	South
Indonesian Tropical Institute (LATIN)	Indonesia	Environment	South
Initiative Tropenwald	Germany	Environment	North
Institute for Sustainable Forestry	US	Economic	North
Institute for Sustainable Forestry	US	Economic	North
Instituto Tecnologico de Costa Rica	Costa Rica	Academic	South
IPEF	Brazil	Academic	South
Iumi Tugetha Holdings Ltd.	Solomon Islands	Economic	South
Iumu Tgetha Holdings/Soltrust	Solomon Islands	Social	South
Knight Associates	UK	Economic	North
KRAV	Sweden	Economic	North
Lignum/Cedotec	Switzerland	Economic	North
Malaysian Timber Industry Development Council	Malaysia	Economic	South
Malaysian Timber Industry Development Council	Malaysia	Economic	South
Manager, Environmental Marketing, Home Depot	US	Economic	North
Masurina PTY Ltd.	Papua New Guinea	Economic	South
Mexican National Institute of Ecology	Mexico	Academia	South
Ministerie Van Landbrouw	Netherlands	Government	North
Nucleus for Indigenous Rights	Brazil	Social	South
Organización Nacional Indígena de Colombia (COICA)	Colombia	Social	South
Pacific Environment & Resources Center	US	Environment	North
Peruvian Foundation for Conservation of Nature	Peru	Environment	South
Private	Brazil	Social	n/a
Private	Canada	n/a	North
Private	Panama	Social	South
Private	Switzerland		North
Proyecto Latifoliado	Honduras	Economic	South
Purde University	US	Academic	North
Rainforest Action Network	US	Environment	North
Rainforest Alliance	US	Economic	North
Rettet den Regenwald e.V.	Germany	Environment	North
Rogue Institute for Ecology and Economy	US	Environment	North
Sarawak Campaign Committee	Japan	Environment	North

School of Forest Resources & Conservation (SFRC)	US	Academia	North/South
Scientific Certification Systems (SCS)	US	Economic	North
Scientific Certification Systems (SCS), (Green Cross)	US	Economic	North
Servicio Holandés de Cooperación Tecnica y Social	Bolivia	n/a	South
SGS Silviconsult Limited	UK	Economic	South
Silva Forest Foundation	Canada	Environment	North
Skephi (Skephi-Support Office)	Netherlands	Environment	North
Sociedad Peruana de Derecho Ambiental	Peru	Environment	North
Steward Associates	Costa Rica	Economic	South
Sylvania Forestry	US	Economic	North
Taiga Rescue Network	Sweden	Social	North
Takoradi Chana	West Africa	n/a	South
Tropical Forest Foundation	US	Environment	North
U.S. Agency for International Development	USA	Government	North
University de los Andes-Las Tapias	Venezuela	Academic	South
University of Tennessee, plus USAID, Dept. of Forestry and Wildlife & Fisheries	US	Academic / Government	North
UTEPA	Ecuador	Government	South
Village Development Trust	Papua New Guinea	Social	South
Vitae Civilis, Institute para of Desenvolvimento	Brazil	Academic	South
Woodworkers Alliance for Rainforest Protection (WARP)	US	Economic	North
Woodworkers Alliance for Rainforest Protection (WARP)	US	Economic	North
Working Tree	UK	n/a	North
World Bank	US	Government / International Organization	North
World Rainforest Movement	UK	Social	North/South
World Resource Institute	US	North	North
WWF Brazil	Brazil	Environment	South
WWF Canada	Canada	Environment	North
WWF International	Switzerland	Environment	North
WWF Malaysia	Malaysia	Environment	South
WWF Sweden	Sweden	Environment	North
WWF UK	UK	Environment	North
WWF UK	UK	Environment	North
WWF UK	UK	Environment	North
WWF USA	US	Environment	North

Notes

CHAPTER 1

1. Private institutions, in contrast to public ones, are formed and managed by nonstate actors often representing a broad range of groups such as social and environmental NGOs, businesses, scientists, and foundations. Of course, there exist many hybrids between purely private and purely public institutions (Hale 2020). This book, however, is specifically concerned with nonstate actors and their entrepreneurial creativity when bringing new institutions into being.

2. The current climate regime features nonstate actors as active and responsible partners (Jernnäs and Lövbrand 2022), and transnational initiatives have skyrocketed since the 1990s (Westerwinter 2021).

3. Global environmental politics scholarship has described intergovernmental negotiations as often being in "gridlock" and transnational governance as moving potentially "beyond gridlock" (Hale and Held 2017; Hale 2020).

4. Maarten Hajer has termed such situations an "institutional void" or "institutional ambiguity" (Hajer 2009, 2003). Neither concept refers to an absence of institutional rules but to the presence of conflicting ideas and practices as to how to organize the institution-making process. An extreme case was the 1952 establishment of the European Coal and Steel Community, which represented the first supranational treaty organization in history (Rittberger 2001).

5. The notion of knowledge about governance is inspired by Jan-Peter Voß and Richard Freeman (2016, 3) who coined the term "knowing governance" for examining "the production and mobilization of ways of knowing about governance."

6. ANT emerged in the 1980s, although in the early days it studied not practices of governing, but the construction of scientific facts (Callon 1986; Latour and Woolgar 1979). I discuss how ANT and governing can be linked in Esguerra 2023.

7. I draw here on governmentality studies that have investigated these translational practices in detail (Lövbrand and Stripple 2011; Jernnäs 2023).

8. Bruno Latour (1999) coined the notion of the chain of translation or translation chain, and Marieke de Goede (2018) mobilized the concept for IR elaborating on a chain of security.

9. I understand microfoundation within an interpretive framework as advanced by Powell and Rerup (2017) and Solomon and Steele (2017).

10. Other scholars when explaining authority emergence point to complex market

demands as well as the influence of institutional forms (Auld 2014) and underline the embeddedness in multilevel institutional landscapes (Bartley 2007b; Pattberg 2007).

11. While actors may recognize an authority's judgment as legitimate, they may also act as if they do not (e.g. with regard to climate change); or they may contest the authoritative claims of international organizations (e.g., of the International Monetary Fund) (Reus-Smit 2007; Zürn 2018).

12. It is important to note that Jessica Green distinguishes further between delegated private authority, in which states delegate a set of tasks to private actors, and entrepreneurial private authority, when nonstate actors strike out on their own (Green 2014, 7). This book only deals with entrepreneurial private authority. Thus, when I speak of private authority I am interested in entrepreneurial private authority.

13. While some of the literature also underlines the moral authority of private governance, I follow Green in focusing on expert knowledge as the main source of legitimizing private authority.

14. For an explicit treatment of expertise and private authority, see Quack 2016.

15. Tobias Berger and I have argued that this constitutive effect of translation could be understood as the construction of relationality (Berger and Esguerra 2018a).

16. On Actor-Network Theory, see Callon (1986); Callon, Lascoumes, and Barthe (2009); Callon and Latour (1981); Latour (1987); Law (2006). For an overview of ANT and translation, see Freeman (2009); Latour (2005); and Michael (2017).

17. Note that ANT deploys the principle of symmetry to give agency to humans as well as to nonhumans (Latour 1991). I recognize the importance of artifacts and materiality but embed ANT's insights into a more conventional sociology of knowledge approach. For an elaboration of this point, see Hilgartner (2000) and Pinch (2009).

18. This constitutive dimension of translation resonates with the mechanism of brokerage. McAdam, Tarrow, and Tilly (2001, 26) define brokerage as "the linking of two or more previously unconnected social sites by a unit that mediates their relations with one another and/or with yet other sites." Translation, however, puts greater stress on the transformation that is necessary for doing the linking (Esguerra, Knappe, and Ziebell 2025).

19. On the notion of productive power in IR, see Barnett and Duvall (2005) and Schindler (2018).

20. I take inspiration from Science and Technology Studies (STS) where closure refers to the stabilization of knowledge claims (see Latour 1987). Stephen Hilgartner (2000) in particular has developed a framework for empirically investigating struggles over the enclosure and disclosure of information.

21. Occasionally, disclosing and enclosing appear together. In these cases, actors make broader statements trying to shift the debate in a specific direction. An example would be "while I think A and B are given, we still lack certainty about C."

22. Goffman's sociology has been mobilized in accounts based on practice theory to rethink agency (Braun, Schindler, and Wille 2019; Ringmar 2018), elaborate on stigma and hierarchy (Zarakol 2010; Pouliot 2016), or study environmental summits (Campbell et al. 2014; Death 2011; Hughes and Vadrot 2023). In particular, Vincent Pouliot (2016) and Eric Ringmar (2012) have employed Goffman for their theorizing of global governance. Maarten Hajer (2009), meanwhile, provides a groundbreaking operationalization of dramaturgy for studying authority.

23. As a result, an actor's performance mediates between "passive structures and active agents" (Ringmar 2012, 2).

24. In the sociology of knowledge, these scripts belong to communicative forms, which are "the major "building blocks" for the construction of reality in that they allow us to coordinate actions and motives. Communicative forms are not only produced by communicative actions. Due to their objectivated character, they also serve as a means to produce order and to orientate action on different scales toward varied goals" (Knoblauch 2013, 306).

25. For instance, Keohane and Nye (1974, 45) cite an official talking about the International Criminal Police Organization (Interpol) who notes, "What's really important here are the meetings on a social level—the official agenda is only for show."

26. How actors accomplish the difficult, yet important task of doing democracy in the realm of the transnational is analytically and normatively of great importance (Dingwerth 2007; Knappe 2017).

27. In negotiation processes, scholars have identified two phases or acts: an opinion-building phase that permits a plethora of diverse opinions to be articulated because of the initial uncertainty and complexity surrounding the issues and procedures, and a decision-making phase that is more restrictive with regard to new issues and reformulations (Holzscheiter 2010, 66).

28. Students of international relations have long recognized that international institutions are stages of world politics where actors arrive at a shared understanding of a problem (Haas and Haas 2002; Johnston 2001). In the absence of established institutions, the chain of meetings and documents provides an iterative structure in which the politics of beginning unfold.

29. Meetings and documents are embedded in structures of knowledge and power. They "internally encode—and at the same time are embedded in—collective modes of information control" (Hilgartner 2000, 17). As in a club, there exists a politics of entry and performance. Not everybody gets in and the repertoire of possible actions is preconfigured. As a result, one should be aware that the full spectrum of historically grown conflicts does not necessarily find expression in meetings and documents. And, once invited, less powerful actors have little chance of integrating their wording in policy documents unless powerful translators make their voices heard. While this study acknowledges this argument, it also shows that meetings and documents form the building blocks of private authority making and thus are worthy of being examined in depth.

30. I thank Marion Karmann from FSC International as well as an FSC founding member who had collected and stored most of the early correspondence.

31. The interviews are referred to in the text using the formula (interview, Fundacion Natura activist, 08/05/2011).

32. The constructivist version of coding acknowledges that "we construct our codes because we are actively naming data—even when we believe our codes form a perfect fit with actions and events in the studied world" (Charmaz 2006, 47).

33. The data sessions mainly took place in the Sociology Department of the Technical University Berlin, where they were led by Hubert Knoblauch, and in the Political Ethnography working group at the Humboldt University Berlin, where they were led by Thomas Scheffer.

CHAPTER 2

1. See Poore (2003) for a detailed genesis of the ITTO.

2. The World Rainforest Movement is an international NGO that works foremost for the respect of local peoples' rights in forest issues. Thus, the quotation comes with a political agenda.

CHAPTER 3

1. For a similar assessment, see Mergen and Vincent 1987.

2. It should be noted that the project also emerged as a local struggle between the Yanesha communities and the Peruvian government's road-building project. Since the US Agency for International Development was providing financial assistance, the project had to consult with the local population, which then led to the transdisciplinary cooperation between the parties (Simeone, Pariona, and Lázaro 1993).

3. Since many of these foresters came to South America via the Peace Corps, some refer to them as the "Peace-Corps-Paraguay mafia." This group formed very strong ties when they were working in the Peace Corps (FSC organizer quoted in Bartley and Smith 2010, 355).

4. Among them Anthony Anderson (Ford Foundation) who had organized the conference in Belém. The Ford foundation also cofunded the conference in London, and later also funded the FSC. There is also an overlap of organizations (National Council of Rubber Tappers, World Bank, Ecological Trading Company, Cultural Survival, WWF, FoE) and individuals (Connor and Christopher) present at the conference in London and at the Founding Assembly of the FSC three years later.

5. The campaign had three major aims: to bring attention to the trade in tropical hardwoods and to try to use consumer and market pressure to move trade toward more sustainable practices; to make public the impact of misconceived aid projects, particularly those of the World Bank; and to engage in public education projects to raise awareness of the tropical forest globally (interview, FoE activist, 08/12/2011).

6. For more information on the guide, see Counsell 1995; Donovan 1996; Thomas 2005.

7. For more examples, see Donovan 1996.

8. World Wildlife Federation UK, "A Brief History of WWF." See https://www.scribd.com/document/132391813/A-Brief-History-of-WWF-WWF-UK

9. The Homeland Foundation was the first of many foundations to fund the nascent FSC (interview, WWF US activist, 06/25/2011).

10. The list of interviewees names one person employed at the United Nations Development Programme.

11. The structure of the study is organized in accordance with a more complicated system that is not reproduced here. Also, the study itself does not relate the perspectives back to the interviewed groups so that it is impossible to reconstruct which actor groups took which perspective.

12. In addition, the study inquires into funding mechanisms, major obstacles, and further steps in an envisioned process.

13. BOSCOSA refers to the the Osa Forest Conservation and Development program in Costa Rica.

14. The list of participants includes participants from the WWF (US), World Rainforest Movement (UK), Fine Timber Ltd. (UK), Homeland Foundation (US), Herman Miller Inc. (US), Green Cross (US), Cultural Survival (US), Ecological Trading Company (UK), Cultural Survival (US), WARP (US), Greenpeace (US), Sylvania Forestry (US), WWF (UK), Smith and Hawken (US), Rainforest Alliance (US), Experience International (US), Rainforest Action Network (US); Sierra Club (US).

15. An eleven-page document protocols some of the themes and controversies that I cite as Tom 1991, a nine-page document processes the notes by Jennifer that I cite as Jennifer 1991, and a three-page report summarizes the main outcomes of the meeting that I cite as Anthony 1991. All of the above authors were present at the meeting.

16. These first ITTO guidelines were presented after a year of negotiation by "a 13-member panel of international experts, composed of representatives from producer and consumer countries in tropical timber, environmental NGOs (WWF), UN Agencies (FAO), the Trade, and other consultants from the ODA, CSIRO and IIED" (ITTO 1990).

17. On the role of foundations in the development of the FSC, see Bartley 2007a.

18. Note that this evaluation is from the coordinator of the consultative process, and is related to the selection of the consultants. Within the countries the process was in part politicized to the extent that some environmental and social NGOs were not willing to sit at the same table with industry representatives (see also next chapter).

19. I examine this draft as the only draft of the FSC Charter that I could find. This draft, with a few changes by Brian, served as a working document at the Founding Assembly.

CHAPTER 4

1. Built in the late 1920s, the hotel was one of the first luxury hotels in Toronto located in the business district (Toronto Modern online). An interview partner recalls the following: "If I remember right, it was a middle-range hotel which had, you know, good facilities, big rooms, and quite a lot of break-out rooms. So there were quite a lot of breakings-out going on to discuss the Principles and Criteria. So, I mean you could do it in a village that would have been very difficult to get everybody there. I guess I did not find the setting offensive. Whereas I did find often the settings of the ITTO really offensive because they were in these luxury hotels like we are today" (interview, World Rainforest Movement activist, 06/29/2011).

2. These theoretical predictions can be found in the empirical world. Regarding symbolic commitments, the "Programme for the Endorsement of Forest Certification Schemes," launched several years after the FSC, clearly has weaker standards. Regarding the decision-making body, the Marine Stewardship Council, launched five years after the FSC, abstained from a multistakeholder board because its founders were shocked by the conflicts that they witnessed at the FSC negotiations.

CHAPTER 5

1. Nominees for the Board of Directors as of Friday evening: William, Brian, Lisa, Carlos, Daniel, Christopher, Ken, Abel, Norberto, Spencer, Henry, Bentley, Maria, Pascal, Gabriel, Anthony, Alonso, Ming (all pseudonyms).

2. He cites several UN reports, and provides statistical data on deforestation; for instance, the assembly learns that, within the last 10 years, deforestation has increased by 50 percent. Further, he engages in historical narration on approaches by the international community to contain deforestation through international initiatives such as the Tropical Forestry Action Plan or the International Timber Organization (see also chapters 2 and 3).

3. These are practices of fact-construction (Latour 1987, chap. 1; Holzscheiter 2010, 75).

4. The notion of balance is threefold. It refers most obviously to the six actor categories that are invited, and which are to be found in the discourse on sustainable development—a discourse that argues in favor of balancing the social, economic, and ecological dimensions of an issue such as forestry. Balance also covers the balance of perspectives on how sustainable forestry should be understood. Third, balance frames the destruction and degradation of forests as a situation that is *out-of-balance*. The "natural balance" has to be restored (Tape 1, Side 2). Hence, the balance approach counters a system that is out of balance, and, in doing so, works as an intertextual mechanism.

5. For instance, Mark tells a well-known multicausal story about skunks in New Hampshire: The local tourism industry, which was heavily dependent on fishing, aggressively eradicated skunks because it thought the skunks would eat all the fish. However, they aggravated the situation because the skunks had been the natural enemy of the snapping turtle, which in turn now ate all the fish eggs. Mark concludes, "For several years the state imported skunks and exported turtles as they tried to reach the natural balance and bring back the fish population" (Tape 1, Side 2).

6. Both speakers have a slightly diverging story to tell. Nicholas acknowledges the differences between the invited groups, and yet asks the participants to make an effort and recognize that they have something in common. Mark, on the other hand, conceptualizes the issue more radically by claiming that differences of opinion are the result of a wrong paradigm. If people deliberate, they will discover that cooperation is not a compromise but a win–win situation. Preserving nature and making a profit is not a contradiction. I have noted earlier how Mark's notion of the paradigm shift excludes, by definition, the possibility of radical difference and conflict.

7. "The United Kingdom colonized Ghana and part of this program was to make sure that we don't destroy our forest resources. And we are most grateful to Britain for this. Forest reserves were created. Conventional wisdom in forestry in those days was applied to our forests.

"Then came independence and the indigenization of the forestry staff, the establishment of our own forestry schools and university in Kumasi until then you had to go either to Edinburgh or Oxford to receive formal forestry education. But still the cooperation continues.

"So, we have [a] forestry commission which seeks to regulate the management and utilization of forest resources. The same goes for fisheries and the other natural resources. Now, I give you this background because this is Ghana. We have had forestry tradition, we have the ITTO to give us green labeling, and now comes FSC and says we can do it better than all the others" (Tape 2, Side 2).

8. This positive labeling is partly qualified by admitting that there was no southern representative on the working group, adding, "But we have had broad geographical input" (Tape 7, Side 1).

9. See chapter 2 on the rubber tappers' movement.

10. See, on positions, Laube, Schank, and Scheffer 2020.

11. When presenting the statement to Connor, he suggested a slight mistake in the transcript. In his view it would make more sense to be quoted as follows: "I take it as a deep insult to hear that there are northern NGOs here who [believe FoE] are opposed to the idea of the FSC." However, the tapes clearly show that his statement appeared as cited above.

12. Gabriel denounces neocolonial practices by some northern NGOs, referring to the critical statement that Connor read out loud in the second act. Whereas one could have assumed that the statement in the second act reflects positions taken by all social and environmental NGOs, Gabriel's denunciation makes clear that there is also antagonism between the views of NGOs from the Global South and the Global North. However, when Connor seeks to respond, the interim board first directs the facilitator to deny the request (the facilitator notes: "I was told that") and then Brian, as a member of the interim board, argues, "I do not believe that your point was in order." Consequently, Connor abstains from voting but stays as an observer.

CHAPTER 6

1. The five positions of round three merged into three motions plus a variant of Motion 3. The economic position of round three became mingled with Motion 1 of round four. The notion of "regional representation," which the Oceania group was still accentuating in round 3, reemerged in Motion 2, while the "Oceania-proposal" itself vanished from the display.

2. Luc Pauwels reminds us that visualization "involves a translation or conversion of some kind . . . whereby the initial source (phenomenon, concept) is captured, transformed, or even (re-)created through a chain of decisions" (Pauwels 2006, 4–5).

3. Since the audio files transmit only a fraction of the communicative practices (which included such things as pointing and air-drawing) that were used in this specific event, an analysis of the full performance of knowledge cannot be carried out. However, the procedural advice offered by Camila, for instance, hints at visual enactments: "Perhaps under C you could put a third option" . . . "No, no under C."

4. "He is saying that for clarity he wants to have it translated by me. And what he is saying is that for the institutions in the South, it is very hard to have negotiations with industry. [*Raimundo speaks Brazilian Portuguese.*] This is especially true in cases where there is conflict and violence especially in terms of logging in many areas. [*Raimundo speaks Brazilian Portuguese.*] On the other hand, it is important to have the participation of a segment of the private sector who is truly committed to changing these policies. [*Raimundo speaks Brazilian Portuguese.*] Therefore, we feel that under certain circumstances we may find a solution that we have the participation of the private sector. [*Raimundo speaks Brazilian Portuguese.*] The idea is in order to avoid bringing the conflict

within the board structure is to have an exclusion of employees and owners of private companies. [*Raimundo speaks Brazilian Portuguese.*] The proposal is that these people would not be employees and they would be affiliated with some way or the other and then would represent the private interest" (Tape 9, Side 2).

5. For instance, the spokesperson from the Oceania group suggests regional representation but fails to provide any operational mechanism for working this into the decision tree. Likewise, the spokesperson for the indigenous groups, Abel, argues in Spanish that the North and South axis is not sufficient since indigenous peoples live in the South as well as in the North. A more appropriate approach to the issue of balance would be, according to him, a differentiation along the axis of the social and environmental interest.

6. Male, UK: "This can be institutionalized, but may I remind voters that the board actually has to do a job as well and that there are going to be a mixture of skills needed on this board. To actually carry out the work! And now here we had a discussion of the actual duties of this board and within all this balance we have to make sure that we have enough skills on the board to carry out the work that they are asked to do."

7. Male: "Excuse me, I'd like to put a decent voice in that simply has not been heard yet. I am sorry to butt in, but I am troubled very much by all this craving for a perfect balance. I am not going to be interested in looking at the board of the FSC and say to myself, OK, am I really satisfied because we have the right balance, the right number of North–South, the right number of women, etc. I am going to be far more interested to see whether we got the right people for the board. that is, people with intelligence, passionate commitment, and foresight to be able to carry the FSC forward, and I don't think that has a great deal to do with which particular region of the world you are born in or which sex you happen to be."

8. In fact, 32 participants were nominated for the board, but the withdrawal of some groups reduced the total number of nominees to 22.

9. Yet, before the assembly conducts a vote, the team creates secret ballots. The ballot is not self-explanatory. In fact, the options to vote have been cut down considerably due to the balance approach. The competition for a seat on the board differs extremely. For instance, the proportion of seats to nominations in the Economic/North fraction is one to six whereas in the Social/North there is only one nominee candidate per seat. A glance into the blurry backstage suggests that the difference can be explained by the fact that in the economic sector individuals may compete against each other. By contrast, in the environmental and social fraction nominees must represent an organization. Illustrative evidence from the interviews hints at there having been intense negotiations behind the scenes between NGO representatives and their constituencies. To give an example, an activist from the Global North representing the Malaysian indigenous peoples' interest within the World Rainforest Movement was nominated for the board but his organizational base in Malaysia refused him permission to actually be a candidate (interview, World Rainforest Movement activist, 06/29/2011). Similarly, an interviee describes how she first sought to be a candidate for the social fraction but later switched to be nominated as environmental candidate for the South. Although heavily involved in work with indigenous people, her organization, Fundacion Natura, is also concerned with environmental issues. During the assembly indigenous groups, however, advocate for a clear-cut commitment to social concerns for those candidates who represent social interest on the board (interview, Fundacion Natura activist, 08/05/2011).

CHAPTER 7

1. Borrowing from legal studies, Sheila Jasanoff defines constitutional moments as "brief periods in which . . . basic rules of political practice are rewritten, whether explicitly or implicitly, thus fundamentally altering the relations between citizens and the state" (Jasanoff 2011, 623).

2. The following information is based on ethnographic observations at the General Assembly in 2011.

3. See https://www.greenpeace.org/international/press-release/15589/greenpeace -international-to-not-renew-fsc-membership/

4. Maarten Hajer (2009) describes such a situation as an "institutional void."

5. Others also point to expert knowledge as a cause for the emergence of private authority (Büthe and Mattli 2013; Hall and Biersteker 2002b; Cutler, Haufler, and Porter 1999a).

6. Recent scholarship has paid close attention to the increasing professionalization of new governing techniques as well as the "new governors"—experts equipped with standardized governance knowledge who move between private and public institutions (Straßheim and Beck 2019; Voß and Freeman 2016).

7. The acronym of REED+ stands for "Reducing emissions from deforestation and forest degradation in developing countries" (see Turnhout and Lynch 2024).

8. The microphone is as much an amplifier of a performed speech act as it is a legitimate position from which to speak. It orders a communicative arena. The chair or facilitator gives the word to a speaker, he or she speaks into the microphone (in contrast to shouting from the back), and thus the order of the arena is reconstituted. Speaking into the microphone, he or she constitutes the front stage with its norms for appropriate behavior. The language adheres, for instance, to the practices of official diplomacy or transnational governance (Sending, Pouliot, and Neumann 2015). Words are chosen carefully because they have to be in line with official policies, whether those of a state or a nonstate actor.

References

Abbott, Kenneth W., and Duncan Snidal. 2009. "The Governance Triangle: Regulatory Standards Institutions and the Shadow of the State." In *The Politics of Global Regulation*, edited by Walter Mattli and Ngaire Woods, 44–88. Princeton: Princeton University Press.

Abraham, Kavi Joseph. 2022. "Modeling Institutional Change and Subject-Production: The World Bank's Turn to Stakeholder Participation." *International Studies Quarterly* 66 (3). https://doi.org/10.1093/isq/sqac032

Adler, Emanuel. 2019. *World Ordering: A Social Theory of Cognitive Evolution*. Cambridge: Cambridge University Press.

Adler-Nissen, Rebecca. 2015. "Conclusion: Relationalism: Why Diplomats Find International Relations Theory Strange." In *Diplomacy and the Making of World Politics*, edited by Ole Jacob Sending, Vincent Pouliot, and Iver B. Neumann, 284–308. Cambridge: Cambridge University Press.

Ahrne, Göran, and Nils Brunsson. 2014. "The Travel of Organization." In *Global Themes and Local Variations in Organization and Management*, edited by Gili S. Drori, Markus A. Höllerer, and Peter Walgenbach. New York: Routledge.

Alexander, Jeffrey C. 2004. "Cultural Pragmatics: Social Performance between Ritual and Strategy." *Sociological Theory* 22 (4): 527–73.

Allan, Bentley B. 2017. "Producing the Climate: States, Scientists, and the Constitution of Global Governance Objects." *International Organization* 71 (1): 131–62.

Allan, Bentley B. 2018. "From Subjects to Objects: Knowledge in International Relations Theory." *European Journal of International Relations* 24 (4): 841–64.

American Woodworker. 1990. "Woodworkers Organize to Protect Rainforests." *American Woodworker*, no. 17 (November/December): 80.

Anderson, Anthony B., ed. 1990. *Alternatives to Deforestation: Steps toward Sustainable Use of the Amazon Rain Forest*. New York: Columbia University Press.

Anthony [pseud.]. 1990a. *Base Issues Document for the Development of a Sustainable Forest Products Certification Process*. Homeland Foundation No. 2-90-27.

Anthony [pseud.]. 1990b. "Memorandum, Ref. Ken [pseud.]'s (Rainforest Alliance) Letter of Dec. 17. 1990, Letter to the Certification Working Group, December 22. 1990." Copy with the author.

Anthony [pseud.]. 1991. "A Report on the Certification Working Group Meeting. Prepared for the Homeland Foundation. San Francisco, April 20th and 21st 1991." Copy with the author.

Arendt, Hannah. 1958. *The Human Condition*. Chicago: University of Chicago Press.

Arnt, Ricardo, and Stephan Schwartzman. 1992. *Um artifício orgânico: Transição na Amazônia e ambientalismo, 1985–1990*. Rio de Janeiro: Rocco.

Arts, Bas. 2021. *Forest Governance: Hydra or Chloris?* Cambridge: Cambridge University Press.

Arts, Bas, and M. Buizer. 2009. "Forests, Discourses, Institutions: A Discursive-Institutional Analysis of Global Forest Governance." *Forest Policy and Economics* 11 (5–6): 340–47.

Asdal, Kristin, and Hilde Reinertsen. 2022. *Doing Document Analysis: A Practice-Oriented Method*. London: Sage.

Auld, Graeme. 2014. *Constructing Private Governance: The Rise and Evolution of Forest, Coffee, and Fisheries Certification*. New Haven: Yale University Press.

Aykut, Stefan C., Felix Schenuit, Jan Klenke, and Emilie d'Amico. 2022. "It's a Performance, Not an Orchestra! Rethinking Soft Coordination in Global Climate Governance." *Global Environmental Politics* 22 (4): 173–96.

Bäckstrand, Karin. 2006. "Multi-Stakeholder Partnerships for Sustainable Development: Rethinking Legitimacy, Accountability and Effectiveness." *European Environment* 16 (5): 290–306.

Bäckstrand, Karin, Jamil Khan, Annica Kronsell, and Eva Lövbrand, eds. 2010. *Environmental Politics and Deliberative Democracy: Examining the Promise of New Modes of Governance*. Cheltenham: Edward Elgar.

Barnett, Michael, and Raymond Duvall. 2005. *Power in Global Governance*. Cambridge: Cambridge University Press.

Barnett, Michael, and Martha Finnemore. 2004. *Rules for the World: International Organizations in Global Politics*. Ithaca: Cornell University Press.

Barry, Andrew. 2012. "Political Situations: Knowledge Controversies in Transnational Governance." *Critical Policy Studies* 6 (3): 324–36.

Bartley, Tim. 2003. "Certifying Forests and Factories: States, Social Movements, and the Rise of Private Regulation in the Apparel and Forest Products Fields." *Politics & Society* 31 (3): 433–64.

Bartley, Tim. 2007a. "How Foundations Shape Social Movements: The Construction of an Organizational Field and the Rise of Forest Certification." *Social Problems* 54 (3): 229–55.

Bartley, Tim. 2007b. "Institutional Emergence in an Era of Globalization: The Rise of Transnational Private Regulation of Labor and Environmental Conditions." *American Journal of Sociology* 113 (2): 297–351.

Bartley, Tim. 2018. *Rules without Rights: Land, Labor, and Private Authority in the Global Economy*. Oxford: Oxford University Press.

Bartley, Tim, and Shawna Smith. 2010. "Communities of Practice as Cause and Consequence of Transnational Governance: The Evolution of Social and Environmental Certification." In *Transnational Communities: Shaping Global Economic Governance*, edited by Marie-Laure Djelic and Sigrid Quack, 347–74. Cambridge: Cambridge University Press.

Beck, Silke, Tim Forsyth, Pia Kohler, Myanna Lahsen, and Martin Mahony. 2017. "The Making of Global Environmental Science and Politics." In *The Handbook of Science and Technology Studies*, 4th ed., edited by Ulrike Felt, Rayvon Fouche, Clark A. Miller, and Laurel Smith-Doerr, 1059–86. Cambridge, MA: MIT Press.

Beck, Silke, Tim Forsyth, and Martin Mahony. 2024. "Climate Change and STS." In *Elgar Encyclopedia of Science and Technology Studies*, edited by Ulrike Felt and Alan Irwin, 451–59. https://doi.org/10.4337/9781800377998.ch47

Beder, Sharon. 1994. "Revoltin' Developments: The Politics of Sustainable Development." *Arena Magazine (Fitzroy, Vic)* 11: 37–39.

Benford, Robert D., and Scott A. Hunt. 1992. "Dramaturgy and Social Movements: The Social Construction and Communication of Power." *Sociological Inquiry* 62 (1): 36–55.

Bennett, Andrew, and Colin Elman. 2007. "Case Study Methods in the International Relations Subfield." *Comparative Political Studies* 40 (2): 170–95.

Berger, Tobias. 2017. *Global Norms and Local Courts: Translating the Rule of Law in Bangladesh*. Oxford: Oxford University Press.

Berger, Tobias, and Alejandro Esguerra. 2018a. "Conclusion: Power, Relationality and Difference." In *World Politics in Translation: Power, Relationality and Difference in Global Cooperation*, edited by Tobias Berger and Alejandro Esguerra, 216–31. London: Routledge.

Berger, Tobias, and Alejandro Esguerra. 2018b. "Introduction. The Objects of Translation." In *World Politics in Translation: Power, Relationality and Difference in Global Cooperation*. London: Routledge.

Berger, Tobias, and Alejandro Esguerra, eds. 2018c. *World Politics in Translation: Power, Relationality and Difference in Global Cooperation*. London: Routledge.

Berger, Tobias, and Alejandro Esguerra. 2025. "Translation." In *Elgar Encyclopedia of International Relations*, edited by Beate Jahn and Sebastian Schindler, 401–3. Cheltenham: Edward Elgar.

Bernstein, Steven F. 2001. *The Compromise of Liberal Environmentalism*. New York: Columbia University Press.

Bernstein, Steven F., and Benjamin William Cashore. 2004. "Non-State Global Governance: Is Forest Certification a Legitimate Alternative to a Global Forest Convention." In *Hard Choices, Soft Law: Voluntary Standards in Global Trade, Environment and Social Governance*, edited by John J. Kirton and Michael J. Trebilcock, 33–63. Aldershot: Ashgate Press.

Best, Jacqueline, and William Walters. 2013. "'Actor-Network Theory' and International Relationality: Lost (and Found) in Translation." *International Political Sociology* 7 (3): 332–34.

Brake, Benjamin, and Peter J. Katzenstein. 2013. "Lost in Translation? Nonstate Actors and the Transnational Movement of Procedural Law." *International Organization* 67 (4): 725–57.

Braun, Benjamin, Sebastian Schindler, and Tobias Wille. 2019. "Rethinking Agency in International Relations: Performativity, Performances and Actor-Networks." *Journal of International Relations and Development* 22: 787–807.

Brook, James. 1990. "Why They Killed Chico Mendes." *New York Times*, August 19. http://www.nytimes.com/1990/08/19/books/why-they-killed-chico-mendes.html?pagewanted=all&src=pm

Bueger, Christian. 2015. "Making Things Known: Epistemic Practices, the United Nations, and the Translation of Piracy." *International Political Sociology* 9 (1): 1–18.

Bueger, Christian, and Frank Gadinger. 2015. "Family Issues: Plurality and Methodology in International Practice Theory." *ISQ Online: International Studies Quarterly* 10

(July 23): 9–15. Available at https://www.dhnexon.net/wp-content/uploads/2020/05/ISQSymposiumBuegerandGadinger.pdf

Büthe, Tim, and Walter Mattli. 2013. *The New Global Rulers: The Privatization of Regulation in the World Economy*. Princeton: Princeton University Press.

Cadman, Timothy. 2011. *Quality and Legitimacy of Global Governance: Case Lessons from Forestry*. New York: Palgrave Macmillan.

Callon, Michel. 1986. "Some Elements of a Sociology of Translation: Domestication of the Scallops and the Fishermen." In *The Science Studies Reader*, edited by Mario Biagioli, 67–83. New York: Routledge.

Callon, Michel, Pierre Lascoumes, and Yannick Barthe. 2009. *Acting in an Uncertain World: An Essay on Technical Democracy*. Cambridge, MA: MIT Press.

Callon, Michel, and Bruno Latour. 1981. "Unscrewing the Big Leviathan: How Actors Macro-Structure Reality and How Sociologists Help Them to Do So." In *Advances in Social Theory and Methodology: Toward an Integration of Micro- and Macro-Sociologies*, edited by Karin Knorr Cetina and Aaron V. Cicourel, 277–303. Boston: Routledge.

Campbell, Lisa M., Catherine Corson, Noella J. Gray, Kenneth I. MacDonald, and J. Peter Brosius. 2014. "Studying Global Environmental Meetings to Understand Global Environmental Governance: Collaborative Event Ethnography at the Tenth Conference of the Parties to the Convention on Biological Diversity." *Global Environmental Politics* 14 (3): 1–20.

Capan, Zeynep Gulsah, Filipe Dos Reis, and Maj Grasten. 2021. "The Politics of Translation in International Relations." In *The Politics of Translation in International Relations*, edited by Zeynep Gulsah Capan, Filipe dos Reis, Maj Grasten, 1–19. Cham, Switzerland: Springer.

Capoccia, Giovanni, and R. Daniel Kelemen. 2007. "The Study of Critical Junctures: Theory, Narrative, and Counterfactuals in Historical Institutionalism." *World Politics* 59 (3): 341–69.

Carlowitz, von, H. C., and J. B. von Rohr. 1732. *Sylvicultura Oeconomica*. Leipzig: Braun.

Cashore, Benjamin, Graeme Auld, and Deanna Newsom. 2004. *Governing through Markets: Forest Certification and the Emergence of Non-State Authority*. New Haven: Yale University Press.

Charmaz, Kathy. 2006. *Constructing Grounded Theory: A Practical Guide through Qualitative Analysis*. London: Sage.

Chilvers, Jason, and Matthew Kearnes. 2019. "Remaking Participation in Science and Democracy." *Science, Technology, & Human Values* 45 (3). https://doi.org/10.1177/0162243919850885

Clarke, John, Dave Bainton, Noémi Lendvai, and Paul Stubbs. 2015. *Making Policy Move: Towards a Politics of Translation and Assemblage*. Bristol: Policy Press.

Cleary, David. 1993. "Review of Alternatives to Deforestation: Steps toward Sustainable Use of the Amazon Rain Forest." *Journal of Latin American Studies* 25 (2): 408–9.

Clement, Charles R., Daniel C. Nepstad, and Stephan Schwartzman. 1993. "Extractive Reserves Examined: Review of *Non-Timber Products from Tropical Forests: Evaluation of a Conservation and Development Strategy*." *BioScience* 43 (9): 644–46.

Colchester, Marcus. 1990. "The International Tropical Timber Organization: Kill or Cure for the Rainforest?" *The Ecologist* 20 (5): 166–73.

Colchester, Marcus, and Larry Lohmann. 1990. *The Tropical Forestry Action Plan: What Progress?* Penang: World Rainforest Movement; The Ecologist.

Colchester, Marcus, and Larry Lohmann. 1993. *The Struggle for Land and the Fate of the Forests*. Penang: World Rainforest Movement.

Corry, Olaf. 2024. "Making the Climate Malleable? 'Weak' and 'Strong' Governance Objects and the Transformation of International Climate Politics." *Global Studies Quarterly* 4 (3). https://doi.org/10.1093/isagsq/ksae062

Counsell, Simon. 1995. "Briefing: Timber: Eco-Labeling and Certification." 1995. http://www.foe.co.uk/resource/briefings/timber_labelling_certification.html (accessed July 2012, no longer available).

Counsell, Simon, and Tim Rice. 1992a. "Preface. The Rainforest Harvest." In *The Rainforest Harvest: Sustainable Strategies for Saving the Tropical Forests? Including the Proceedings of an International Conference Held at the Royal Geographical Society, London 17–18th May 1990*, edited by Simon Counsell and Tim Rice, 17–19. London: Friends of the Earth Trust.

Counsell, Simon, and Tim Rice, eds. 1992b. *The Rainforest Harvest: Sustainable Strategies for Saving the Tropical Forests? Including the Proceedings of an International Conference Held at the Royal Geographical Society, London 17–18th May 1990*. London: Friends of the Earth Trust.

Cox, Chris. 1992. "First Experiences: Trading in Sustainable Rainforest Timbers." In *The Rainforest Harvest: Sustainable Strategies for Saving the Tropical Forests? Including the Proceedings of an International Conference Held at the Royal Geographical Society, London 17–18th May 1990*, edited by Simon Counsell and Tim Rice, 109–13. London: Friends of the Earth Trust.

Cutler, A. Claire, Virginia Haufler, and Tony Porter. 1999a. "Private Authority and International Affairs." In *Private Authority and International Affairs*, edited by A. Claire Cutler, Virginia Haufler, and Tony Porter, 3–30. Albany: State University of New York Press.

Cutler, A. Claire, Virginia Haufler, and Tony Porter. 1999b. *Private Authority and International Affairs*. Albany: State University of New York Press.

Czarniawska, Barbara, and Guje Sevón. 1996. *Translating Organizational Change*. Berlin: Walter de Gruyter.

Davis, Alexander E., Vineet Thakur, and Peter Vale. 2020. *The Imperial Discipline: Race and the Founding of International Relations*. London: Pluto Press.

Death, Carl. 2011. "Summit Theatre: Exemplary Governmentality and Environmental Diplomacy in Johannesburg and Copenhagen." *Environmental Politics* 20 (1): 1–19.

Deitelhoff, Nicole. 2009. "The Discursive Process of Legalization: Charting Islands of Persuasion in the ICC Case." *International Organization* 63 (1): 33–65.

Dingwerth, Klaus. 2007. *The New Transnationalism. Transnational Governance and Democratic Legitimacy*. Basingstoke: Palgrave Macmillan.

Dingwerth, Klaus. 2017. "Field Recognition and the State Prerogative: Why Democratic Legitimation Recedes in Private Transnational Sustainability Regulation." *Politics and Governance* 5 (1): 75–84.

Dingwerth, Klaus, and Philipp Pattberg. 2009. "World Politics and Organizational Fields: The Case of Transnational Sustainability Governance." *European Journal of International Relations* 15 (4): 707–43.

Djelic, Marie-Laure, and Sigrid Quack. 2010. *Transnational Communities: Shaping Global Economic Governance*. Cambridge: Cambridge University Press.

Doerr, Nicole. 2018. *Political Translation: How Social Movement Democracies Survive*. Cambridge: Cambridge University Press.

Domask, John. 2003. "From Boycotts to Global Partnership: NGOs, the Private Sector, and the Struggle to Protect the World's Forests." In *Globalization and NGOs: Transforming Business, Government, and Society*, edited by Johanthan Doh and Hildy Teegen. Westport, CT: Praeger.

Donovan, Richard. 1996. "Role of NGOs." In *Certification of Forest Products: Issues and Perspectives*, edited by Virgilio M. Viana, Jamison Ervin, Richard Donovan, Chris Elliott, and Henry Gholz, 93–110. Washington, DC: Island Press.

Draude, Anke. 2017. "Translation in Motion: A Concept's Journey towards Norm Diffusion Studies." *Third World Thematics: A TWQ Journal* 2 (5): 588–605.

Elliott, Christopher. 2000. *Forest Certification: A Policy Perspective*. Bogor, Indonesia: Center for International Forestry Research. https://www.cifor-icraf.org/publications /pdf_files/Books/BCIFOR0004.pdf

Ervin, Jamison. 1996. "The Consultative Process." In *Certification of Forest Products: Issues and Perspectives*, edited by Virgilio M. Viana, Jamison Ervin, Richard Donovan, Chris Elliott, and Henry Gholz, 13–41. Washington, DC: Island Press.

Esguerra, Alejandro. 2023. "An Actor-Network Perspective on Polycentric Governing." In *Polycentrism: How Governing Works Today*, edited by Frank Gadinger and Jan Art Scholte, 260–80. Oxford: Oxford University Press.

Esguerra, Alejandro. 2024. "Objects of Expertise. The Socio-Material Politics of Expert Knowledge in Global Governance." *Global Studies Quarterly* 4 (3) (July). https://doi .org/10.1093/isagsq/ksae060

Esguerra, Alejandro, Silke Beck, and Rolf Lidskog. 2017. "Stakeholder Engagement in the Making: IPBES Legitimization Politics." *Global Environmental Politics* 17 (1): 59–76.

Esguerra, Alejandro, Henrike Knappe, and Lukas Ziebell. 2025. "Representing across Scales: How Do Indigenous Youth Activists Translate Claims to International Institutions?" *Globalizations* 22 (3): 472–87.

Falkner, Robert. 2022. *Environmentalism and Global International Society*. Cambridge: Cambridge University Press.

Fierke, Karin. 2004. "World or Worlds? The Analysis of Content and Discourse." *Qualitative Methods* 2 (1): 36–39.

Finger, Matthias, and Thomas Princen, eds. 1994. *Environmental NGOs in World Politics: Linking the Local and the Global*. London: Routledge.

Fioretos, Orfeo. 2011. "Historical Institutionalism in International Relations." *International Organization* 65 (2): 367–99.

Freeman, Richard. 2008. "Learning by Meeting." *Critical Policy Analysis* 2 (1): 1–24.

Freeman, Richard. 2009. "What Is 'Translation'?" *Evidence & Policy: A Journal of Research, Debate and Practice* 5 (4): 429–47.

Freeman, Richard. 2012. "Reverb: Policy Making in Wave Form." *Environment and Planning A* 44 (1): 13–20.

Freeman, Richard. 2019. "Meeting, Talk and Text: Policy and Politics in Practice." *Policy & Politics* 47 (2): 371–88.

Freeman, Richard. 2021. *Doing Politics*. Available at https://doingpolitics.space/

Freeman, Richard, and Jo Maybin. 2011. "Documents, Practices and Policy." *Evidence & Policy: A Journal of Research, Debate and Practice* 7 (2): 155–70.

FSC. 1993a. "Working Draft of the Principles and Criteria (Draft 7A, July 1993)." Copy with the author.

FSC. 1993b. "Forest Stewardship Council Principles and Criteria as of September 1993. After the Blue Moon Meeting." Copy with the author.

Gadinger, Frank. 2023. "Fields, Trajectories, and Symbolic Power." In *Polycentrism: How Governing Works Today*, edited by Jan Aart Scholte and Frank Gadinger. Oxford: Oxford University Press.

Gale, Fred P. 1998. *The Tropical Timber Trade Regime*. New York: Macmillan.

Geis, Anna, Frank Nullmeier, and Christopher Daase. 2012. *Der Aufstieg der Legitimitätspolitik*. Baden-Baden: Nomos Verlagsgesellschaft.

Genette, Gérard. 1997. *Paratexts: Thresholds of Interpretation*. Lincoln: University of Nebraska Press.

Goede, Marieke de. 2018. "The Chain of Security." *Review of International Studies* 44 (1): 24–42.

Goffman, Erving. 1959. *The Presentation of Self in Everyday Life*. London: Penguin Books.

Goffman, Erving. 1981. *Forms of Talk*. Philadelphia: University of Pennsylvania Press.

Goffman, Erving. 1983. "The Interaction Order: American Sociological Association, 1982 Presidential Address." *American Sociological Review* 48 (1): 1–17.

Goldhill, Simon. 2013. "The Greek Chorus: Our German Eyes." In *Choruses, Ancient and Modern*, edited by Joshua Billings, Felix Budelmann, and Fiona Macintosh, 35–52. Oxford: Oxford University Press.

Graz, Jean-Christophe. 2019. *The Power of Standards*. Cambridge: Cambridge University Press.

Graz, Jean-Christophe. 2021. "Grounding the Politics of Transnational Private Governance: Introduction to the Special Section." *New Political Economy* 27 (2): 1–11. https://doi.org/10.1080/13563467.2021.1881472

Green, Jessica F. 2014. *Rethinking Private Authority: Agents and Entrepreneurs in Global Environmental Governance*. Princeton: Princeton University Press.

Green, Jessica F., and Thomas N. Hale. 2017. "Reversing the Marginalization of Global Environmental Politics in International Relations: An Opportunity for the Discipline." *PS: Political Science & Politics* 50 (2): 473–79.

Gulbrandsen, Lars H. 2010. *Transnational Environmental Governance: The Emergence and Effects of the Certification of Forest and Fisheries*. Cheltenham: Edward Elgar.

Haas, Peter M. 1992. "Introduction: Epistemic Communities and International Policy Coordination." *International Organization* 46 (1): 1–35.

Haas, Peter M. 2017. "The Epistemic Authority of Solution-Oriented Global Environmental Assessments." *Environmental Science & Policy* 77: 221–24.

Haas, Peter M., and Ernst B. Haas. 2002. "Pragmatic Constructivism and the Study of International Institutions." *Millennium—Journal of International Studies* 31 (3): 573–601.

Habermas, Jürgen. 1981. *Theorie des Kommunikativen Handelns*. Frankfurt am Main: Suhrkamp.

Hajer, Maarten A. 1995. *The Politics of Environmental Discourse: Ecological Modernization and the Policy Process*. New York: Oxford University Press.

Hajer, Maarten A. 2003. "Policy without Polity? Policy Analysis and the Institutional Void." *Policy Sciences* 36 (2): 175–95.

Hajer, Maarten A. 2009. *Authoritative Governance: Policy-Making in the Age of Mediatization*. New York: Oxford University Press.

Hajer, Maarten A., and Peter Pelzer. 2018. "2050—an Energetic Odyssey: Understanding "Techniques of Futuring" in the Transition towards Renewable Energy." *Energy Research & Social Science* 44: 222–31.

Hale, Thomas. 2020. "Transnational Actors and Transnational Governance in Global Environmental Politics." *Annual Review of Political Science* 23: 203–20.

Hale, Thomas, and David Held. 2017. *Beyond Gridlock*. Cambridge: Polity Press.

Hall, Bruce R., and Thomas J. Biersteker, eds. 2002a. *The Emergence of Private Authority in Global Governance*. New York: Cambridge University Press.

Hall, Bruce R., and Thomas J. Biersteker. 2002b. "The Emergence of Private Authority in the International System." In *The Emergence of Private Authority in Global Governance*, edited by Bruce R. Hall and Thomas J. Biersteker, 3–22. New York: Cambridge University Press.

Hanrieder, Tine. 2015. *International Organization in Time: Fragmentation and Reform*. Oxford: Oxford University Press.

Hartshorn, Gary S. 1989. "Application of Gap Theory to Tropical Forest Management: Natural Regeneration on Strip Clear-Cuts in the Peruvian Amazon." *Ecology* 70 (3): 567–76.

Hartshorn, Gary S. 1990. "Natural Forest Management by the Yanesha Forestry Cooperative in Peruvian Amazon." In *Alternatives to Deforestation: Steps toward Sustainable Use of the Amazon Rain Forest*, edited by Anthony B. Anderson. New York: Columbia University Press.

Hel, Sandra van der, and Frank Biermann. 2017. "The Authority of Science in Sustainability Governance: A Structured Comparison of Six Science Institutions Engaged with the Sustainable Development Goals." *Environmental Science & Policy* 77 (November): 211–20.

Hilgartner, Stephen. 2000. *Science on Stage: Expert Advice as Public Drama*. Stanford: Stanford University Press.

Höhler, Sabine. 2014. "Von Biodiversität zu Biodiversifizierung: Eine Neue Ökonomie der Natur?" *Berichte zur Wissenschaftsgeschichte* 37 (1): 60–77.

Höhler, Sabine, and Rafael Ziegler. 2010. "Nature's Accountability: Stocks and Stories." *Science as Culture* 19 (4): 417–30.

Holly [pseud.]. 1993a. "Memo to All Charter and Statutes Working Group Members and Advisors." Copy with the author.

Holly [pseud.]. 1993b. "Summary of the Forest Stewardship Council Consultative Process." Copy with the author.

Hölzl, Richard. 2010. "Historicizing Sustainability: German Scientific Forestry in the Eighteenth and Nineteenth Centuries." *Science as Culture* 19 (4): 431–60.

Holzscheiter, Anna. 2010. *Children's Rights in International Politics: The Transformative Power of Discourse*. Basingstoke: Palgrave Macmillan.

Holzscheiter, Anna. 2017. "Was vom arguing übrigblieb. . . ." *ZIB Zeitschrift für Internationale Beziehungen* 24 (1): 143–59. https://doi.org/10.5771/0946-7165-2017-1-143

Huber, Joseph. 2011. "Umweltbewegung: Vom Outsider-Protest zur Assimilation." In

Allgemeine Umweltsoziologie, edited by Joseph Huber, 109–33. Wiesbaden: VS Verlag.

Hughes, Hannah, and Alice B. M. Vadrot. 2023. *Conducting Research on Global Environmental Agreement-Making*. Cambridge: Cambridge University Press.

Hulme, Mike. 2010. "Problems with Making and Governing Global Kinds of Knowledge." *Global Environmental Change* 20 (4): 558–64.

Human Rights Watch and Natural Resources Defense Council. 1992. *Defending the Earth: Abuses of Human Rights and the Environment*. New York: Human Rights Watch.

Humphreys, David. 2004. "Redefining the Issues: NGO Influence on International Forest Negotiations." *Global Environmental Politics* 4 (2): 51–74.

Humphreys, David. 2012. *Logjam: Deforestation and the Crisis of Global Governance*. London: Earthscan.

ITTO. 1990. "ITTO Guidelines for the Sustainable Management of Natural Tropical Forests. ITTO Policy Development Series 1." Yokohama: ITTO.

Jackson, Patrick Thaddeus. 2010. *The Conduct of Inquiry in International Relations: Philosophy of Science and Its Implications for the Study of World Politics*. Abingdon: Routledge.

Jackson, Patrick Thaddeus. 2015. "Making Sense of Making Sense: Configurational Analysis and the Double Hermeneutic." In *Interpretation and Method: Empirical Research Methods and the Interpretive Turn*, edited by Peregrine Schwartz-Shea and Dvora Yanow, 267–83. Abingdon: Routledge.

Jacobs, Michael. 1999. "Sustainable Development as a Contested Concept." In *Fairness and Futurity*, edited by Andrew Dobson, 21–45. Oxford: Oxford University Press.

Jacques, Peter. 2016. "Autonomy and Activism in Civil Society." In *New Earth Politics: Essays from the Anthropocene*, edited by Simon Nicholson and Sikina Jinnah, 221–46. Cambridge, MA: MIT Press.

Jasanoff, Sheila. 2004. *States of Knowledge: The Co-Production of Science and Social Order*. London: Routledge.

Jasanoff, Sheila. 2011. "Constitutional Moments in Governing Science and Technology." *Science and Engineering Ethics* 17 (4): 621–38.

Jennifer [pseud.]. 1991. "Certification Working Group Meeting Notes—April 20th-21st 1991." Copy with the author.

Jernnäs, Maria. 2023. "Governing through the Nationally Determined Contribution (NDC): Five Functions to Steer States' Climate Conduct." *Environmental Politics* 33 (3): 530–51.

Jernnäs, Maria, and Eva Lövbrand. 2022. "Accelerating Climate Action: The Politics of Nonstate Actor Engagement in the Paris Regime." *Global Environmental Politics* 22 (3): 38–58.

Johnston, Alastair Iain. 2001. "Treating International Institutions as Social Environments." *International Studies Quarterly* 45 (4): 487–515.

Johnstone, Ian. 2011. *The Power of Deliberation: International Law, Politics and Organizations*. Oxford: Oxford University Press.

Keck, Margaret E. 1995. "Social Equity and Environmental Politics in Brazil: Lessons from the Rubber Tappers of Acre." *Comparative Politics* 27 (4): 409–24.

Keck, Margaret E. 2001. "Dilemmas for Conservation in the Brazilian Amazon." *Environmental Change and Security Project Report*, no. 7: 32–46.

Keck, Margaret E., and Kathryn Sikkink. 1998. *Activists beyond Borders: Advocacy Networks in International Politics*. Ithaca: Cornell University Press.

Keohane, Robert O., and Joseph S. Nye. 1974. "Transgovernmental Relations and International Organizations." *World Politics: A Quarterly Journal of International Relations* 27 (1): 39–62.

Kilian [pseud.]. 1990. "Memorandum to the Certification Working Group." Copy with the author.

Kill, Jutta. 2016. "The Role of Voluntary Certification in Maintaining the Ecologically Unequal Exchange of Wood Pulp: The Forest Stewardship Council's Certification of Industrial Tree Plantations in Brazil." *Journal of Political Ecology* 23 (1): 434–45.

Knappe, Henrike. 2017. *Doing Democracy Differently: Political Practices and Transnational Civil Society*. Leverkusen-Opladen: Budrich Press.

Knappe, Henrike. 2022. "Temporalities in Translation: Anthropocene Futures, the SDGs and Justice in Baltimore." *Millennium* 51 (1): 330–53.

Knoblauch, Hubert. 2005. "Focused Ethnography." *Forum Qualitative Sozialforschung/Forum: Qualitative Social Research* 6 (3). https://doi.org/10.17169/fqs-6.3.20

Knoblauch, Hubert. 2013. "Communicative Constructivism and Mediatization." *Communication Theory* 23 (3): 297–315.

Knoblauch, Hubert. 2020. *The Communicative Construction of Reality*. Abingdon: Routledge.

Knorr-Cetina, Karin. 1981. *The Manufacture of Knowledge*. Oxford: Pergamon Press.

Kolk, A. 1996. "The Limited Returns of Dutch Rainforest Policy." *International Environmental Affairs* 8 (1): 41–49.

Krasner, Stephen D. 1976. "State Power and the Structure of International Trade." *World Politics* 28 (3): 317–47.

Krisch, Nico. 2017. "Liquid Authority in Global Governance." *International Theory* 9 (2): 237–60.

Kunz, Rahel. 2021. "De/Colonising through Translation? Rethinking the Politics of Translation in the Women, Peace and Security Agenda." In *The Politics of Translation in International Relations*, edited by Zeynep Gulsah Capan, Filipe Dos Reis, and Maj Grasten, 111–29. Cham, Switzerland: Springer.

Kustermans, Jorg, and Rikkert Horemans. 2022. "Four Conceptions of Authority in International Relations." *International Organization* 76 (1): 204–28.

Latour, Bruno. 1983. "Give Me a Laboratory and I Will Raise the World." Repr., in *The Science Studies Reader*, edited by Mario Biagioli, 141–70. New York: Routledge, 1999.

Latour, Bruno. 1987. *Science in Action: How to Follow Scientists and Engineers through Society*. Cambridge: Harvard University Press.

Latour, Bruno. 1991. "The Berlin Key or How to Do Things with Words." In *Matter, Materiality and Modern Culture*, edited by P. M. Graves-Brown, 10–21. London: Routledge.

Latour, Bruno. 1999. *Pandora's Hope: Essays on the Reality of Science Studies*. Cambridge: Harvard University Press.

Latour, Bruno. 2005. *Reassembling the Social: An Introduction to Actor-Network Theory*. Oxford: Oxford University Press.

Latour, Bruno, and Steve Woolgar. 1979. *Laboratory Life: The Social Construction of Scientific Facts*. London: Sage.

Laube, Stefan, Jan Schank, and Thomas Scheffer. 2020. "Constitutive Invisibility: Exploring the Invisible Work of Staff Advisers in Political Position Making." *Social Studies of Science* 50 (2): 292–316.

Law, John. 2006. "Traduction/Trahison: Notes on ANT." *Convergencia. Revista de Ciencias Sociales* 13 (42): 47–72.

Law, John. 2009. "Actor Network Theory and Material Semiotics." In *The New Blackwell Companion to Social Theory*, edited by Bryan S. Turner, 141–58. Oxford: Wiley-Blackwell.

Leander, Anna. 2021. "Locating (New) Materialist Characters and Processes in Global Governance." *International Theory* 13 (1): 157–68.

Littoz-Monnet, Annabelle. 2024. "Knowledge Machineries and Their Objects of Expertise: Knowing Bodies, Moves, and Moods through 'Mobile Health' Data." *Global Studies Quarterly* 4 (3). https://doi.org/10.1093/isagsq/ksae061

Littoz-Monnet, Annabelle. 2025. "The Co-Production of Expertise in Global Governance." In *Knowledge and Expertise in International Politics: A Handbook*, edited by Berit Bliesemann de Gueveara, Katarzyna Kaczmarska, Xymena Kurowka, Birgit Poopuu, and Andrea Warnecke. Oxford: Oxford University Press.

Logan [pseud.]. 1990. "Letter to Anthony and others. Memorandum, Forest Products Certification Ideas, Dec. 2nd." Copy with the author.

Lövbrand, Eva, and Johannes Stripple. 2011. "Making Climate Change Governable: Accounting for Carbon as Sinks, Credits and Personal Budgets." *Critical Policy Studies* 5 (2): 187–200.

Lynch, Michael. 1985. *Art and Artifact in Laboratory Science: A Study of Shop Work and Shop Talk in a Research Laboratory*. London: Routledge & Kegan Paul.

Marres, Noortje. 2012. *Material Participation: Technology, the Environment and Everyday Publics*. London: Macmillan.

Mathews, Andrew S. 2011. *Instituting Nature: Authority, Expertise, and Power in Mexican Forests*. Cambridge, MA: MIT Press.

McAdam, Doug, Sidney Tarrow, and Charles Tilly. 2001. *Dynamics of Contention*. Cambridge: Cambridge University Press.

Meegdenburg, Hilde van. 2023. "Process Tracing: An Analyticist Approach." In *Routledge Handbook of Foreign Policy Analysis Methods*, edited by Patrick A. Mello and Falk Ostermann. London: Routledge.

Mergen, François, and Jeffrey R. Vincent. 1987. *Natural Management of Tropical Moist Forests: Silvicultural and Management Prospects of Sustained Utilization*. New Haven: Yale University, School of Forestry and Environmental Studies.

Michael, Mike. 2017. *Actor-Network Theory: Trials, Trails and Translations*. London: SAGE.

Miller, Clark A. 2017. "Engaging with Societal Challenges." In *The Handbook of Science and Technology Studies*, edited by Ulrike Felt, Rayvon Fouche, Clark A. Miller, and Laurel Smith-Doerr, 4th ed., 909–13. Cambridge, MA: MIT Press.

Miller, Clark A., and Paul N. Edwards. 2001. *Changing the Atmosphere: Expert Knowledge and Environmental Governance*. Cambridge, MA: MIT Press.

Montana, Jasper. 2019. "Co-Production in Action: Perceiving Power in the Organisational Dimensions of a Global Biodiversity Expert Process." *Sustainability Science* 14 (6): 1581–91.

Nadim, Tahani. 2016. "Biodiversität Erfassen: Von Suppen und Satelliten." In *Diversität: Geschichte und Aktualität Eines Konzepts*, edited by V. Barras, A. Blum, Hans-Jörg Rheinberger, and N. Zschoke. Würzburg: Königshausen & Neumann.

Nepstad, Daniel C., and Stephan Schwartzman. 1992. *Non-Timber Products from Tropical Forests: Evaluation of a Conservation and Development Strategy.* Bronx: New York Botanical Garden.

Neumann, Iver B. 2013. *Diplomatic Sites: A Critical Enquiry.* Oxford: Oxford University Press.

Nye, David, and Robert Emmett. 2017. *The Environmental Humanities: A Critical Introduction.* Cambridge, MA: MIT Press.

ODA. 1989. "Letter from the Minister of the Overseas Development Administration to Ken [pseud.] (FoE), 19 May 1989." Copy with the author.

O'Neill, Kate, and Peter M. Haas. 2019. "Being There: International Negotiations as Study Sites in Global Environmental Politics." *Global Environmental Politics* 19 (2): 4–13.

Oomen, Jeroen, Jesse Hoffman, and Maarten A. Hajer. 2021. "Techniques of Futuring: On How Imagined Futures Become Socially Performative." *European Journal of Social Theory* 25 (2). https://doi.org/10.1177/1368431020988

Pachirat, Timothy. 2018. *Among Wolves: Ethnography and the Immersive Study of Power.* Abingdon: Routledge.

Pantzerhielm, Laura. 2023. "On Multiple Objects and Ontic Fixes: Human Rights and the 'Forgotten' Politics of the United Nations' Human Rights-Based Approach." *Millennium* 51 (2): 519–51.

Pantzerhielm, Laura. 2024. "Objects in Relations: Competing Visions of International Order at the Nexus of Human Rights and Development." *Global Studies Quarterly* 4 (3). https://doi.org/10.1093/isagsq/ksae058

Pattberg, Phillipp. 2007. *Private Institutions and Global Governance: The New Politics of Environmental Sustainability.* Cheltenham: Edward Elgar.

Pauwels, Luc. 2006. "A Theoretical Framework for Assessing Visual Representational Practices in Knowledge Building and Science Communications." In *Visual Cultures of Science: Rethinking Representational Practices in Knowledge Building and Science Communication*, edited by Luc Pauwels. Hanover: University Press of New England.

Pinch, Trevor. 2008. "Technology and Institutions: Living in a Material World." *Theory and Society* 37 (5): 461–83.

Pinch, Trevor. 2009. "On Making Infrastructure Visible: Putting the Non-Humans to Rights." *Cambridge Journal of Economics* 34 (1): 77–89.

Poore, Duncan. 2003. *Changing Landscapes: The Development of the International Tropical Timber Organization and Its Influence on Tropical Forest Management.* London: Earthscan Publications.

Poore, Duncan, Peter Burges, John Palmer, Simon Rietbergen, and Timothy Synnott. 1989. *No Timber without Trees: Sustainability in the Tropical Forest.* London: Earthscan.

Pouliot, Vincent. 2016. *International Pecking Orders: The Politics and Practice of Multilateral Diplomacy.* Cambridge: Cambridge University Press.

Pouliot, Vincent, and Jean-Philippe Thérien. 2018. "Global Governance in Practice." *Global Policy* 9 (2): 163–72.

Powell, Walter W., and Claus Rerup. 2017. "Opening the Black Box: The Microfoundations of Institutions." In *The SAGE Handbook of Organizational Institutionalism*, edited by Royston Greenwood. Vol. 2. London: Sage.

Prior, Lindsay. 2008. "Repositioning Documents in Social Research." *Sociology* 42 (5): 821–36.

Pülzl, H. 2010. *Die Politik des Waldes*. Vienna: Böhlau.

Quack, Sigrid. 2016. "Expertise and Authority in Transnational Governance." In *Authority in Transnational Legal Theory*, edited by Roger Cotterrell and Maksymilian Del Mar. Cheltenham: Edward Elgar.

Quack, Sigrid, and Olga Malets. 2014. "Projecting the Local into the Global: Trajectories of Participation in Transnational Standard-Setting." In *Global Themes and Local Variations in Organization and Management*, edited by Gili S. Drori, Markus A. Höllerer, and Peter Walgenbach. New York: Routledge.

Raz, Joseph. 1990. *Authority*. New York University Press.

Reus-Smit, Christian. 2007. "International Crises of Legitimacy." *International Politics* 44 (2): 157–74.

Rheinberger, Hans-Jörg. 1997. *Toward a History of Epistemic Things: Synthesizing Proteins in the Test Tube*. Stanford: Stanford University Press.

Riles, Annelise, ed. 2006. *Documents: Artifacts of Modern Knowledge*. Ann Arbor: University of Michigan Press.

Ringmar, Erik. 2012. "Performing International Systems: Two East-Asian Alternatives to the Westphalian Order." *International Organization* 66 (1): 1–25.

Ringmar, Erik. 2014. "The Search for Dialogue as a Hindrance to Understanding: Practices as Inter-Paradigmatic Research Program." *International Theory* 6 (1): 1–27.

Ringmar, Erik. 2016. "How the World Stage Makes Its Subjects: An Embodied Critique of Constructivist IR Theory." *Journal of International Relations and Development* 19 (1): 101–25.

Ringmar, Erik. 2018. "The Problem with Performativity: Comments on the Contributions." *Journal of International Relations and Development* 22 (4): 899–908.

Risse, Thomas. 2000. "Let's Argue! Communicative Action in World Politics." *International Organization* 54 (1): 1–39.

Risse, Thomas. 2016. *Domestic Politics and Norm Diffusion in International Relations: Ideas Do Not Float Freely*. London: Routledge.

Risse, Thomas. 2017a. "Human Rights in Areas of Limited Statehood: From the Spiral Model to Localization and Translation." In *Human Rights Futures*, edited by Jack Snyder, Leslie Vinjamuri, and Stephen Hopgood, 135–58. Cambridge: Cambridge University Press. https://doi.org/10.1017/9781108147767.006

Risse, Thomas. 2017b. "Reden ist (immer noch) nicht billig." *Zeitschrift für Internationale Beziehungen* 24 (1): 189–97.

Risse, Thomas, and Mareike Kleine. 2010. "Deliberation in Negotiations." *Journal of European Public Policy* 17 (5): 708–26.

Rittberger, Berthold. 2001. "Which Institutions for Post-War Europe? Explaining the Institutional Design of Europe's First Community." *Journal of European Public Policy* 8 (5): 673–708.

Sachs, Jeffrey D. 2015. *The Age of Sustainable Development*. New York: Columbia University Press.

Santiago [pseud.]. 1993. "Forest Stewardship Council. Principles and Criteria: Country Assessment in Peru. Peruvian Foundation for the Conservation of Nature." Copy with the author.

Scheffer, Thomas. 2023. "Studying Legal Courts Trans-Sequentially." In *Courtroom Eth-*

nography: Exploring Contemporary Approaches, Fieldwork and Challenges*, edited by Lisa Flower and Sarah Klosterkamp, 75–91. Cham, Switzerland: Springer.

Schindler, Sebastian. 2018. "What Is Wrong with the United Nations? Cynicism and the Translation of Facts." In *World Politics in Translation: Power, Relationality and Difference in Global Cooperation*, edited by Tobias Berger and Alejandro Esguerra, 95–112. London: Routledge.

Schwartzman, Stephan. 1984. "Linguistic Humor and the Maintenance of Krenakore Identity under Contact." *International Journal of American Linguistics* 50 (2): 232–37.

Schwartzman, Stephan. 1986. *Bankrolling Disasters: International Development Banks and the Global Environment: A Citizens' Environmental Guide to the World Bank and the Regional Multilateral Development Banks*. San Francisco: Sierra Club Books.

Schwartzman, Stephan. 1988. "The Panara of the Xingu National Park: The Transformation of a Society." PhD thesis, University of Chicago.

Schwartzman, Stephan. 1989. "Extractive Reserves: The Rubber Tappers' Strategy for Sustainable Use of the Amazon Rainforest." In *Fragile Lands of Latin America: Strategies for Sustainable Development*, edited by John O. Browder, 150–63. Boulder: Westview.

Schwartzman, Stephan. 1991. "Deforestation and Popular Resistance in Acre: From Local Social Movement to Global Network." *Centennial Review* 35 (2): 397–422.

Schwartzman, Stephan. 1992. "Social Movements and Natural Resources Conservation in the Brazilian Amazon." In *The Rainforest Harvest: Sustainable Strategies for Saving the Tropical Forests? Including the Proceedings of an International Conference Held at the Royal Geographical Society, London 17–18th May 1990*, edited by Simon Counsell and Tim Rice, 207–12. London: Friends of the Earth Trust.

Scott, James C. 1998. *Seeing Like a State: How Certain Schemes to Improve the Human Condition Have Failed*. New Haven: Yale University Press.

Sending, Ole Jacob. 2015. *The Politics of Expertise: Competing for Authority in Global Governance*. Ann Arbor: University of Michigan Press.

Sending, Ole Jacob. 2017. "Recognition and Liquid Authority." *International Theory* 9 (2): 311–28.

Sending, Ole Jacob, Vincent Pouliot, and Iver B. Neumann. 2015. *Diplomacy and the Making of World Politics*. Cambridge: Cambridge University Press.

Shiva, Vandana. 1993. *Monocultures of the Mind: Perspectives on Biodiversity and Biotechnology*. Basingstoke: Palgrave Macmillan.

Simeone, Robert, Mario Pariona, and Manuel Lázaro. 1993. "A Natural Harvest: The Yanesha Forestry Cooperative in Peru Combines Western Science and Indigenous Knowledge." *Cultural Survival Quarterly* 17 (1): 48–51.

Solomon, Ty, and Brent J. Steele. 2017. "Micro-Moves in International Relations Theory." *European Journal of International Relations* 23 (2): 267–91. https://doi.org/10.1177/1354066116634442

Sontag, Susan. 2002. "The World as India: The St. Jerome Lecture on Literary Translation." October 3. Available at http://www.susansontag.com/prize/onTranslation.shtml

Steinberg, Richard H. 2002. "In the Shadow of Law or Power? Consensus-Based Bargaining and Outcomes in the GATT/WTO." *International Organization* 56 (2): 339–74.

Stirling, Andy. 2008. "'Opening Up' and 'Closing Down' Power, Participation, and Pluralism in the Social Appraisal of Technology." *Science, Technology, & Human Values* 33 (2): 262–94.

Stocks, Anthony, and Gary S. Hartshorn. 1992. "The Palcazu Project: Forest Management and Native Yanesha Communities." *Journal of Sustainable Forestry* 1 (1): 97–123.

Straßheim, Holger, and Silke Beck. 2019. *Handbook of Behavioural Change and Public Policy*. Cheltenham: Edward Elgar.

Stritzel, Holger. 2014. *Security in Translation: Securitization Theory and the Localization of Threat*. London: Palgrave Macmillan.

Susskind, Lawrence, Sarah McKearnan, and Jennifer Thomas-Larmer. 1999. *The Consensus Building Handbook: A Comprehensive Guide to Reaching Agreement*. Thousand Oaks, CA: SAGE.

Taggart, Todd, and John Curtis. 1993. "Alternatives to Rainforest Destruction." *The Luthiers' Mercantile Catalog* (blog). 1993. http://members.shaw.ca/strings/forestdestr .htm

Takacs, David. 1996. *The Idea of Biodiversity: Philosophies of Paradise*. Baltimore: Johns Hopkins University Press.

Taggart, Jack, and Kavi Joseph Abraham. 2023. "Norm Dynamics in a Post-Hegemonic World: Multistakeholder Global Governance and the End of Liberal International Order." *Review of International Political Economy* 31 (1): 1–28

Thomas [pseud.]. 1988. "Letter to Ken Regarding Meeting and Study." Copy with the author.

Thomas [pseud.]. 1991. "Forest Stewardship Standards as of December 10th." Copy with the author.

Thomas [pseud.]. 2005. "Some Notes on the Early Years of FSC." Copy with the author.

Thomas [pseud.], Ken [pseud.], and Connor [pseud.]. 1989. "Pre-Project Proposal for the ITTO. Labeling Systems for the promotion of Sustainably produced tropical timber." Copy with the author.

Tom [pseud.]. 1991. "Report on the Meeting of the Certification Working Group, Held in April 20-21-1991 at Greenpeace Office, San Francisco." Copy with the author.

Tsing, Anna Lowenhaupt. 2005. *Friction: An Ethnography of Global Connection*. Princeton: Princeton University Press.

Turnhout, Esther. 2018. "The Politics of Environmental Knowledge." *Conservation and Society* 16 (3): 363–71.

Turnhout, Esther, and Casey R Lynch. 2024. "Raising the Carbonized Forest: Science and Technologies of Singularization." *Environment and Planning F*, 26349825241255685.

United Nations. 1992. "Report of the United Nations Conference on Environment and Development. A/CONF.151/26 (Vol. I)."

United Nations Conference on Environment and Development (UNCED). 1992. "Agenda 21." Rio de Janeiro. https://sustainabledevelopment.un.org/content/docum ents/Agenda21.pdf

Upton, Christopher, and Stephen Bass. 1996. *The Forest Certification Handbook*. Delray Beach, FL: St. Lucie Press.

Uribe, Juanita. 2024. "Governing on Par with States: Private Power and Practices of

Political Normalisation." *Review of International Studies*, 1–20. https://doi.org/10.10 17/S0260210524000780

Van der Heijden, H. A. 1999. "Environmental Movements, Ecological Modernisation and Political Opportunity Structures." *Environmental Politics* 8 (1): 199–221.

Van der Ven, Hamish, and Benjamin Cashore. 2018. "Forest Certification: The Challenge of Measuring Impacts." *Current Opinion in Environmental Sustainability* 32: 104–11.

Voß, Jan-Peter, and Richard Freeman. 2016. *Knowing Governance: The Epistemic Construction of Political Order*. London: Palgrave Macmillan.

Voß, Jan-Peter, and Arno Simons. 2018. "A Novel Understanding of Experimentation in Governance: Co-Producing Innovations between 'Lab' and 'Field.'" *Policy Sciences* 51 (2): 213–29.

WARP. 1993. "Woodworkers Alliance for Rainforest Protection." *The Luthiers' Mercantile Catalog* (blog). 1993. http://members.shaw.ca/strings/warp.htm

Washington Post. 1988. "Thousands in Brazil Attend Slain Ecologist's Funeral." December 26.

Weber, Max. 1921. *Wirtschaft und Gesellschaft*. 5th ed. Tübingen: Mohr Siebeck.

Wellner, Pamela, and Eugene Dickey. 1991. *The Wood Users Guide*. San Francisco: Rainforest Action Network.

Westerwinter, Oliver. 2021. "Transnational Public-Private Governance Initiatives in World Politics: Introducing a New Dataset." *Review of International Organizations* 16 (1): 137–74.

Wigen, Einar. 2018. *State of Translation: Turkey in Interlingual Relations*. Ann Arbor: University of Michigan Press.

Wigen, Einar, and Mauro J. Caraccioli. 2026. *Interlingual Relations: Global Politics in a Polyglot World*. Ann Arbor: University of Michigan Press.

Wilson, Edward Osborne. 1988. *Biodiversity: Papers from the National Forum on Biodiversity, Held Sept. 21–25, 1986 in Washington, D.C.* Washington, DC: National Academy Press.

Wodak, Ruth. 2000. "From Conflict to Consensus? The Co-Construction of a Policy Paper." In *European Union Discourses on Un/Employment: An Interdisciplinary Approach to Employment Policy-Making and Organizational Change*, edited by Peter Muntigl, G. Weiss, and Ruth Wodak, 73–114. Amsterdam: John Benjamins.

Wodak, Ruth. 2009. *The Discourse of Politics in Action: Politics as Usual*. Basingstoke: Palgrave Macmillan.

World Wildlife Federation UK. "A Brief History of WWF." Available at https://www.scri bd.com/document/132391813/A-Brief-History-of-WWF-WWF-UK

Yanow, Dvora, and Peregrine Schwartz-Shea, eds. 2015. *Interpretation and Method: Empirical Research Methods and the Interpretive Turn*. Abingdon: Routledge.

Zarakol, Ayşe. 2010. *After Defeat: How the East Learned to Live with the West*. Cambridge: Cambridge University Press.

Zimmermann, Lisbeth. 2017. *Global Norms with a Local Face: Rule-of-Law Promotion and Norm Translation*. Cambridge: Cambridge University Press.

Zürn, Michael. 2018. *A Theory of Global Governance: Authority, Legitimacy, and Contestation*. Oxford: Oxford University Press.

Zwingel, Susanne. 2016. *Translating International Women's Rights*. London: Palgrave Macmillan.

Index